Encountering God
in the Psalms

Encountering God *in the* Psalms

Michael E. Travers

Kregel
Publications

Encountering God in the Psalms

Published by Kregel Publications, a division of Kregel, Inc., P.O. Box 2607, Grand Rapids, MI 49501.

Library of Congress Cataloging-in-Publication Data
Travers, Michael E.
Encountering God in the Psalms / by Michael E. Travers.
   p. cm.
Includes bibliographical references.
   1. Bible. O.T. Psalms—Criticism, interpretation, etc.
2. Bible. O.T. Psalms—Theology. 3. God—Biblical
teaching. I. Title.
II. Title.
BS1430.52.T73   2003
223'.206—dc21   2003012167

ISBN 0-8254-3842-x

Printed in the United States of America

03 04 05 06 07 / 5 4 3 2 1

For
Barbara, Stephen, and Elizabeth

Contents

7

Acknowledgments

MY DEBTS ARE MANY, AND I acknowledge them gratefully. Jim Weaver, my editor from the initial discussions about this book to its publication. Jim is a consummate editor and godly counselor. Thank you for your friendship as well as your professional guidance. Richard D. Patterson, Old Testament and Hebrew scholar and longtime friend. Dr. Patterson made many valuable comments on the manuscript, especially in regard to the nuances of the Hebrew text. Dr. Patterson is more than a scholar; he is a Christian gentleman who lives his faith.

Kathy Baughman, secretary to the English Department at Mississippi College. Kathy typed the texts of the Psalms and provided assistance in countless details as I wrote.

Dr. Gene Fant, formerly chair of the Department of English at Mississippi College, who provided resources and time in my teaching schedule to finish the manuscript.

Katie Barr, graduate research assistant at Mississippi College, who did the bibliographical work. I could not have asked for a kinder and more thorough assistant.

Phyllis Keith, faculty secretary at Southeastern Baptist Theological Seminary, who helped me with the final manuscript and bibliographical details.

Dr. Paige Patterson, former president of Southeastern Baptist

Theological Seminary, who hired an English professor who was writing a book on the Psalms and encouraged me in my work.

Barbara, my wife, and Stephen and Elizabeth, my children, who saw the value of the book and encouraged me to carry on when I faltered. Thank you for your godly witness.

The Psalms: An Encounter Between God and Man

As the deer pants for streams of water,
  so my soul pants for you, O God.
My soul thirsts for God, for the living God.
When can I go and meet with God?

—Psalm 42:1–2

WHY ARE THE PSALMS A FAVORITE portion of Scripture for so many Christians today as well as those throughout the ages? Anyone who has attended church for any length of time can quote verses from the Psalms, and even whole psalms, from memory. Who of us does not know Psalm 23 by heart? We sing psalms or verses taken from them in our church services, focusing our corporate worship on the Lord and drawing the congregation into the experience of the service. We sometimes use the Psalms in benedictions to conclude our services. Apart from our love of the Psalms in our church services, we read them in our own private devotional lives. Some Christians make it a practice to read five psalms a day and thus read through the Psalms every month. When we face a difficult situation—such as a family member's illness, slander in the marketplace, or uncertainty about the Lord's leading in our lives—we turn to the Psalms for comfort, peace, and direction. When we sin, the

Psalms give us words of confession to ask for God's forgiveness. We love the Psalms because they are so relevant to us.

No matter what we face in our lives,
the Psalms have something to say to us.

Over the years, scholars and laypeople alike have written hundreds of scholarly and devotional books on the Psalms. When Augustine wrote about his conversion to faith in Christ, the Psalms came to his mind. When in his *Confessions* Augustine writes, "However, when I call to mind the tears I shed at the songs [Psalms] of thy church at the outset of my recovered faith," he testifies to the effect the Psalms had on him.[1] He wept for joy that the Lord inspired such a beautiful book of devotion for us to enjoy. Calvin, Luther, Spurgeon, and countless other pastors and ministers have written commentaries on the Psalms. C. S. Lewis, the great twentieth-century creator of Narnia, English professor at Oxford and Cambridge, and apologist for the Christian faith, wrote only one book on a portion of Scripture—the Psalms.

One reason we love the Psalms is because they tell us so much about God. The Psalms give us a dialogue with God in which we speak our joys and sorrows to God, and God for his part meets our needs and receives our praise. In fact, because the Psalms record the psalmists' expressions of their own emotions and experiences, and because God inspired them, they become God's words to us too. We might say there is a dual focus to the Psalms—God and man in dialogue—for in the Psalms we encounter Yahweh (or the LORD) in every area of life. God inspires the psalmists to write, and we use the Psalms to speak our feelings and thoughts back to God.

It has long been recognized that the Psalms express a broad range of human experiences, emotions, and reflections. For example, in Psalm

---

1. Augustine, *Confessions and Enchiridion*, vol. 7 of *The Library of Christian Classics*, bk. 10, trans. and ed. Albert C. Outler (Philadelphia: Westminster, 1955), 186.

42 the writer longs for God with all his being. "As the deer pants for streams of water, so my soul pants for you, O God," the psalmist proclaims (v. 1). In Psalm 69, David cries to God in fear, "Save me, O God, for the waters have come up to my neck" (v. 1). When everything seems to be against him, in Psalm 73, the psalmist speaks his faith: "My flesh and my heart may fail, but God is the strength of my heart and my portion forever" (v. 26). When sin overwhelms his soul, David repents and acknowledges in Psalm 51 that God is justified when he speaks and just when he judges (vv. 3–4); in turn, his sin is forgiven. The Psalms portray human experiences that range from exuberant joy to profound despair, from fear to hope, from anger to love, and from doubt to faith. John Calvin begins his commentary on the Psalms by calling them "An Anatomy of all the Parts of Soul."[2] In the same passage, Calvin goes on to say that "there is not an emotion of which any one can be conscious that is not here represented as in a mirror."[3] Leland Ryken lists the range of different emotions in the Psalms, among them, "praise, adoration, awe, terror, joy, sorrow, fear, depression."[4] The more we read the Psalms, the more we find that they contain every emotion we could ever experience. The psalms put our own deepest feelings into words, and when we read them we direct God's words back to him.

Praise and Prayer

In broadest terms, we might classify the range of human emotions in the Psalms in two categories: prayer and praise. When we praise God, or Yahweh, we acknowledge that he is at the center of the Psalms. In praise, we lift our hearts to God, thanking and worshiping him for who he is and what he has done in our lives. The psalmists praise God for his creation (e.g., Pss. 8; 19; 97; 104), his rule as King of Kings (e.g.,

---

2. John Calvin, *Commentary on the Book of Psalms*, trans. James Anderson (Grand Rapids: Baker, 1998), 1:xxxvii.
3. Ibid.
4. Leland Ryken, *Words of Delight: A Literary Introduction to the Bible* (Grand Rapids: Baker, 1992), 228.

Pss. 2; 45; 110), his mercy and unfailing love (e.g., Pss. 51; 103; 105), and his protection and provision (e.g., Pss. 57; 77; 86; 88). Most of all, they praise God simply for who he is—Yahweh, the one true God (e.g., Pss. 33; 67; 97; 149). As Ronald Allen phrases it, praise in the Psalms reflects "our excited boastings in the wonder of knowing the living God."[5] Praise expresses our overflowing adoration of God. With the psalmists we should not be able to contain our praise; we should burst forth in lyrical worship of Yahweh. When was the last time the public worship of God brought you to tears of joy? The psalmists see praise as essential to a healthy spiritual life.

*When was the last time you were moved emotionally
in your personal devotions?*

Complementing praise in the Psalms are the prayers that the psalmists raise to God in the daily experiences of life. The psalmists pray when their enemies surround them (e.g., Pss. 3; 41; 109), when they are exiled in a foreign land (e.g., Ps. 137), and when they sin and need forgiveness (e.g., Pss. 6; 32; 39; 51; 102). Implicit in these psalms of prayer is the psalmists' faith that God will answer; in prayer, they express their confidence and trust that God will fulfill his promises and meet their needs as his people. Calvin reminds us, "Genuine and earnest prayer proceeds first from a sense of our need, and next, from faith in the promises of God."[6] Here again is the dual focus on God and man. Prayers in the Psalms originate from our human needs and express our dependence on God for all of life. Paradoxically, prayer also gives testimony to our faith in God. Does not the very act of prayer testify to our trust in God? Why would we pray at all if we did not think God would answer? The deists of the eighteenth century saw no need to pray because they believed in a God who created the world

---

5. Ronald Allen, *And I Will Praise Him: A Guide to Worship in the Psalms* (Grand Rapids: Kregel, 1999), 72.
6. Calvin, *Commentary on the Book of Psalms,* 1:xxxvii.

and then stood aside from it, uninvolved with his creation or his people's lives. Christians, on the other hand, believe God is involved personally with his people (and the creation at large, for that matter); we are theists, not deists. Prayer testifies to who God is and acknowledges what he does.

When we pray, we testify to God's sovereignty and our dependence on him for everything in life.

An Encounter with God

Both prayer and praise in the Psalms begin with God and describe man in relation to him. Again we are reminded of the dialogue, or the conversation, with God in the Psalms—man speaking to God the words God has inspired the writers of old to say. God is the alpha and the omega, the beginning and the end of our reading in the Psalms; he is the subject of all the Psalms, no matter what they say about our human experience. In one way or another, every psalm expresses something about God. We learn about his sovereignty, his mercy and loving-kindness, his care and protection of his people, and his great majesty as Creator of all things and King of Kings. It is fitting then that praise focuses on God first. In Ronald Allen's words, praise "must come from a genuine and vital relationship with God."[7] Prayer raises our human concerns to God by acknowledging first that only God can meet our needs and then asking him to meet those needs according to his will. The pattern is always the same: God first and man in relation to him. This is not to say that the human emotions and feelings expressed by the psalmists are not important. More than any other book in the Bible, the Psalms express human feelings and reflections on the experiences of daily life. They do so, however, in the light of God's revelation of himself to the psalmists. There is a paradox at work

---

7. Allen, *And I Will Praise Him*, 58.

in our dialogue with God: the more we focus on God, the more he fulfills the desires of our hearts (Ps. 37:4); the more we give ourselves to him, the more we are fulfilled. The dialogue is grounded in God, and human experience takes on significance in relation to God. The psalmists place God before themselves, and so should we.

The Plan of This Book

There are two parts to this book. Part One, "How to Read the Psalms," introduces the poetry of the Psalms and demonstrates how to read the Psalms as they were written. We do not read poetry the same way we read prose, and we cannot read the Psalms the way we do the book of Romans, for instance. When we read Hebrew poetry we need to pay attention to figures of speech, different types of parallelism, and the various genres (or types) of psalms in the Bible. Chapters 1 through 3 provide useful tools for reading the Psalms the way they were written.

Part Two, "God in the Psalms," begins by turning our attention to God's meetings with Moses on Mount Sinai. In these meetings, God—or Yahweh—tells Moses who he is and what he is like; he gives Moses a character sketch of himself. Chapter 4 thus provides a picture of the God we will meet in the Psalms. Part Two then turns to the Psalms themselves and examines them in light of the material in Part One. Because the Psalms are so rich and varied, scholars have approached them in different ways. Some approach the Psalms through their types, or "genres" (e.g., Longman, Ryken), while others see the Psalms as songs of worship and praise (Allen). I have approached the Psalms with an emphasis on God because he is the primary focus of all 150 psalms. I have divided the Psalms into several themes, each presented in a separate chapter.

Chapter 5 presents God as Creator for, if we are to understand who God is, we must begin with his work of creation. Chapter 6 turns from God's work as Creator to his special love and care for his people. Chapter 7 considers God as the sovereign King who rules the nations and individual lives. Chapter 8 examines some of the Psalms that speak of the coming Messiah, Jesus Christ. Chapter 9 considers some of the dilemmas and problems in which we find ourselves and promises the help of God in those difficult times. Chapter 10 turns our attention to the difficult psalms in which the psalmist curses his enemies and offers some answers as to how the Christian is to think about these psalms. Chapter 11 shows how we can use the Psalms to help us confess our sins to God and receive his forgiveness. Chapter 12 shows us the character of God and the character of the godly person, giving us a picture of the wisdom of the Psalms about living the godly life. Chapter 13 serves as a conclusion, answering the question, "What Have We Learned?" This chapter will answer questions like, "What have we learned about reading the Psalms?" "What have we learned about Yahweh?" and "What have we learned about living the God-centered Christian life?"

Reading the introductory material in Part One before reading about particular psalms in Part Two will help readers understand the interpretations of the Psalms in Part Two. In Part Two, readers can choose any theme of interest and read one, or more than one, psalm on that subject. After I analyze each psalm, I suggest some devotional thoughts.

My analyses of individual passages in the Psalms and devotional applications of those psalms are based on the English translation in the *New International Version* of the Bible. Accordingly, I do not comment on the Hebrew texts, nor do I address the textual difficulties the Hebrew sometimes presents in the Psalms.

My prayer is that this book will help you to know and love God more and that you will find help for daily living in the Psalms.

Part One

How to Read
the Psalms

Chapter 1

The Poetry of the Psalms

My heart is stirred by a noble theme
as I recite my verses for the king;
my tongue is the pen of a skillful writer.

— Psalm 45:1

The Psalms Are Poems

MANY PEOPLE FIND POETRY difficult to understand. As modern people, we tend toward the pragmatic and the profitable. Poetry strikes many of us as superfluous, too "pretty" for serious consideration, and certainly not likely to increase our financial position. Ironically, however, we are surrounded by more poetry than we realize, even in our daily lives. If you listen to music with lyrics, you are listening to poetry. When you speak in figures of speech (as in "I see what you mean," or "Turn on the light," or "Take the picture"), you are speaking poetically. If you find it easier to remember a proverb than a sentence in a textbook, you are responding to the mnemonic (or "remembering") qualities of poetry. In fact, it is difficult to escape poetry in our daily lives; we use poetry every day, and we hear poetry every day. We do not have the option to ignore poetry; we only have the options of knowing how to read poetry well or missing much of what poetry has to say to us. The psalms are poems, and to read them well we will have to learn something about reading poetry.

The Psalms Are Inspired Writings

Most evangelical Christians, at least those who hold to the inspiration of Scripture, would agree that the theology of the Psalms is inspired by God and therefore true. When the Psalms speak, for instance, of the godly man as one who separates himself from sinners, as in Psalm 1, we presume the theology to be true and should attempt to pattern our lives after the admonition to separate ourselves from sin. What the Psalms say is inspired by God, and we would never question their truthfulness.

The Psalms Are Inspired as Poems

If we do not find it difficult to accept the idea that the theology of the Psalms is inspired by God, why do we find it difficult to think of the form in which the theology is expressed as equally inspired by God?

The psalms are poems, and we must read them as such. If we read the Psalms the way we read biblical prose, such as the narratives of Genesis, Exodus, the Gospels, and the Acts of the Apostles, we are not reading the Psalms the way they were written. In *Reflections on the Psalms,* C. S. Lewis emphasizes the point that we must read the Psalms as poetry. Lewis writes, "the Psalms must be read as poems; as lyrics, with all the licences [sic] and all the formalities, the hyperboles, the emotional rather than logical connections, which are proper to lyrical poetry."[1]

Take just one feature of poetry as opposed to narrative prose. Po-

---

1. C. S. Lewis, *Reflections on the Psalms* (New York: Harcourt, Brace, Jovanovich, 1958), 3.

etry is a more concentrated form of writing than prose, more intense and patterned. When we read poetry, we sense quickly that the unit of expression is the verse (or colon, as we call it in Hebrew poetry), not the sentence. Consider the first verse of Psalm 1:

> Blessed is the man
> who does not walk in the counsel of the wicked
> or stand in the way of sinners
> or sit in the seat of the mockers.

Note how deliberately patterned the verse is, paralleling the three statements about the godly man: he does not walk, he does not stand, he does not sit with sinners. Consider how carefully structured the verse is, expressing each statement about the godly man in almost parallel grammatical structures. Then think of the linear progression of the verbs in this verse—walk, stand, sit—to point out the fact that the godly man does not allow himself to become increasingly comfortable with sinners. The Psalms are inspired not only because *what* they say is God-breathed but also because *how* they say it is God-breathed: that is, the poetic form, as well as the theological content, of the Psalms is inspired.

What Is Poetry?

If the Psalms are inspired poems, what do we need to know about poetry to read and appreciate them? We do not have the option of ignoring the poetic form of the Psalms if we wish to gain the fullest benefits from reading them. If we are to read the poetry of the Psalms well, we need to think correctly about how poetry works. To know how poetry works, we will have to correct some misconceptions about poetry that are prevalent in our culture. The first misconception we sometimes have about poetry is that its verses rhyme. While many poems have rhyme, not all poems contain rhyme. Many modern poems do not rhyme at all, and Old English poems had no rhyme. The only "rhyme" Hebrew poetry has is what Claus Westermann calls "thought rhymes" or "sentence rhymes," by which he indicates that the meanings of sentences are repeated.[2] Poems are not identified by rhyme, though some poems do indeed rhyme. We cannot identify a poem by rhyme because rhyme is not a necessary characteristic of poetry. Biblical Hebrew poetry seldom uses sound rhyme (though it does at times), and for this reason we cannot depend on sound rhyme alone to help us recognize poetry in the Bible.

A second mistaken way we sometimes think of poetry is to assume that only poetry uses figures of speech like simile, metaphor, image, or personification. It is true that most poems contain these figures of speech, but so does much prose. Think of the many kingdom parables that Jesus begins with "The kingdom of heaven is like . . ." These parables are not poems, but they do contain similes, images, and sometimes allegories—all figures of speech. In everyday, informal conversation, we use figures of speech more than we realize. For instance, we speak of the sun "rising" in the east and "setting" in the west, when in fact it is the earth that rotates in reference to the sun, and not the sun rising or setting in relation to the earth at all. We find figures of speech in prose as well as poetry, and in everyday speech as well as in books. Poetry is not distinguished from other forms of language by its figures of speech, though it does use such figures more regularly than any other form of language.

A third error we sometimes fall into is the idea that poetry can be distinguished by the way its lines appear on the page. Certainly most of the poems we are used to are patterned visually on the page in verses; their appearance is often the first indication that they are poems. However, even the appearance of language does not necessarily denote poetry. The book of Job is intensely poetical, as are even the parts of Revelation that are not specifically poetry, and the writing in these sections does not "look like" poetry. Poetry is not distinguished by the appearance of its verses on the page.

If we cannot distinguish poetry from other uses of language by

---

2. Claus Westermann, *The Psalms: Structure, Content and Message* (Minneapolis: Augsburg, 1980), 23–24.

rhyme, figures of speech, or appearance, how can we recognize a poem? Poetry is distinguished from other uses of language in at least four ways, each of which we will consider in turn.

1. Poetry Communicates Experience

Most of the writing we read every day in the marketplace communicates information. Reports, manuals, school textbooks, and the many "how-to" books all deliver information of one kind or another. We read these books for the facts and data they provide. Typically, we do not read these books word for word, from cover to cover, first page to last page in sequence; rather, we read only for the information we need. Poetry does not work this way.

Poetry communicates experience, not just information. We do not read a poem on fences (e.g., Robert Frost's poem, "Mending Wall") to learn how to build or maintain a fence, though Frost's poem presents a scene in which farmers mend their mutual stone wall in springtime. Nor do we read a poem about war (e.g., Tennyson's "The Charge of the Light Brigade") to learn how to wage war. We read poetry to experience the essential human dimension to life, to see what is important in the human condition. Frost's poem communicates the experience of living with neighbors and building positive relations with them. Tennyson's poem communicates the human toll of war in the dramatic image of the numberless cavalry riding to certain death. Neither poem is primarily informational, but both express something of the human condition and show us something of what it means to be human.

Poetry communicates experience, not just information.

The desire to see life from a human perspective is what literary critic Northrop Frye calls "the motive for metaphor" (borrowing a phrase from a title of one of Wallace Stevens's poems). Frye states that literature begins in the impulse to identify ourselves with the "other"—nature, people, God. When we use metaphors, we unite things that are normally separate from each other.[3] That is what metaphors do; they bring together what is normally disconnected. When we use metaphors, we put our own human image on the "other." Hence, we use metaphors in which one object or idea is seen in and through another. For example, think of the opening verse of Psalm 23: "The LORD is my shepherd, I shall not be in want." In this metaphor, David compares God (the "other" in the comparison) to a shepherd (the "human") who cares and provides for his "sheep" (or people). By making this comparison, David uses human terms to express God's loving care and provision for us. Every Christian knows the experience David is describing, a difficulty or sorrow out of which only God can deliver us. David gives God's provision a human face, that of a shepherd. Poetry communicates experiences from the human perspective.

As the illustrations from the poetry of Frost, Tennyson, and David all suggest, poets do not *tell* us about experience; they *show* us experience. Poetry uses concrete images to give "the experience of experience." Poets use specific, concrete details that embody (or "incarnate," to use a more accurate term) the experience they wish to express. Informational language, such as manuals and reports, tells us what we need to know; poetry shows us experience. In a little essay titled "Meditation in a Toolshed," C. S. Lewis clarifies the difference between telling information and showing experience.[4] Lewis asks his readers to imagine they are in a toolshed with the door closed; little rays of sunlight come in through a gap between the door and the frame. Lewis suggests there are two ways of "looking" in this situation. We can "look at" or we can "look along." When we "look at" the sunbeam, we see it as a ray of light in the darkness of the shed; we analyze it as such. When we "look along" the ray, on the other hand, we see what the sunbeam shows us—perhaps a treetop or a house roof that is visible outside in the sun. The difference between "looking at" and "looking along" is the difference between in-

---

3. Northrop Frye, *The Educated Imagination* (Toronto: CBC Publications, 1963), 6.
4. C. S. Lewis, "Meditation in a Toolshed," in *God in the Dock: Essays on Theology and Ethics* (Grand Rapids: Eerdmans, 1970), 212–15.

formation ("looking at") and experience ("looking along"), the difference between telling and showing. In poems, we "look along" life to experience it. Poetry communicates experience with a human face.

2. The Language of Poetry Is Concentrated and Heightened

In informational prose, the unit of expression is the sentence or the paragraph.[5] In English, it takes a complete sentence, or at least a principal clause, to express a complete thought, and sometimes a whole paragraph to fit the thought into its logical context. Think of the Epistles in the New Testament, where the writers take several verses, and sometimes multiple chapters, to express their thought. The New Testament Epistles, as well as the language of our daily communication, use the individual sentence as the building block. We express ideas in sentences. Poetry, on the other hand, uses individual words and figures of speech, not just sentences, as the basic building blocks of meaning. This is not to say that poetry does not make "sentence sense"; it usually does. However, poetry concentrates more on individual words and figures of speech and the way they relate to each other than does prose. As one editor of a college literature anthology puts it, "Poetry is the most condensed and concentrated form of literature. It is language whose individual lines, either because of their own brilliance or because they focus so powerfully on what has gone before, have a higher voltage than most language."[6]

Consider the following example of a poetic use of language in the Psalms:

> Love and faithfulness meet together;
> righteousness and peace kiss each other.
> —Psalm 85:10

---

5. Leland Ryken, *Words of Delight: A Literary Introduction to the Bible* (Grand Rapids: Baker, 1992), 159.
6. Thomas R. Arp, *Perrine's Literature: Structure, Sound, and Sense,* 7th ed. (Fort Worth: Harcourt Brace College Publishers, 1998), 567.

This verse gives us four characteristics of God in concentrated form. The psalmist personifies love and faithfulness by depicting their first meeting. He also personifies righteousness and peace, suggesting that they kiss. The picture of love and faithfulness meeting is an image of friendship, suggesting that the two characteristics of God belong together, as friends. As for God's righteousness and peacefulness, they belong together too. This may strike the reader as odd; at first glance, it appears that righteousness and peacefulness do not belong together in the same person. The psalmist is telling us, however, that God is not either holy or merciful; he is both holy and merciful. In fact, this image is rather startling, suggesting that God's righteousness and peace are so far from being antithetical, they are unified as one. Though we have not exhausted the verse with this brief analysis, the psalmist teaches us the theological truth that God's mercy is based on his truthfulness (or faithfulness)—a message of great comfort to those who call out for the mercy of the Lord. In this short example, we can see the intense, focused use of words that characterizes poetry. Words in poems are more concentrated and heightened than in other uses of language, and we must read them more closely if we are to hear what they say.[7] When we read the Psalms this way, we will be rewarded with deep spiritual blessings.

> *It is by understanding the literary figures of speech in*
> *Psalm 85:10 that we realize that, even though God is righteous,*
> *we can still have peace with him.*

This concentrated use of words in poetry is reflected in the opening verses from one of William Wordsworth's sonnets:

> It is a beauteous evening, calm and free,
> The holy time is quiet as a Nun
> Breathless with adoration.[8]

7. Ibid., 563.
8. William Wordsworth, "Sonnet XXX," in *Poetical Works: Wordsworth* (London: Oxford University Press, 1967), 205.

In these verses, the speaker is overwhelmed with the beauty and peacefulness of a sunset; in fact, he finds the experience to be a spiritual one, as his reference to a nun's devotion attests. To paraphrase, or perhaps summarize, the verses this way, however, strips the poem of much of its effect and much of what it is actually saying.

After establishing in the opening verse that he is writing about an evening, the poet uses words in the next two verses that suggest the experience is one of deep religious emotion for him. Notice that he calls the time "holy," suggesting its spiritual character. The word *holy* denotes purity and separation; that is, an experience that is holy is one set apart from, or distinct from, other experiences. The poet continues his religious imagery with the reference to the nun at devotions. Notice how the words deepen the religious experience significantly in this image. The nun is not just going through the perfunctory motions of her devotional duty. She is overwhelmed with awe at the one she worships; she is "breathless with adoration," we are told—entirely overcome with the object of her devotion. These words—*holy* and *breathless with adoration*—show how poetry deepens meaning and experience by concentrating our emotions, thoughts, and imaginations. In just a few short verses the poet in Wordsworth's sonnet expresses what would take paragraphs in analytical prose.

One feature of the poetry of the Psalms that contributes to its concentrated effect is what Tremper Longman calls its terseness.[9] Longman remarks that the terseness of Hebrew poetry intensifies the effect in the poem;[10] he identifies ellipsis and the lack of conjunctions or particles as two methods of terseness. Longman cites Psalm 33:12 as an example of ellipsis:

> Blessed is the nation whose God is the LORD,
>   the people he chose for his inheritance.

---

9. Tremper Longman, *Literary Approaches to Biblical Interpretation* (Grand Rapids: Zondervan, 1987), 121–22.
10. Ibid., 122.

The verb from the first colon is understood but not explicitly stated in the second. Psalmists often omit such conjunctions and markers as *then, when, therefore,* and *because.* The effect of both ellipsis and omission of conjunctions is to intensify or heighten what is being said. The terse way of making the point emphasizes it; the omission of normally included words encourages readers to participate actively in the reading because they must provide what is missing.

When we read poetry we must pay careful attention to individual words and phrases, for they often carry more meaning and significance in poetry than they do in informational prose. In Psalm 85:10 the psalmist teaches a theology of God's holiness and faithfulness on the one hand, married to his love and mercy on the other. God is both just and forgiving; in fact, he could not be the one without the other. The opening verses of Wordsworth's sonnet show us that we cannot "skim read" poetry. If we read poetry carelessly, not paying due attention to individual words and phrases, we will miss much of the intended meaning. When we remember that God has inspired the Psalms, we must assume that we were intended to understand the meanings communicated through the psalmists' concentrated use of individual words.

3. Poetry Is Consciously Structured and Patterned

Complementing the close reading of individual words and phrases is the careful, conscious structure of poetry. Poems display structure and pattern in a variety of ways. Just as we read carefully for words, so we need to read for structure, for it too helps us understand poetry. An example of patterning is the use some poems make of stanzas, or "paragraphs" of verses, which display the same rhythms and rhymes. Some poets use rhymes to structure their poems. Poets often combine rhyme and stanzaic structure to pattern their poems. Consider the concluding stanzas from a poem many of us likely read in school, William Blake's "Tyger, Tyger":

When the stars threw down their spears,
And water'd heaven with their tears,
Did he smile his work to see?
Did he who made the Lamb make thee?

Tyger! Tyger! Burning bright
In the forests of the night,
What immortal hand or eye
Dare frame thy fearful symmetry?[11]

Blake's poem uses a traditional rhyme scheme of A-A-B-B. That is, the first two verses of the stanza rhyme, as do the last two: "spears . . . tears" (A-A) and "see . . . thee" (B-B). The same pattern is repeated in every stanza ("bright . . . night" and "eye . . . symmetry"—this last rhyme is a poetic license). The effect of the rhyme and stanzaic structure is to provide repetition and pattern, within which the poet can develop his thought and not lose his reader. Stanzas and rhymes provide a recognizable, repeated pattern that frees us to appreciate the experiences the poet wishes to communicate. Music uses repetition in much the same way.

Biblical poetry, especially the poetry in the Psalms, does not use stanzas and repeated rhymes as patterning devices. The Psalms do, however, use a repeating pattern to help readers follow the writer's thoughts and feelings. Hebrew poetry is patterned in at least two specific ways, one in regard to the psalm as a whole, and one in regard to the smaller units within the psalm. To structure the smaller units (or "cola," as we call them, "colon" for singular), Hebrew poetry uses parallelism, a patterning technique with which most Christians are somewhat familiar. We might call parallelism the "microcosmic" structure of the Psalms, for it provides the pattern for the smaller units within the poem. The other way the Psalms are patterned is in regard to the pattern of the psalm as a whole. We might call this structure the

---

11. William Blake, "Tyger, Tyger," in *The Poetical Works of William Blake,* ed. John Sampson (London: Oxford University Press, 1941).

"macrocosmic," referring to the organization of the entire psalm. Put more precisely, the macrocosmic structure of the Psalms refers to the genres, or types, of psalms—such as the Hymn, Lament, Royal, Thanksgiving, and Wisdom Psalms. We will consider the genres of the Psalms in the next chapter and turn our attention at this point to the techniques of parallelism.

Though not limited to poetry, parallelism is certainly one of the primary patterning devices of the Psalms. Parallelism is the repetition of the same idea in different words in two or more phrases (or cola) in the poem; often the repetition of the idea modifies the original idea. Tremper Longman defines parallelism as "the correspondence which occurs between the phrases of a poetic line."[12] In Longman's terminology, which we will use in this book, a line is one complete parallelism, and a phrase is one of the parts of the parallelism. To be more precise, a phrase is a colon (cola for the plural), and two or more cola go together to make one line. For example, David thanks God in Psalm 8 that he has elevated mankind to a position of honor:

> You made him ruler over the works of your hands;
>   you put everything under his feet.
>
> —verse 6

In the first colon, David reminds us that humans are stewards over everything God made; in the second colon, David repeats the idea of man's responsibility but shifts the emphasis. In the first colon, part of the emphasis is on God's creative work ("the works of your hands"); in the second colon, the emphasis is on man's stewardship of God's creation, for everything in creation is "under his feet."

For our purposes, we will identify four types of parallelism in the Psalms.[13] The first type of parallelism, *synonymous parallelism,* is the

---

12. Tremper Longman, *How to Read the Psalms* (Downers Grove, Ill.: InterVarsity, 1988), 95.

13. I follow the classification of types of parallelism outlined in Ryken's *Words of Delight,* 181–82. Though Ryken's is not the only classification of the types of parallelism, his types relate well to the parallelisms in the Psalms.

simplest form. As its name implies, synonymous parallelism is a device in which the poet says the same thing in successive cola (or phrases). For example:

> Praise the LORD with the harp;
>   make music to him on the ten-stringed lyre.
>   —Psalm 33:2

Both cola say essentially the same thing: use stringed instruments to praise the Lord. The second colon does not seem to add anything significant to the first, though it does change the instrument from harp to lyre. Even so, the change does not seem to affect the quality of praise in any significant way. In synonymous parallelism, the second part repeats the first part in different words and emphasizes the point being made.

The second type of parallelism Leland Ryken identifies is *antithetic parallelism*. In antithetic parallelism, the idea of the first colon is reiterated in an antithetical, or contrasting way. Consider the well-known admonition from the book of Proverbs:

> Righteousness exalts a nation,
>   but sin is a disgrace to any people.
>   —Proverbs 14:34

In the first colon, the writer states positively that holy living results in blessing. In the second colon, the same idea is stated negatively—namely, sin dishonors a people. Stated in opposite ways—first positively, then negatively—righteous living lifts a people up, whereas sin degrades them.

The third type of parallelism is *climactic parallelism*. Other names sometimes used for climactic parallelism are "stepladder," "staircase," and "repetitive" parallelism.[14] In this type of parallelism, the second colon repeats part of the first and adds something to it. A good example

---

14. Longman, *How to Read the Psalms*, 101.

of climactic parallelism is found in the encouragements to praise that open Psalm 96:

> Sing to the LORD a new song;
>   sing to the LORD, all the earth.
> Sing to the LORD, praise his name;
>   proclaim his salvation day after day.
>
> —verses 1–2

In these opening verses, the psalmist begins by asking his readers to sing a new song to God; he then extends his call to sing to all people ("all the earth"). Next, he instructs his readers to praise God's name; finally, he admonishes them to give daily witness to the salvation of the Lord. The effect of the parallelisms is to graduate the call to praise incrementally. That is, the psalmist expands his initial call to sing to the Lord's glory by adding that it extends to everyone everywhere, that we are to praise God's name, and that we are to proclaim his salvation. The parallelisms "climax" in that they build to a crescendo in declaring God's salvation.

Ryken's fourth type of parallelism is *synthetic parallelism*. In this form of parallelism, the second colon "completes or expands the thought introduced in the first line."[15] As Ryken suggests, synthetic parallelism may not be a pure parallelism. However, the structure in this type is indeed parallel, and the thought from the first colon is completed and extended in the second colon. Consider this example:

> The LORD Almighty is with us;
>   the God of Jacob is our fortress.
>
> —Psalm 46:7

The first colon tells us that the omnipotent God of the universe is "with" us, or close to us. The second colon informs us that the covenant God, or the "God of Jacob," is our defense ("fortress"). In both

---

15. Ryken, *Words of Delight*, 182.

cola, it is God himself who is present, but the second phrase completes the first by clarifying that the specific way in which God is present with us is as a defense for us against enemies. The parallelism is "synthetic" in that part of the first is included in the second.

We cannot overlook parallelism in the Psalms, not because it is a biblical Hebrew poetic ornament that we no longer use. Rather, parallelism is a poetic device with which the psalmists express their thoughts, and their thoughts cannot be understood properly any other way. C. S. Lewis concludes his comments on parallelism in the Psalms by noting, "If we have any taste for poetry we shall enjoy this feature of the Psalms. Even those Christians who cannot enjoy it will respect it."[16] As we look at the Psalms, we will notice examples of parallelism and how they contribute to our understanding and experience of God.

4. Poetry Uses Figures of Speech

The fourth characteristic of poetry is its use of figures of speech. Poetry certainly is not the only form of language that uses figures of speech. Many modern novels use figures of speech, some even building their whole structure on a primary image. Joseph Conrad's *Heart of Darkness* employs the image of the Congo River in Africa as a symbol for the evil inherent in the human heart.[17] Chinua Achebe's book, *Things Fall Apart,* is a novel with a dominating image of disintegration.[18] Even so, poetry uses figures of speech more frequently than other forms of language, and often a figure of speech provides the key to what a poem says.

A figure of speech is a device in which a comparison occurs. A figure of speech contains two terms, A and B, which are compared to each other. We should notice at least two important points about figures of speech at the outset of our discussion. First, the two terms are logically separate; that is, A is not in fact B, or else we could not see

---

16. Lewis, *Reflections on the Psalms,* 5.
17. Joseph Conrad, *Heart of Darkness* (New York: Penguin, 1983).
18. Chinua Achebe, *Things Fall Apart* (New York: Random House, 1992).

them as separate. When Shakespeare says that love "is the star to every wandering bark, / Whose worth's unknown, although his height be taken,"[19] he is comparing two distinct objects. In this example, he compares true love to the star a mariner would use to guide his ship ("bark") at sea; the star and true love are far from being the same thing. The second point we need to underscore about figures of speech is that, though the terms are logically distinct, they are brought together in the comparison. That is, the poem suggests a way, or ways, in which the two distinct terms are alike. In the example from Shakespeare's Sonnet 116, the star and true love are alike in that they are permanent, always the same, reliable; they are guides in life. In a figure of speech, then, two objects or ideas that are logically distinct are found imaginatively to have something significant in common.

> *God inspired the figures of speech in the Psalms as much*
> *as he did their theology. We will benefit immensely if we read*
> *the figures of speech in the Psalms the way the psalmists—*
> *and God—intended them to be read.*

Many readers are likely to think of figures of speech as poetic decorations that help the poem along. Nothing could be further from the truth. The thought or experience they suggest can be understood only as it is presented in the comparison. They are necessary in that they frame the idea or experience in the poem. As a result of the similarity in the comparison, readers see things in a way they had not seen them before; they are given a new insight, a significant experience. Before Shakespeare's sonnet, we might not have thought of love as a permanent, exalted guide in life; now we do. Another way in which figures of speech are indispensable to the poem is that they involve readers actively in the process of reading. When we find a figure of speech, we have to make the imaginative leap to understand what is being said.

---

19. William Shakespeare, "Sonnet 116," in *The Riverside Shakespeare* (Boston: Houghton Mifflin, 1974), 1770.

Reading poetry is no spectator sport; we must become active readers if we are to experience what the poem offers.

The most frequent figures of speech in the Psalms are simile, metaphor, image, symbol, personification, metonymy, and synecdoche. A simile is a comparison of two objects using *like* or *as*. Speaking of the godly man who trusts in the Lord, David writes:

> But I am like an olive tree
> flourishing in the house of God;
> I trust in God's unfailing love
> for ever and ever.
>
> —Psalm 52:8

The two terms of the simile are the olive tree (term A) and the godly man (term B). What do the two terms have in common? How are they compared? Just as an olive tree thrives, so the godly man thrives in God's "unfailing love," or *ḥesed,* the word used here to denote God's particular love for his own people. In this brief, focused simile, David shows us with a concrete object (the flourishing olive tree) that the life of faith is one of great spiritual joy and security.

Before we move on to the other figures of speech, we should note two further considerations about figures of speech on the basis of David's simile. Notice first that the similes (and all other figures of speech along with the simile) are intense, concentrated forms in which a poet can say a great deal with a few words. The comparison of faith to a flourishing olive tree teaches us an important theological truth: we have an abundant life that the world cannot give ("flourishing"). When we find figures of speech in the Psalms, we will have to slow down and read closely to hear what the psalmist—and God—is saying. The second consideration from David's simile comes as a further implication of the point just made. When we find a figure of speech, we have to become active readers and interpret it. That is, we must participate in understanding and experiencing what the figure is saying. To do this, we must identify the two terms (A and B), discover what they have in common (in this example, prosperity), and note the context in which the comparison is found. In the context of our example simile from Psalm 52, David is contrasting the wicked (vv. 1–5) and the righteous (vv. 6–9): the wicked will perish (v. 5), but the righteous will live forever (v. 8). Figures of speech say a great deal in a short space. No wonder the Psalms appeal to so many Christians; we find so much in them.

The second figure of speech is the metaphor. A metaphor is a comparison without using *like* or *as*. Metaphor is the imaginative identification of two dissimilar terms. In a simile, "A is like B"; in a metaphor, "A is B." A metaphor is a tighter and stronger comparison than a simile. We might think of a metaphor as a mathematical equation; in a metaphor, "A = B." A brief example of a metaphor in the Psalms is found in Psalm 115, a psalm of public worship and praise:

> O house of Israel, trust in the LORD—
>   he is their help and shield.
>
> —verse 9

The metaphor in this verse is the comparison of the Lord to a shield. What the psalmist is saying, of course, is that the Lord protects his people. In the ancient world, the shield covered a warrior from head to foot; it was full-length protection from arrows and darts. By comparing God to such a shield, the psalmist shows us that God protects us completely. This verse is found in a psalm of public worship in which the Levitical priest speaks, promising the congregation God's protection in time of trouble, and the congregation responds. One further note about the immediate context of this metaphor is that the priest tells the people that the Lord is a help as well as a shield. In a positive sense, God provides what we need ("help"), and in a negative sense, he wards off attacks. Again, we can see how the metaphor shows us much in a few words and involves us actively in interpreting the meaning.

The third figure of speech in the Psalms is personification. Personification is a special type of metaphor in which a nonhuman object is compared to a person. To use our formula again, "A (nonhuman) is B (human)." The effect of personifying something is to make it more accessible and close to us. The most obvious example of personification in the Psalms is "The LORD is my shepherd." The rest of Psalm 23 plays out the variations on this comparison. What does it mean that the Lord is the believer's "shepherd"? It means that he will meet our needs (v. 2); he will encourage us spiritually (v. 3a); he will sanctify us (v. 3b); he will comfort us in sorrow (v. 4); he will provide abundant spiritual blessings now and forever (vv. 5–6). Psalm 23 is about the Lord first, believers second; it is about the shepherd first, the sheep second. One reason why the psalm is so comforting to us is that it paints a picture of the Lord and shows what he does for us. In the personification here, God is brought close to us as a shepherd constantly tending his sheep.

The fourth figure of speech that finds frequent expression in the Psalms is the image. An image is a word picture. As such, images use concrete objects, things we can perceive with our senses. In an image, we see, taste, touch, smell, or hear an object; the object in turn suggests something more. Often in images only one of the two terms is developed at length; sometimes, the second term remains implicit. In all cases, images concentrate attention on the tangible object and present it in such a way that it obviously suggests something more. Psalm 97, a Royal Psalm, gives us an image of God's reign as the King:

> Clouds and thick darkness surround him;
> righteousness and justice are the foundations of his throne.
> Fire goes before him
> and consumes his foes on every side.
> His lightning lights up the world;
> the earth sees and trembles.
> The mountains melt like wax before the LORD,
> before the Lord of all the earth.
> The heavens proclaim his righteousness,
> and all the peoples see his glory.

—verses 2–6

In this image we "see" clouds and darkness veiling God, fire destroying his enemies, and lightning melting mountains. We "hear" the heavens proclaiming God's glory. What does the imagery here mean? All of these images point to God's righteousness and justice and suggest his glory. Clouds and darkness imply God's transcendent holiness; lightning and melting mountains speak of God's sovereign power over the universe; and the heavens give testimony to God's glory. The imagery here shows us in pictorial form God's transcendent holiness, sovereignty, and majesty. God reigns because of who he is; he is righteous, just, and omnipotent. Psalm 97 shows us something of the glory of God as a great King above all kings. The images present God to our senses, better enabling us to experience what the psalmist is saying about God and uniting experience with doctrine.

> *Imagery allows us to participate experientially*
> *in the theology of the Psalms. This way, doctrine and*
> *experience are united.*

It may well be that the images and metaphors of the Psalms do even more than I have suggested so far. They may point to the fact that God is so far above us that we can only approximate his glory. In *How to Read the Psalms,* Tremper Longman makes this point well:

> Images, particularly metaphors, help to communicate the fact that God is so great and powerful and mighty that he can't be exhaustively described. Metaphor . . . may be accurate, but is less precise than literal language. Metaphor preserves the mystery of God's nature and being, while communicating to us about him and his love for us.[20]

In the metaphors and images of the Psalms, the psalmists are not showing off their artistry or abilities; rather, they are demonstrating

20. Longman, *How to Read the Psalms,* 121.

that the consummate glory of God is too great for human words to capture. In this way, the images and metaphors the psalmists use glorify God.

There are two other figures of speech that occur periodically in the Psalms. These two devices are likely less recognizable to most readers, but the psalmists use them often to suggest many important characteristics of God. They are metonymy and synecdoche. Metonymy is a device in which an idea or object closely associated with another object stands for that object. For example, when journalists speak about the president of the United States, they may say something like, "The White House reported today . . ." Of course the White House itself does not speak; we use it as a metonymy to represent the president who lives there. The White House is closely related to the president and stands for him. Synecdoche is a similar device. In synecdoche, a part represents the whole. For instance, "All hands on deck." When a ship's captain gives this order, he does not expect his sailors to send the hands at the ends of their arms to the deck; he means for the sailors to present themselves on deck. A part—the hand—stands for the whole person in this case.

We find examples of both metonymy and synecdoche in Psalm 45, that great wedding song that speaks of our Lord Jesus Christ. The psalmist uses a synecdoche to speak of God's great power:

> In your majesty ride forth victoriously
>   in behalf of truth, humility and righteousness;
>   let your right hand display awesome deeds.
>
>   —verse 4

God's omnipotence is given a military image in the first part of this verse; the synecdoche occurs at the end of the verse with the hand. The hand is used to represent God's great power over the nations of the earth, as if he were a great military general who did awesome things. A further effect of the synecdoche is to show how insignificant human power is; all it takes is God's hand to destroy those who stand against him. We find the metonymy two verses later:

> Your throne, O God, will last for ever and ever;
>   a scepter of justice will be the scepter of your kingdom.
> —verse 6

Here, the throne and the scepter are metonymies for God's righteous reign. A throne is closely associated with a king, and so God's reign (as represented in the metonymy of the throne) will last forever. The scepter is closely associated with a king's absolute power over his subjects. When an ancient Near Eastern king extended his scepter, a subject could approach the king; if he did not extend the scepter, the subject could die for his temerity. We see an example of this use of the scepter in the book of Esther (5:1–3), when the king extends his scepter to Esther and allows her to speak. In the example from Psalm 45, the scepter stands as a metonymy for God's perfect justice.

When we read the Psalms, we need to know something about figures of speech—what they are, how they work, and why they are important. Figures of speech find similarities in objects or ideas we would not normally find similar. They use concrete objects that appeal to our senses and thereby show rather than tell. They appear in even the strongest theology in the Bible (consider the image of slavery either to sin or to God in Rom. 6:15–23, for example). Furthermore, they provide the form in which their theology is set; they are indispensable to meaning. Because they use a concentrated and heightened form of language, figures of speech require the reader to participate actively in the reading process, interpreting what they mean based on the terms of the comparison itself and the context in which the figure is found. For all these reasons, we cannot overlook figures of speech when we read the Psalms. In fact, it is more proper to say that we must respond to figures of speech if we are to gain the experience and theology that the Psalms were intended to convey. Again, we must remember that God inspired the figures of speech in the Psalms, as much as he did their theology. For all these reasons, we can enjoy the figures of speech in the Psalms and learn from them, not dread them.

Summary

1. The Psalms are poems. God inspired them in that form, and we must read them as poems if we are to read them as they were written.
2. Poetry has four primary characteristics:
   A. Poetry communicates experience, not just information. Poetry expresses what is important in human experience, and the Psalms tell us what is important in human experience from God's perspective.
   B. The language of poetry is concentrated and heightened. Poetry focuses on words in relation to each other, not just sentence sense. When we read the Psalms, we must pay attention to individual words and phrases and note their nuances.
   C. Poetry is consciously structured and patterned. Because the Psalms are so obviously structured, it will be easy for us to follow the psalmists' ideas and feelings. The structure of an individual psalm will help us understand what the psalmist is saying.
   D. Poetry uses figures of speech. We need to recognize figures of speech in the Psalms to gain a fuller experience of what the psalmist is trying to express.

Reading the Psalms as poems is actually an enjoyable experience. When we read the Psalms the way they were written, we will begin to appreciate the beauty God inspired in the Bible. In fact, reading the Psalms as poetry will give us a fuller appreciation of who God is and what he has done for his people.

Chapter 2

Genres, or Types, of Psalms

ONE OF THE CHARACTERISTICS OF poetry we discussed in the previous chapter was structure. In this chapter, we will consider poetic structure under two headings, the "microcosmic" and the "macrocosmic." The microcosmic structure has to do with the pattern of the small units contained within the poem—parallelism, for instance. The macrocosmic relates to the structure and design of the whole psalm. The design of the psalm at large tells us what type—or *genre,* to use the proper word—of psalm we are reading. Because we do not always know the author or the historical context of any given psalm, it is helpful to know its type, or genre.[1] Most important for our encounter with God in the Psalms, genre gives us a clue as to how to approach God in any given psalm.

Genres in Everyday Life

You are likely more familiar with genre than you think, for we find genres all around us in our daily lives. In a newspaper, for example, there are different types of writing. News stories are the most obvious type of writing in newspapers. When you read a news story, you ex-

---

1. For a further discussion of the place of genre in classifying the Psalms, see Leland Ryken, *Words of Delight: A Literary Introduction to the Bible* (Grand Rapids: Baker, 1992), 227ff.

pect information, and, in good journalism, the writer puts the most important information in the first three paragraphs. But newspapers also run letters to the editor. In letters to the editor, you read for the writer's opinion, not news facts. We have no trouble making the switch from news stories to letters to the editor. News stories and letters to the editor are genres, and they make it possible for us to read the newspaper efficiently and accurately.

When you turn on the TV, you find genres too. Two typical TV genres are the sitcom and the news. In a sitcom, you know the characters and their relationships from previous episodes. It does not take long to figure out the conflict or dilemma, such as it is, that forms the mainspring of the plot for the episode you are watching. You know as well that the conflict will be resolved within the half hour of the episode. Even commercials are a genre, triggering recognition of what to expect even if we do not need a new car or "whiter whites." In TV news, you expect to hear short accounts, along with appropriate video, of the day's events. We would like to think we are hearing only the facts of the events reported and do not expect the anchorperson's political views to bias the reporting. We find genres in our everyday lives from TV to newspapers to letters. Even emails, whether they are on the job or private, are a genre, though a recent one. With genre all around us, we should not be surprised to find different genres in literature and the Bible.

How Do We Use Genre in Understanding the Psalms?

The Bible contains a compendium of literary genres.[2] We might think of the Epistles, or letters, in the New Testament as an obvious example of literary genre. Each epistle is written to a particular person (or persons, or even a church) and addresses a particular issue (and often more than one issue). That is, each epistle has a particular

---

2. Again, Ryken is helpful in this regard. His *Words of Delight* provides a useful overview of the various literary genres of the Bible and gives the reader helpful guidance on how to read the Bible with an awareness of literary genres.

context and purpose that we must consider if we expect to interpret it correctly. Paul addresses 1 Corinthians, for instance, to the church at Corinth; in this epistle, Paul seeks to correct error and reprove specific sins among the members of the church. Other New Testament genres include narrative (as in the Acts of the Apostle) and apocalypse (the book of Revelation). In the Old Testament, we find similar genres—narrative in the history books; poetry in the Psalms, Proverbs, Ecclesiastes, and Song of Solomon; and apocalypse in Daniel and Ezekiel. Though this is not a complete list of genres in the Old and New Testaments, these examples serve to illustrate the point that the Bible is written in a variety of literary forms. The important point is that we should not read the different genres of the Bible the same way; we must read poetry differently than we do an epistle and both differently than we do narratives. If we do not read the Bible with an eye to genre, we risk misreading it, perhaps with serious consequences.

Reading the Bible with an understanding of genre will help us avoid misinterpreting what the writer intended to say.

Reading the Bible with an eye to genre will help us interpret the Bible correctly. In the book of Revelation, for instance, we need to distinguish between the genre of the letters in chapters 2 and 3 and the visions of the later chapters. Understanding the apocalyptic genre that John is using in the book of Revelation helps us avoid serious misinterpretation of the symbols in the book. In fact, reading with the apocalyptic genre in mind will give us guidance in deciding which references are symbols and which are not, helping us understand the book as it was intended.

So too in the Psalms, reading with an eye to genre will help us understand and experience what the psalmist—and God—intend. Claus Westermann goes so far as to say that genre is "the first and most important step toward interpreting the Psalms. . . . An individual psalm can be adequately understood only in context—in connection with the group to which it belongs, i.e. by comparing it with psalms of the same genre."[3] Genre is indispensable to appropriate interpretation, particularly in the Psalms, where we have such a variety of backgrounds and where we do not always know the author or historical context of the writing. If we are to interpret correctly what the psalmists say about God, we will need to know the genres of the Psalms.

Genre helps us experience the full intent of a given psalm in another way. Recognizing the particular genre of the psalm we are reading helps us participate actively in the psalm from its earliest verses. For instance, one of the types of psalms is the Hymn. A typical Hymn begins with a call to praise God; the call to praise is followed by a middle section that enumerates reasons to praise God; the Hymn ends with a further call to praise. When you pick up a psalm like Psalm 103, which begins with the liturgical "Praise the LORD, O my soul," you expect a Hymn. What comes next? You know that the reasons for praising God are to follow. Knowing the genre—which we might think of as a "family resemblance" among psalms of the same type—will help us understand the psalm more fully. Genre helps us enter the world of the particular psalm we are reading and gives us a quick understanding of how to approach God in the psalm; in the case of Psalm 103, we are to approach Yahweh with praise. So it is with the other genres of the Psalms; each helps us understand what a particular psalm says about God.

The Genres of the Psalms

In the 150 psalms in the Bible, we find five main genres. These are the Hymn (sometimes called the Psalm of Praise), the Lament, the Royal (or Kingship) Psalm, the Thanksgiving, and the Wisdom Psalm.[4]

---

3. Claus Westermann, *The Psalms: Structure, Content and Message* (Minneapolis: Augsburg, 1980), 29.
4. The commentators on the Psalms do not agree on the number or even the specific genres of the Psalms. The reader should consult the books by Allen, Longman, Ryken, and Westermann listed in the bibliography. The five genres I have chosen seem to reflect the Psalter accurately; they certainly all provide ways of approaching and understanding Yahweh in the Psalms.

Each of these genres has its own structure, and each has its own tone. It is these characteristics—structure and tone—that help us identify which genre a particular psalm belongs to. As you can imagine, the Hymn and the Lament, for instance, display different tones (or attitudes) toward God; in fact, the Hymn and Lament provide the two basic tones in the Psalter—praise and petition. In a Hymn we praise God for who he is and what he has done; in a Lament, we cry to Yahweh in our distress and ask (or petition him) for his help. When we know the genre of a psalm, we can organize our own reading of the psalm accurately and join with the psalmist in the particular approach he takes to Yahweh. The Psalms are organized in different ways and express various attitudes toward God. Genre helps us understand what the psalmist is trying to do and helps us participate with him in the psalm. Let us consider each of the five genres of the Psalms in turn.

The Hymn

In the Hymn, the psalmist lifts his voice in praise to God for who he is and what he has done. Hymns are psalms of worship and praise and, as such, focus our attention on Yahweh himself. These psalms worship God for who he is—the sovereign Lord of the universe—and what he has done—his loving acts on behalf of his people or his sovereign rule over the nations and creation. Hymns are altogether theocentric; that is, they are God-centered. They focus our attention on God in such a way that they encourage us to praise and worship him. In fact, because praise is so clearly the focus of the Hymn, Leland Ryken calls the Hymn a "Psalm of Praise."[5] Ryken's designation of the Hymn as a Psalm of Praise underscores the primary theme of the Hymn and reminds us that our attitude toward God in these psalms is one of adoration.

Hymns are psalms of praise and worship.

---

5. Ryken, *Words of Delight*, 244–50.

Within the general attitude of praise to God in the Psalms, the Hymn focuses on praise, and praise alone. The Hymn offers praise in a formal worship of God. As a psalm of praise and worship, the Hymn glorifies God for who he is and what he has done. As we might expect in psalms so obviously focused on the praise of Yahweh, Hymns have a recognizable structure that sets them apart as a genre in their own right. The structure of the Hymn assists the congregation to praise God and helps the individual to organize her or his praise in private devotion. Hymns contain three sections:

1. Formal call to praise Yahweh
2. Reasons to praise Yahweh
3. Concluding resolution to praise Yahweh

The tripartite structure of Hymns makes them easy to recognize. In the first section, a Hymn establishes a tone of praise and worship; it then goes on in the second section to list reasons for the praise of Yahweh; and it ends in the third section with a renewed call to praise the Lord.

This simple structure, not to mention their focus on praising Yahweh, makes Hymns particularly useful in both corporate worship and private devotion . In Old Testament times, Hymns were a regular part of corporate worship.[6] The Israelites of old sang these psalms of praise during their worship at the temple, and even as they approached the temple, as the Songs of Ascent (Pss. 120–134) suggest. The congregation in Old Testament times, many of whom would not have had a written text in front of them, could recognize a Hymn as soon as the priest began to sing. The call to praise Yahweh that begins a Hymn would help the worshipers put themselves in the proper frame of mind for what was to follow; they could join in the praise of Yahweh, often because they would have memorized the words. In private devotion, believers are able to compose their minds and hearts to praise from

---

6. Ronald Allen, *And I Will Praise Him: A Guide to Worship in the Psalms* (Grand Rapids: Kregel, 1999), 70–72; Tremper Longman, *How to Read the Psalms* (Downers Grove, Ill.: InterVarsity, 1988), 46–49.

the very beginning of the Hymn because it announces its intention so clearly in the opening verses. Whether we are in church or in our prayer closet, Hymns focus our attention on God and help us to offer him the praise he alone deserves.

The Lament

Hymns offer praise to Yahweh; Laments ask Yahweh for help of one kind or another. In the Hymn, the psalmist thinks of God's character and great works and is prompted to praise. In the Lament, the psalmist finds himself in difficulty and turns to God for relief. Enemies may surround and threaten the writer of a Lament (as in Ps. 56), others may falsely accuse him (Ps. 35), or he may need to confess his sin (Ps. 51). In some Laments, the psalmist calls down judgment on his enemies (as in Ps. 59). Whatever the specific situation, Psalms of Lament, by their very nature, acknowledge Yahweh as the only one who can answer the prayer and deliver the writer. In effect, Laments offer praise to Yahweh. As Ronald Allen reminds us, "Perhaps the most important observation you should make in reading these Psalms of Lament is that *finally they too lead to praise*" (emphasis Allen's).[7] In one way or another, all of the Psalms praise Yahweh, even the Laments that call upon him for help. In fact, "the praise of God is the central issue of the book of Psalms."[8] Whether the psalmist asks for forgiveness, praises God in the sanctuary, or asks for God's help in a difficult situation, he is praising God. He praises God by acknowledging that Yahweh alone is worthy of praise or that he alone can answer prayer. The Lament, as well as the Hymn, directs our attention toward Yahweh and acknowledges him to be the sovereign and loving Lord who answers prayer. When we realize that there are more Laments than any other type of psalm, it is helpful to remember that the Psalms of Lament offer praise to God, even if only implicitly; they are as theocentric as the Hymn.

---

7. Ibid., 34.
8. Ibid., 72.

The Psalm of Lament has a more complex structure than the Hymn, and it is written with more parts. There are so many Laments and they address so many different situations that the structure of the Lament may vary from example to example. In fact, the commentators and scholars find no absolute agreement in their analysis of the Lament structure.[9] I would suggest the following structure for the Psalm of Lament because it takes into account the variety of situations we find in Laments:

1. Invocation, or a call to praise Yahweh
2. The lament or complaint
3. Petition or supplication
4. Curse of enemies, or imprecation (in some Laments, not all)
5. Confession of sin (in some Laments, not all)
6. Statement of confidence in Yahweh
7. Vow to praise Yahweh

As this complex structure suggests, the Psalm of Lament begins with an acknowledgment of the importance of Yahweh, for he is addressed and called upon to assist the psalmist. The second and third sections accomplish two ends: they state the psalmist's dilemma or problem, and they tacitly acknowledge that Yahweh alone can meet his need. The final two sections conclude the psalm by recognizing explicitly that Yahweh is sovereign in the difficulty and that he alone can resolve the matter. The sections of imprecation and confession do not appear in every Lament and deserve special comment.

Some Psalms of Lament include a section in which the psalmist confesses his sin to Yahweh and asks for forgiveness. Seven of these Laments focus so exclusively on confession that we call them the

---

9. Ryken offers a five-part structure for the Lament (*Words of Delight,* 239–45); Allen suggests a six-part structure (*And I Will Praise Him,* 34–35); and Longman proposes a seven-part structure (*How to Read the Psalms,* 26–30). For my part, I have followed Ryken's suggestions with some modifications from Longman.

Penitential Psalms (Pss. 6; 32; 38; 51; 102; 130; 143). The Penitential Psalms are a subgenre of the Lament. They are "Laments" because they petition God for help, in this case the forgiveness of acknowledged sin; they are a special type of Lament in that they focus so exclusively on repentance. Tremper Longman suggests that the psalmist may protest his innocence in a Psalm of Lament or confess his sin.[10] It is this latter group, the one in which the writer confesses his sin to Yahweh, that we call the Penitential Psalms. Psalm 51, David's confession of his sins of adultery and murder, is likely the most familiar Penitential Psalm, and we will examine it later in the book.

In some Psalms of Lament, we find the opposite attitude from confession and repentance. Some Laments contain a section of imprecation in which the psalmist calls down curses on his (or God's) enemies. The whole idea of condemning our enemies strikes us as inconsistent with New Testament teaching. As Christians called upon to love our enemies (Matt. 5:43–48), we find the imprecatory sections of the Psalms difficult to understand. Even in the Old Testament, the Israelites are urged to love and forgive (cf. Exod. 23:4–5; Prov. 24:17; 25:21). When Old and New Testaments alike enjoin us to love and forgive, we have to wonder how we are to respond to the attitude of cursing on the psalmist's part. We will save our discussion of the curses and imprecations in the Psalms for chapter 10, for it is an important issue. Suffice it to say here, however, that imprecations are found in the Psalms of Lament where Longman places them.[11]

How do Christians, commanded to love their neighbors as themselves, read the cursing sections of the Psalms?

Apart from those Laments in which we find confession of sin or imprecatory curses, all Psalms of Lament offer a "complaint" to God.

---

10. Longman, *How to Read the Psalms*, 28–29.
11. Ibid., 139.

They are all prayers. As prayers, we find one further distinction in the Laments, just as we do in our own prayers today. Laments can be identified as individual or communal Laments, the prayer of one person or the prayer of a group of people. In the individual Laments, the psalmist voices his own complaint to Yahweh and asks for help in his personal life (e.g., Pss. 57; 64; 77; 86). Tremper Longman calls these Laments "Individual Laments"[12] and Ronald Allen calls them "Laments of the Individual."[13] In other Laments, the psalmist voices the complaint of the congregation or community (e.g., Pss. 74; 80). Longman calls these "National Laments,"[14] and Allen refers to them variously as "Laments of the People" or "Laments of the Community."[15] It is safe to assume that the ancient Israelites used these psalms in their corporate worship. Emphasizing the public use of these psalms in ancient times, these psalms may also be called "Corporate Laments." As Christians today, we can use either the Individual or the Corporate Lament to speak our prayers to God.

The Hymn and the Lament show us the two primary attitudes in the Psalms—praise and prayer. Hymns offer praise to Yahweh for who he is and what he has done. Laments bring us before Yahweh in petition and prayer, asking for his aid. In one sense, all 150 psalms offer either praise or prayer; many do both. Still, we recognize the separate genres of the Hymn and Lament in part by their emphasis on praise or prayer, and in part by their different structures. We need to remind ourselves, however, that both the Hymn and the Lament focus on Yahweh and relate us to him in prayer or praise. In both types of psalms, what we learn about Yahweh and how he relates to us is the most important consideration.

---

12. Ibid., 29.
13. Allen, *And I Will Praise Him*, 34.
14. Longman, *How to Read the Psalms*, 29.
15. Allen, *And I Will Praise Him*, 34.

Other Genres in the Psalms

Apart from the two primary genres of Hymn and Lament, we can identify at least three other genres in the Psalms: the Royal Psalm, the Thanksgiving Psalm, and the Wisdom Psalm. We identify these genres more by their subject matter and theme than by their structures.

As the name implies, Royal Psalms focus on the king and depict him in his splendor and majesty. They show the king's reign and power and are sometimes called Kingship Psalms. Royal Psalms fall into two categories. The first group is the Psalms about the human king of Israel. These psalms often point toward David as the king of Israel, in part because he is so important in Old Testament history, and in part because his is the messianic line leading to Jesus Christ. The second type of Royal Psalm is the psalm that depicts God as King. These psalms point toward Jesus Christ who is the King of Kings and who will one day reign over the earth, and both show that Yahweh is the ultimate and sovereign Ruler of the nations as well as Israel. Claus Westermann characterizes the Royal Psalms as psalms of "exuberant praise" to the king.[16] Royal Psalms include Psalms 2; 20; 21; 45; 72; and 132.

Thanksgiving Psalms are closely related to Hymns in that the primary focus of both is praise. In fact, Westermann regards Psalms of Thanksgiving to be a subtype of the Hymn.[17] In the Hymn, the psalmist worships God for who he is and what he has done. In the Psalm of Thanksgiving, the writer offers gratitude to God for something he has done on his behalf or for his people in general. According to Tremper Longman, Psalms of Thanksgiving are structured much like the Hymn. They begin with an announcement of praise, and sometimes call upon the congregation to join in the thanksgiving; they then list God's acts on behalf of his people and conclude with another call on others to praise Yahweh.[18] With the structure and tone of the Psalm of Thanks-

---

16. Claus Westermann, *Praise and Lament,* trans. Keith R. Crim and Richard N. Soulen (Atlanta: John Knox, 1981), 23.

17. Ibid., 25–30.

18. Longman, *How to Read the Psalms,* 30–31.

giving so close to that of the Hymn, it is easy to see the close connection of the two. However, the Psalm of Thanksgiving may be distinguished from the Hymn because it focuses on particular answers to prayer and thanks Yahweh for them. Psalms of Thanksgiving include Psalms 34; 40; and 69.

Wisdom Psalms also have distinct characteristics that set them apart from the others. While we speak of the wisdom books of the Bible, such as the Psalms, Proverbs, and Ecclesiastes, we will use the term *Wisdom Psalms* to refer to a specific group of psalms that teach us how to live godly lives. These psalms show the sharp contrast between the godly man and the ungodly man. We might think of the Wisdom Psalms as "character sketches" because they present a portrait of the character of the godly man, often in sharp opposition to the ungodly man. Leland Ryken calls this type of portrait "the character"[19] and illustrates it with a description of the ungodly man from Psalm 10:

> He boasts of the cravings of his heart;
>   he blesses the greedy and reviles the LORD.
> In his pride the wicked does not seek him;
>   in all his thoughts there is no room for God.
>
> —verses 3–4

The godly man is shown to have a heart for God and a wish to shun evil, whereas the wicked turn away from God. The contrast of the two is always clear. Wisdom Psalms do not follow a particular structure other than contrasting the two types of people, the godly and ungodly. Typical Wisdom Psalms are Psalms 1; 111; and 112. Psalms 111 and 112 are paired Wisdom Psalms, with Psalm 111 painting a picture of God and Psalm 112 a portrait of the godly man in whom the grace of God is at work. We recognize Wisdom Psalms, then, by the contrast of the wicked and godly and, as Tremper Longman puts it, by the fact that they "reveal God's will in the nitty-gritty and difficult areas of our lives."[20]

---

19. Ryken, *Words of Delight*, 242.
20. Longman, *How to Read the Psalms*, 33.

Some Final Thoughts on Genre

A few words more are necessary before we leave the genres of the Psalms. The psalmists do not always follow the structure of a genre in exact detail. We have already noted that the Lament may or may not contain a section in which the psalmist confesses his sin, or another section in which he curses his enemies, but not all Laments contain these sections. Some Laments are personal; others are for the congregation to sing. Psalms of Thanksgiving sometimes begin much as a Hymn does, inviting the congregation to praise Yahweh. Wisdom Psalms hardly follow any particular pattern, apart from the obvious contrast of the godly and ungodly. Some psalms combine genres, as when a Royal Psalm may sometimes contain elements of praise and worship. Claus Westermann tells us, "In the case of many psalms a clear-cut categorization into one of these genres is impossible because they are composites of mixed genres."[21] In short, we must be flexible as we assign a particular genre to a psalm; psalms simply will not be forced into preconceived molds. Tremper Longman cautions us: "Genres are not written on tablets of stone; they are flexible."[22]

With that said, however, understanding genre in the Psalms is useful in many ways. It helps us enter the world of the psalmist quickly and accurately. When we can recognize a psalm as a Hymn, for instance, we are immediately put in the proper frame of mind and heart to praise Yahweh; when we enter the congregation, a Hymn is one of the best ways to sing praises to God. When we are burdened with problems in our lives, we naturally turn to a Lament to voice our concern to God and to ask for his help. When we see a Royal Psalm that praises the king, we can participate in the psalm because Jesus Christ is our Prophet, Priest, and King. David's reign anticipates Christ's reign. If we think about the blessings that we enjoy every day, we should be encouraged to turn to a Thanksgiving Psalm and rehearse it to God as a prayer of gratitude. Finally, when we need to know God's will, the

---

21. Westermann, *The Psalms*, 27.
22. Longman, *How to Read the Psalms*, 35.

Wisdom Psalms tell us how to live to God's glory. We learn how to respond to God in a variety of ways when we read the different genres of the Psalms, and daily life will show us how important each of these ways of responding to God really is.

Chapter 3

How to Read the Psalms

To get the most from reading the Psalms, we must read them as poetry; this much we have established in the previous chapters. We do a disservice to the inspiration of Scripture if we do not read the books of the Bible according to their genres. Hence, in the Old Testament we need to read Genesis, Exodus, the books of history, and in the New Testament the Gospels and the book of Acts as narratives; we should read the Psalms, Proverbs, Ecclesiastes, and the Song of Solomon as poetry. Reading the Psalms as poetry is the first step toward understanding and experiencing what the psalmists intended, for the Psalms are written in poetry and they are inspired in poetic form. What is more, we will gain a deeper and more accurate appreciation of the character and actions of God in the Psalms if we read them this way. The question remains, however: how do we read the Psalms as poems? This chapter provides a practical guide for reading the Psalms as they were written and seeing how they point to God as their primary subject.

A Fourfold Approach to Reading the Psalms

When we read a psalm, we should approach it with four questions in mind. I prefer to frame this approach to reading the Psalms in the form of questions, not as rules for interpretation. As we have already seen, the Psalms require active, participatory reading. Asking questions of the Psalms as we interpret them will keep us dynamically (or actively) involved in the reading process, which is the way they were meant to be read. There is no magic formula for reading the Psalms, no "how-to" method that will yield automatic results every time. If we take these four questions together, however, we will be going in the right direction.

The Questions

1. What is the overall effect of the psalm?

With the first question, we are asking what experience or experiences the psalm expresses. We are looking for the impression that the psalm gives. Is it joyous and full of praise? Are we drawn upward to contemplate the glories of Yahweh or to worship him? In some psalms, the writers are overwhelmed with the glory and majesty of God; they simply stand in awe of God. In other psalms, we see the opposite emotions. Are we cast down at what appears to be the silence of God, as in the Psalms that ask, "How long, O God?" Are we admonished to examine ourselves? Do we see the wicked prospering and have to curb our jealousy at the sight? Our first question then is "What is the overall impression or effect of the psalm?" To answer this question we should look at the type of subject matter in the psalm and the tone (or attitude) the psalm conveys. Asking a question encourages us to become active readers.

2. What is the structure of the psalm?

This question directs our attention to the macrostructure of the poem and to its parts. We find an answer to this question in the type, or genre, of psalm. Is it a Hymn or a Lament? Is it a Royal or Messianic Psalm? Is it a Wisdom Psalm? While these five types of psalms are not the only genres that scholars have identified, they are the primary genres and will help us understand most of the Psalms. As we have seen in the previous chapter, genre governs the structure of the poem, though structure is by no means absolute in all examples of any one genre. Knowing the structure of the psalm will help us follow the psalmist's thoughts, aiding us in determining transitions and indicating the steps in the psalmist's thought process. Once we know the genre and structure of a psalm, we will have a good idea of what to expect in the psalm. Knowing structure will free us to pay attention to details we might otherwise miss.

3. What are the figures of speech in the psalm, and what effects do they have?

Figures of speech often carry the burden of theology in the Psalms. Some psalms rely on figures of speech more than others do, but most psalms contain some figurative language. Knowing how to read figures of speech is not a matter of guesswork. Rather, knowing the figures of speech in a psalm is a necessary part of understanding what the psalm is saying. The more fully we can interact with the figurative language in a psalm, the more we will understand and experience what the psalmist—and God—intended.

We considered the types of parallelism in chapter 1. Here we suggest that it is best to consider parallelism under this question about figures of speech because it is so closely involved with the particular details of the poem.

4. What are the themes and theology in the psalm?

Once we have considered overall effect, structure, figures of speech, and parallelism, we need to ask about themes and theology. All of the Psalms show us something about God and ourselves; they teach us spiritual truths. The time to ask questions about theme and theology is after we have answered the three other questions. This way we will be less likely to jump to conclusions that may not be warranted in the psalm. In asking questions about theme and theology, we need to pay attention to the experiences expressed in the psalm (overall effect), the development of thought in the psalm (structure), and the details within the psalm (figures of speech and parallelism). The theology of a psalm is expressed in its details and pattern, and we will be wise to take these factors into consideration when we are interpreting a psalm thematically or theologically.

An "Applications" section follows the four questions. How we read a psalm will result in practical spiritual applications in our lives. In our reading, we must never lose sight of God, even though we pay proper attention to the poetic features of the psalm. In fact, reading the Psalms as poetry will lead us to see more of who God is and what he does. In turn, we should apply those lessons to our own Christian lives.

The Four Questions Applied to a Psalm

By way of application, I wish to examine Psalm 97 in the light of these four questions. Because it is short, and it teaches much about the character and actions of God, Psalm 97 will illustrate how we read a psalm effectively.

Psalm 97
LET THE EARTH BE GLAD

¹The LORD reigns, let the earth be glad;
    let the distant shores rejoice.
²Clouds and thick darkness surround him;
    righteousness and justice are the foundation of his throne.
³Fire goes before him
    and consumes his foes on every side.
⁴His lightning lights up the world;
    the earth sees and trembles.
⁵The mountains melt like wax before the LORD,
    before the Lord of all the earth.
⁶The heavens proclaim his righteousness,
    and all the peoples see his glory.

[7]All who worship images are put to shame,
    those who boast in idols—
    worship him, all you gods!
[8]Zion hears and rejoices
    and the villages of Judah are glad
    because of your judgments, O LORD.
[9]For you, O LORD, are the Most High over all the earth;
    you are exalted far above all gods.
[10]Let those who love the LORD hate evil,
    for he guards the lives of his faithful ones
    and delivers them from the hand of the wicked.
[11]Light is shed upon the righteous
    and joy on the upright in heart.
[12]Rejoice in the LORD, you who are righteous,
    and praise his holy name.

What Is the Overall Effect of the Psalm?

Psalm 97 glorifies the name of Yahweh, exalting him as the one true God and Ruler of the nations of the earth. The opening verses show God's sovereign power over the universe. They do so by means of a rapid succession of images taken from nature, the effect of which is to overwhelm the reader with the glory and majesty of Yahweh as the one who rules everything by his power. Though God is the primary subject of Psalm 97, he is not alone in the psalm. Whenever God reveals himself in Scripture, he does so to seek a response from people. In this psalm, people respond in two ways to the sovereign Lord. They either turn from him to make idols, or they rejoice in Yahweh and reap the benefits of his grace. Half the psalm (the first six verses) paints a picture of the sovereign Lord; the other half shows how people respond to him. The psalm moves from the universe as a whole to the worship of God in the congregation of the faithful—from macrocosmic to microcosmic. In both the natural creation and the worship of his people, God is glorified. By moving from God's sovereignty over the earth in the first part of the psalm to his worship in the congregation in the second section, the psalmist puts the reader in a position of choice. We must either reject Yahweh or worship him; there is no middle ground. If we read the psalm with spiritual eyes, we will choose to worship him. Psalm 97 glorifies God and calls us to his worship.

Whenever God reveals himself in Scripture, he does so to seek a response from his people. How do you respond to Psalm 97?

What Is the Structure of the Psalm?

Psalm 97 is a Hymn. More precisely, it is a Hymn of Public Praise that describes the character and actions of Yahweh as the reasons for praising him. As we said in the previous chapter, Hymns typically follow a three-part structure: they begin with a call to praise; they express the reasons why we should praise; and they conclude with an exhortation or resolution to praise God. Psalm 97 follows this typical structure in general, but it does so with what appears to be a minor variation in verse 7. We can outline Psalm 97 as follows.

 I. Verse 1: Call to Praise Yahweh
 II. Verses 2–9: Yahweh's Praiseworthy Attributes and Acts
 III. Verses 10–12: Exhortation to Praise Yahweh in the Sanctuary

We will examine each section of the psalm more closely.

In the call to praise, the psalmist tells us that we should praise Yahweh because he reigns over the whole earth; he is sovereign. The psalmist also encourages everyone throughout the earth to praise God. The reference to the "distant shores" suggests that the psalmist is calling for universal praise from all nations, not just Israel's worship. This conclusion is supported by verse 7, which makes mention of those who do not believe, as well as verses 8–12, which refer to God's people. Though the call to praise is brief, it is universal; everyone is admonished to praise Yahweh. In passing, it is worth noting that the reference to

gladness in verse 1 is paralleled to rejoicing in verse 12: the opening
and closing verses of the psalm are a framing device that begins and
ends the psalm on the same theme.

The middle section, which is the longest in the psalm, lists the reasons why we should praise Yahweh. In verses 2–6, the psalmist paints a
series of pictures (or images) of God's omnipotence and holiness. God's
power finds expression in the natural images of lightning and the
melting mountain, his holiness in the clouds and fire. We should praise
God because he rules the universe with absolute sovereignty and the
nations with justice. After these six verses, however, verse 7 appears to
provide a brief departure from the typical praise pattern, for it introduces the unbelieving pagan who worships idols, not Yahweh. What
place does such a reference have in this section of the psalm that lists
God's character and actions? Verse 7 is a hinge verse, following five
verses that impress us with God's great power and majesty. It suggests
that it should be incomprehensible that anyone would reject God. After
all, look at the litany of great things we have just read about God; how
could anyone not worship him? Verse 7 shows the depravity of the
human heart: even when people are faced with the majesty of God,
some still choose to reject him. The middle section of the psalm concludes by turning our attention from God as the Creator and Ruler of
the earth and the nations to the Lord as the loving God of his people.
Here we see the Lord as a provider for his people and a protector for
them. Even in the list of God's attributes and actions, the psalmist
moves from macrocosmic (the God of the whole earth) to microcosmic (the God of his people). The patterning of the middle section,
along with its message, puts the reader in a position of having to respond to God.

The psalm concludes with an exhortation to praise God in the congregation of the faithful (vv. 10–12). This section shifts the emphasis
from God's sovereignty back to his holiness. By so doing, the psalmist
brings his poem full circle, returning us to the emphasis we saw earlier in the psalm in verses 2 and 3. We should note, however, that the
psalmist is not just repeating himself here for effect. Rather, with this
reference to God's holiness, the psalmist calls on the faithful to be

holy, as God is holy. In other words, the psalmist reminds us of an earlier thought but does so to encourage a response from us. A second effect of the concluding exhortation is a reminder of the blessings the faithful enjoy in worshiping God.

Structured like a typical Praise Psalm, Psalm 97 glorifies God and calls on readers to see him as he really is. The structure moves from macrocosmic to microcosmic in an echo of the basic purpose of the psalm, which is to encourage us to lift our praises to Yahweh.

What Are the Figures of Speech in the Psalm, and What Effects Do They Have?

With this section, we come to the close reading of the psalm that is so necessary to understanding and experiencing what the writer intended. This is the point in our reading when we do the detail work; it is also a rewarding and spiritually encouraging part of the process. Psalm 97 contains many figures of speech and examples of parallelism, all of which are focused on Yahweh.

Throughout the psalm, the psalmist depicts the Lord as a King. He "reigns" (v. 1), he has a throne (v. 2), he is "Most High" (v. 6), and he provides for his people (v. 10). The predominant image in the psalm is this picture of Yahweh as King. Complementing this image of God as a King is a series of other images and parallelisms in verses 2–6 that show God's sovereign power over the earth and its peoples. Likewise, verses 10 and 11 use images and parallelisms to show God's particular care for his people. We will examine the figures of speech in each of the three sections of the psalm and see how they contribute to our understanding of Yahweh.

In the brief first section, the call to praise, the writer uses metonymy and parallelism to exhort his readers to glorify God. With the references to the "earth" and the "distant shores," the psalmist uses metonymies to represent the peoples of the world. We know these are figures of speech because neither the literal earth nor the shores can display emotion of any kind. What the psalmist is suggesting is that the peoples of the earth, and specifically those in distant places, should rejoice in God's sovereign reign. Assisting these metonymies is the synonymous parallelism of verse 1, in which the writer calls on the "earth" in the first colon to rejoice and then parallels the earth with the "distant shores" in the second colon. It is likely that the distant shores represent the Gentile nations; the emphasis at the end of the psalm on the nation of Israel, God's own people, may well indicate that the distant shores in verse 1 refer to the nations of the world at large. In any event, the metonymies and parallelism in the call to praise make it quite clear that all people are to praise the Lord.

The long middle section, which lists God's praiseworthy attributes and actions, contains a number of images and examples of parallelism that underscore God's glory and our need to worship him. The section begins with a compelling series of images that show God's greatness as the Creator and Ruler of the universe. The "clouds and thick darkness" of verse 2 show God's glory by veiling him from us; the implication is that God is too glorious to look at, and he must be separated from us as he was from Moses on Mount Sinai (Exod. 33:21–23). In the same verse, two attributes of God, his righteousness and justice, are depicted as if they were the throne on which he sits. The image suggests that God's rule or reign, as pictured in his throne, reflects his character—as indeed it does. What God does always expresses his character. The three images of the fire, lightning, and melting mountains all show God's awesome power over nature and the nations. The fire likely suggests God's holiness, for it consumes the ungodly who oppose him; the lightning pictures God's power over creation; and the melting mountains attest to God's ability to de-create as well as create. In short, God is sovereign. The writer uses a synthetic parallelism in verse 3, for the second colon extends the thought of fire from the first to judgment on the ungodly of the earth. The image may remind us of Sodom and Gomorrah and the destruction of this earth and heaven in the book of Revelation. In verse 5, the psalmist uses a climactic parallelism; it repeats "before the LORD" but extends

God's power from the mountains to the whole earth. The combined images and parallelisms in these verses give vivid testimony to God's sovereign power over nature and the nations. Dull would the reader be who could read these verses and not be awestruck.

The middle section of the psalm (vv. 2–9) turns on verse 7. Before verse 7, the psalm emphasizes God's power over everything; after the verse, it emphasizes his love for his special people. In verse 7, the psalmist makes the transition between these two aspects of God's reign by using an antithetic parallelism. Notice in the first two cola of the verse that the ungodly worship idols, but that in the last colon of the verse, they are admonished to worship Yahweh. More pointedly yet, the psalmist calls on the idols to worship God! This brief verse shows man's depraved heart. He will not acknowledge God, sometimes even when he is invited to do so. What horror attends this verse!

With verses 8 and 9, the psalmist turns from God as Ruler over all to God as King over his people. Zion and Judah (v. 8) are used as metonymies to represent the whole of God's people. After the reigns of David and Solomon, the nation was divided into two parts—the southern portion (Judah) and the northern portion (Israel). The references to Zion and Judah here are to be seen in contrast to the pagan nations of the world (those "distant shores" of v. 1), not as competing parts of the Jewish nation each seeking God's favor over against the other. Verse 9 uses a climactic parallelism to show God's glory over everything. It begins with Yahweh's control over the earth and extends to his control over even the gods of the pagan nations. We might think of the plagues God brought on Egypt for Pharaoh's refusal to let God's people go. The idea in this verse is that, if even their gods must bow down to Yahweh, how much more will they. The list of God's praiseworthy acts in the middle section of the psalm begins with multiple images and ends with very few figures of speech. As the focus narrows from the universe at the beginning of the section to God's own people at its end, so too God's worthiness becomes increasingly clear.

In the concluding section we do not see many figures of speech. Verse 11 uses the imagery of light upon the righteous as a reference to God's blessing on his people. God is light, and he sheds his light on his people.

The writer omits the verb ("is shed") in the second half of verse 11, for it is understood that joy "is shed" on God's people as well. The omission of the verb makes the verse more concise and requires readers to supply the verb. It is as if we are invited to participate in the light and joy of the faithful by our actively participating in the reading.

As this brief analysis shows, Psalm 97 uses the poetic devices of imagery and parallelism in two ways. First, the figures of speech show God's glory pictorially. Images of fire, lightning, and mountains melting give a visual picture of God's great power over the earth. The image of light and joy shed upon believers shows God's tender love and care for his people. Second, the images and parallelisms in this psalm require active reading. We cannot read the psalm without experiencing something of God's glory and something of the joy it is to be a believer.

What Are the Themes and Theology in the Psalm?

After asking and answering the first three questions,
it becomes readily apparent what the psalm teaches
thematically and theologically.

Psalm 97 teaches two closely related theological truths. First, God reigns. He is the sovereign Lord of the universe whose reign is awesome and holy. Nature trembles before his majesty, and nations will ultimately bow down to him. The second theme of the psalm comes as a direct consequence of the first; we should gladly praise God for his righteous rule. Because of who God is—the sovereign Lord of the universe—and because of what he has done—invited us to love him—we should willingly bow before him. To bow to him is to praise him, and that is what Psalm 97 does. An invitation to public praise, Psalm 97 exalts the Lord.

Applications

1. Because God is sovereign, we can rest assured that he controls everything. He superintends the affairs of nations and is never surprised at the shifting balances of power in the world. He controls the circumstances in our lives—all of them. When we experience difficulty, illness, or sorrow, we can know that God is doing what he is doing for our good as well as his glory. God's sovereignty relates to our everyday lives. We are not in control; God is.

2. God does not wish any to perish in unbelief (2 Peter 3:9). If you have unsaved loved ones and friends, pray for them. Only God can save them, just as he saved you. In Psalm 97, he invites even the idol worshipers to come to him.

3. If you have responded to the gospel of grace by faith in Jesus Christ, you are to grow in grace. God's will for us is our sanctification; he wants us to be holy, as he is holy. Psalm 97 is an encouragement to become more like Christ (Rom. 12:1–2).

4. God wants our praise. He wants us to think about his glory, and when we do, we will be filled with light and joy.

Summary Thoughts

My hope is you will see that this fourfold approach to reading the Psalms is not a literary exercise for people in ivory towers. It is the right way to read the Psalms, and it is infinitely practical. We read the Psalms the right way when we read to find what they say about God, and when we pay enough attention to their poetic qualities to help us understand them correctly. When we pay appropriate attention to the poetic features of the Psalms, as we have done in our analysis of Psalm 97, we read the Psalms the way they were written. Our study of the literary features of Psalm 97 has resulted in some very practical applications of the psalm to our own lives. When we read the Psalms to see what they say about God, we learn about ourselves as well. In Psalm 97, we discover that God's righteous reign over the universe expresses his holiness and sovereignty and that the blessings we enjoy as Christians come from our relationship with God. If God were not sovereign, he could not direct human history for his glory and our good; if he were not sovereign, we could not enjoy the blessings we do. Studying the poetic qualities of the Psalms will teach us about God—and ourselves.

Part Two

God in the
Psalms

Chapter 4

Moses Meets God:
A Pattern for the Psalms

If you are pleased with me, teach me your ways so I may
know you and continue to find favor with you.

—Exodus 33:13

BEFORE WE TURN TO THE PSALMS, we need to know how God reveals himself. If there were an Old Testament passage in which God communicates something about himself and tells us what he is like, such a passage would give us a starting point for seeing God in the Psalms. In this chapter we will look at three times in Moses' life when God reveals explicitly who he is (his attributes) and what he does (his actions). Then we will consider parts of four psalms in which God reveals his characteristics to the psalmists. These references will give us a good idea of what to look for when we read the Psalms.

Moses' Encounters with God

Moses is the author of the Pentateuch in which he recounts the story of creation and begins the story of redemption. Moses meets God on several occasions, beginning with his encounter at the burning bush. At these meetings Yahweh tells Moses about himself and

73

promises that he will be close to Moses just as he had been present with Abraham, Isaac, Jacob, and Joseph in earlier days. Early in the Exodus account, Moses and Aaron meet with the elders of the Israelites in Egypt to tell them that Yahweh has heard their cry for deliverance and will redeem his people; the elders believe the promise and worship God (Exod. 4:29–31). However, after Moses and Aaron visit Pharaoh the first time to ask that their people be freed, Pharaoh responds in anger, forcing the Israelite slaves to gather their own straw and yet not diminishing their quota of bricks. At this point in the narrative, Moses complains to God that he has brought trouble, not redemption, on his people (Exod. 5:22–23). God's response to Moses reveals his grace and sovereignty, two attributes we will find repeated throughout the Old Testament in general and in the Psalms in particular. God says in part to Moses:

> Therefore, say to the Israelites: "I am the LORD, and I will bring you out from under the yoke of the Egyptians. I will free you from being slaves to them, and I will redeem you with an outstretched arm and with mighty acts of judgment. I will take you as my own people, and I will be your God. Then you will know that I am the LORD your God, who brought you out from under the yoke of the Egyptians. And I will bring you to the land I swore with uplifted hand to give to Abraham, to Isaac and to Jacob. I will give it to you as a possession. I am the LORD."
>
> —Exodus 6:6–8

While Moses might have expected an angry response for his complaint, God responds graciously with numerous promises of rescue and redemption. Notice the "I wills" of God's answer to Moses. God promises he will free the Israelites from slavery, redeem them, make them his people, be their God, and give them the land he promised to their fathers. God gives Moses a brief glimpse of himself, emphasizing that he is quick to redeem and provide for his people. Part of God's graciousness to Moses involves his sovereignty over the nations in general and Egypt in particular. If God does not have the power to make things happen the way he wishes, he could not fulfill the promises he makes to Moses in this passage. God's gracious help for his people presumes his sovereignty, or his ability to carry out his promises. How often did Moses need to remember these promises as the people wandered in the wilderness? How often do the psalmists call on God for redemption and provision? Yahweh is sovereign and quick to provide for his people; these are two important characteristics of God in the Psalms.

A second occasion in which God reveals something of himself is his meeting with Moses on Mount Sinai. The attributes that God reveals to Moses in this scene are the same as those he discloses to the psalmists, for God is consistent in his character and in the way he treats his people. One reason the Mount Sinai meeting of Moses and God in Exodus is so important is that Moses asks God directly who he is and what he is like, and in his grace, God answers Moses' question explicitly. In reporting this story under the inspiration of the Holy Spirit, Moses records one of the great self-revelations of God in the Old Testament, parallel in importance to the passage in Deuteronomy in which God tells his people that he alone is God (Deut. 6:4–9).

The scene is the one in which Moses meets with God to receive the second set of tablets with the Ten Commandments (Exod. 33–34). Earlier in the Exodus narrative, Moses had destroyed the first set of tablets in a fit of anger over the people's idolatry in making the golden calf. In chapter 33, God calls Moses back to receive the Ten Commandments again, and Moses stands "face to face" with God and speaks with him (v. 11). During their conversation, Moses asks to know something about Yahweh so that he can tell the people who God is and what he is like. Boldly Moses states: "If you are pleased with me, teach me your ways so I may know you and continue to find favor with you. Remember that this nation is your people" (Exod. 33:13).

In this request, Moses identifies two reasons why he wants God to reveal himself to him. First, Moses wants to "know" God; that is, he wants to have a personal relationship with God, as distinct from the vague sense that the surrounding pagans had of their gods. These nations lived in fear of their gods. Their gods were silent; if the people "heard" from their gods, it was only through the secret mediation of their priests or a belief that every natural disaster was the gods' reaction to their behavior. These pagans lived in ignorance, never knowing whether their gods would be kind or cruel, never certain of their gods' favor or curses. Moses knows Yahweh is not like the gods of the pagans; Yahweh has met with him on numerous occasions, and he has seen his sovereignty, especially in the plagues that fell only on Egypt and not on the Israelites in Goshen. Now he is standing face-to-face with him on Mount Sinai. Still, if he is to communicate God's words to his people, he needs to be able to tell the people who has sent him.

Second, Moses wishes that he and the people might "find favor" in God's sight. When we remember that he has just seen the Israelites fashion the idolatrous golden calf, Moses' wish to find favor with God during this second meeting shows his desire to purify himself of the people's earlier sin. Moses' request to find God's favor underscores his longing to serve him faithfully. Before we leave this verse, we should note that Moses is not suggesting that we can earn God's grace. Far from it; he is asking God to bestow his grace even though the people are sinful. He is asking for mercy.

The third reason Moses gives for why he wishes to know God is so that God's people may be "distinguish[ed]" from all other peoples (v. 16). How can the Israelites show God's glory to a godless world if they do not know who he is and what he is like? Moses wishes God's people, the Israelites, would be a testimony of God's grace to those around them. He wants God's people to be distinct enough from the other nations that they would take note of Yahweh, the one true God. Believers today are to do the same; they are to have a testimony that separates them from the world to such an extent that non-Christians take notice of them. In the New Testament, Peter speaks of "a people belonging to God" (1 Peter 2:9) who are distinct enough to show God's glory. Moses wants to know God and, on the basis of knowing him, to experience his favor. How bold is Moses' request that he should ask such a thing of the sovereign Lord of the universe!

More remarkable than Moses' request that God would reveal himself explicitly to him is the fact that God graciously answers Moses directly. God first establishes his holiness when he separates both Moses and himself from the people by calling Moses to ascend the mountain. No one is to touch the mountain because it is holy (Exod. 34:3). There, on Mount Sinai, Moses listens as God tells him who he is and what he is like. The central statement of God's character is given in chapter 34:

> And he passed in front of Moses, proclaiming, "The LORD, the LORD, the compassionate and gracious God, slow to anger, abounding in love and faithfulness, maintaining love to thousands, and forgiving wickedness, rebellion and sin. Yet he does not leave the guilty unpunished; he punishes the children and their children for the sin of the fathers to the third and fourth generation."
>
> —verses 6–7

*The removal to the mountain is an object
lesson of God's holiness.*

This passage is full of glorious truths about God, only some of which we can consider here. God opens the dialogue with Moses by telling him his name—"the LORD, the LORD." With this name God tells Moses two important truths about himself. First, the name *Yahweh* points to God's eternal existence; he always was and always will be. Second, Yahweh is the name God uses to establish his special relationship with his people, Israel. In effect, the name God uses here, "Yahweh," combines his eternal power with his special love for Israel. Even in his name, God comforts Moses, for his name speaks of his sovereign power on the one hand and his special love for his people on the other. Moses learns all this because God revealed his character to him on Mount Sinai.

It is important for us to note that we, like Moses, must begin with God, not ourselves. As humans we tend to think of ourselves as the center of things. By contrast, God would have us place him at the center of our lives. This is the first lesson Moses learns from God, and we would be wise to learn the lesson with Moses.

What follows God's announcement of his name is a glorious catalog of some of his greatest attributes. First, God is "compassionate and gracious" because he forgives the sins of his people. What an encouragement that the first quality God teaches Moses is his mercy; it is the sinner's first understanding of God's grace. Second, God is "slow to anger"; that is, he is patient and long-suffering. His patience relates to his mercy in that he is not quick to condemn the sinner; he is willing to give adequate time for the sinner to repent. In this regard, we are reminded in the New Testament that God "is patient with [us], not wanting anyone to perish, but everyone to come to repentance" (2 Peter 3:9). Third, God's character overflows with love. This word—*hesed,* or "unfailing love" in the NIV translation—refers to God's special love for his people, and it includes a range of characteristics and attitudes, from forgiveness of sin to provision and protection. We will find God's unfailing love repeated so frequently in the Psalms that it becomes one of the psalmists' great sources of comfort. Fourth, God is faithful. God's faithfulness carries with it the idea of truthfulness. Truth is that which is consistent with a standard. God himself is the standard; he is truth. When he says in his Word that he will do something, we can know that word to be true because it reflects God's righteous and holy character.

We will find ḥesed, *God's loving-kindness for his people,*
to be one of the most important and comforting characteristics
of God in the Psalms.

With the mention of his truthfulness, God's self-revelation takes a significant turn, moving from mercy and love to justice and righteousness. In verse 7, God states that he is just. God's justice is predicated on his righteousness, which Moses realizes when God separates himself and Moses from the people and takes him up the mountain (33:17–34:3). Furthermore, God's justice in no way countermands his compas-

sion and love (34:6). In fact, we will find repeatedly in the Psalms that
God's righteousness provides the only reliable foundation for his mercy.
As Paul affirms in the New Testament, God "demonstrate[s] his justice
at the present time, so as to be just and the one who justifies those who
have faith in Jesus" (Rom. 3:26). God's justice and mercy go hand in
hand. If God were not righteous and true, we could not rely on his promises of mercy and love. How could we know that he would do what he
promised? Righteousness and loving-kindness are inseparable attributes
of God here when he speaks to Moses on Mount Sinai, as they are
throughout the Bible in general and in the Psalms in particular.

In this dialogue with Moses, God reveals his goodness and love on
the one hand and his righteousness on the other. Both of these attributes
are essential characteristics in his dealings with his people. At first reading, we are likely to be encouraged by the reminder of God's mercy and
perhaps a bit frightened at God's righteousness. However, righteousness and mercy complement each other, for God's righteousness guarantees his mercy. Paul teaches the same truth even more explicitly in his
epistle to the Romans, where he states that God justifies the believer and
satisfies his righteousness by pouring out his wrath against sin on his
Son, Jesus Christ, at Calvary (Rom. 3:21–24). God's righteousness, not
just his loving-kindness, finds expression in the gospel of salvation by
grace through faith in Jesus Christ. It is this truth that we must take to
the Psalms if we wish to know Yahweh as he reveals himself there.

Toward the end of his life, Moses shows that he has learned what
God had been teaching him all along. He has followed God out of
Egypt and through the wilderness; the land of promise is before the
Israelites, though Moses will not enter into it. Having seen God's faith-
fulness in every circumstance of his life, Moses pens his beautiful song
in which he says of Yahweh:

> He [Yahweh] is the Rock, his works are perfect,
>   and all his ways are just.
> A faithful God who does no wrong,
>   upright and just is he.
>
> —Deuteronomy 32:4

As so many writers of Scripture do, Moses speaks of God's attributes and actions when he describes what God is like. This reference to Moses' life does not involve a revelation of God to the prophet; rather, it is Moses' final poem about God. In this verse taken from his song, Moses describes God first as the strength and foundation of his people's lives; the image of God as a Rock suggests his power on behalf of those who "stand" on the "Rock." Moses has seen God's power numerous times during the plagues in Egypt and throughout the wilderness wanderings. Now he describes God as the Rock of his people, signifying that God uses that same power on their behalf. To prove his point about God, Moses makes three statements about God's actions and three about his character. God's actions are perfect, just, and right (i.e., he "does no wrong"). God's actions, so described, reflect his character, which is faithful, upright, and just. The point is that God can be trusted. He has the power to carry out his plans; he does what is just and good; and he is always faithful to his people. Moses talked with God on Mount Sinai, and then he walked with God in the wilderness for forty years. At the end of his life, when he reflects on God, Moses remembers his faithfulness, his goodness, and his power.

Taken together, these three incidents in Moses' life reveal a great deal about Yahweh and much that is repeated and emphasized in the Psalms. God tells a discouraged Moses after his first meeting with Pharaoh that he—Yahweh—will faithfully fulfill the promises he had made to Abraham, Isaac, and Jacob: he would be their God and would bring them to the land of promise, just as he said he would. Underlying these promises is God's sovereignty, for he could not fulfill his promises if he did not have the power to do so. The second example, Yahweh's meeting with Moses on Mount Sinai, points to two great pillars of God's character—his righteousness and his unfailing love. The important lessons for Moses in this encounter with God are that God's character is consistent, and his holiness does not abrogate his love. Finally, toward the end of his life Moses' song emphasizes God's faithfulness, goodness, and power. Inherent in all of Moses' encounters with God are two truths that permeate Old and New Testaments alike: God's character is consistent, and he reveals his character in the way he treats his people.

Encounters with God in the Psalms

When we turn to the Psalms, we find that God communicates with the psalmists the same way he does with Moses. The Psalms, however, present human circumstances and situations with much greater variety and depth than Moses' meetings with God do. In fact, one of the main reasons Christians love the Psalms so much is because they hold a mirror up to the human condition we all share. What is more, the Psalms show God's involvement in human lives. We love the Psalms because they are relevant to us; we benefit by reading them because they show us what the Lord is like. In effect, the Psalms show how the character and actions of God are relevant to our lives, just as they were to Moses and the psalmists.

A brief look at four representative psalms will provide some of the typical features of God's character in the Psalms.

Psalm 18 is a glorious Psalm of Praise (or Hymn) to Yahweh that David sang when the Lord had delivered him from his enemies. As such, it is a psalm of private praise that gives thanks to the Lord for his kindness to David as the king. David begins and ends the psalm by noting similar characteristics of God. In this way David frames his praise to God by repeating certain important attributes of God. David praises the Lord for rescuing him from his enemies and showing his special love to him and his descendants. David speaks of God first as a "Rock," or place of refuge, and then as a "shield" of protection against his enemies (v. 2). Both of these images evoke the ideas of strength and invulnerability, characteristics of God the beleaguered David was certain to appreciate. Again at the conclusion of the psalm, David speaks of God as his "Rock" (v. 46) and expresses his gratitude to God for his having delivered him from his enemies (vv. 47–49). Though he does not repeat the image of the shield in the concluding verses, he thanks God for the protection he offers.

The other recurring characteristic of God in Psalm 18 is his unfailing love to his people. David mentions God's love in his references to God's protection of him against his enemies. Why does God favor David and not the other nations? Simply because he loves him. David comments on God's unfailing love in his references to salvation (v. 2), the author-ity God gives him over other nations (vv. 43–45), and most important, in his "unfailing kindness" to "David and his descendants forever" (v. 50). Here in Psalm 18 we see God's love for his people demonstrated in his kindness to them and protection of them. Though an ancient Israel-ite king wrote Psalm 18, it is directly relevant to our lives today. We always need God's kindness, and there are many times—perhaps more than we sometimes realize—that we need his protection.

No mention of God's involvement in the Psalms would be com-plete without Psalm 23, perhaps the best-loved psalm of all. Many Christians have memorized this psalm—and with good reason, for it is full of promises of help based on the character of God. Psalm 23 is another one of David's Hymns, or Psalms of Private Praise to God. Though some people think of the psalm as focusing on the "sheep" (or God's people), Psalm 23 actually focuses primarily on the "shep-herd" (the Lord). In so doing, it enumerates several attributes of God and shows how they relate to believers, especially in times of distress. The psalm begins with Yahweh as a provider and protector. These two ideas are inherent in the image of the shepherd, of course, for the shepherd protects the sheep from danger and leads them to the best pastures. In the same way, the Lord provides for his people by protect-ing them from danger and giving them in abundance what they need (vv. 1–2). The image of the spread table also suggests the ample sup-ply God gives his people (v. 5). In this psalm, God is more than a protector from enemies, however, for he is close to his people when they must face death (v. 4). Just as the Holy Spirit is called in the New Testament the *parakletos,* or "the one who comes alongside," so the Lord in Psalm 23 is close to his people in the hours of darkness and death. What better encouragement can there be than protection from Satan's power over believers in death?

Not only does God supply the needs of this life and protection in death, he guides his people through this life in "paths of righteous-ness" (v. 3). When we read the Psalms and realize how full of signifi-cance the "paths of righteousness" are, we come to appreciate the benefit this guidance is. Living a righteous life is a benefit in itself, but it is also an indication of God's love. Notice too that God leads his people in righteousness not only for their benefit but also for his glory, or, as David puts it, "for his name's sake" (v. 3). We would do well to meditate on the truth that God's glory and our good go hand in hand; when we seek God's glory, we add to our good (though our motive should be God's glory, not our benefit). Finally, Psalm 23 concludes with the promise of eternity with God. In sum, Psalm 23 presents a picture of God's guidance, protection, and provision in this life; his faithfulness in the hour of death; and the promise of an eternity of glory with the Lord. No wonder Psalm 23 has sustained so many believers through the ages. It does so by enumerating the attributes of God and showing how they relate to believers' lives.

Both Psalm 18 and Psalm 23 are Hymns, or Psalms of Praise, in which it is to be expected that the psalmists would seek to glorify God by praising his attributes and actions. What do we find when we turn to a Psalm of Lament, where we might expect the writer who is in a difficult situation to be less inclined to offer praise to God? There are more Psalms of Lament than there are Hymns. Do the writers of the Laments refer to God the same ways the writers of the Psalms of Praise do? Or do they concentrate on their own predicaments and not acknowledge the Lord? In fact, the writers of the Psalms of Lament always turn to God's attributes and actions as the answer to their dilemmas.

Psalm 89 is a Psalm of Lament in which the psalmist, in this case Ethan, still finds reason to praise Yahweh for his goodness to him. Ethan's complaint (simply another word for "lament") comes because he has been attacked on all sides and apparently is deserted by God (see vv. 38–51). Characteristic of a Lament in which the psalmist fears that the Lord has forsaken him is the rhetorical question, "How long, O LORD? Will you hide yourself forever?" (v. 46). Though the psalmist knows that God has not deserted him, in fact it feels at times as if he has. A careful reading of Psalm 89, however, shows that, even though Ethan is in distress and complains to God about his situation, he praises God far more than he complains.

Ethan praises Yahweh in Psalm 89 for at least six reasons. First, Ethan praises God for his love. He begins his psalm with the words, "I will sing of the LORD's great love forever" (v. 1). Frequently throughout the psalm, he returns to the theme of God's love for him. Consider some of the many references to God's love in the psalm. Ethan says that he will "declare" God's love (v. 2), that love is the "foundation" of God's throne (v. 14), and that God's love for his people will not be taken away from them (v. 33). Finally, he calls on God at the end of the psalm to restore his "former love" (v. 49) and rescue him. Though he complains to God about his distress, Ethan has the confidence that God loves him, and that he does so eternally. The second great theme of the psalm is God's faithfulness to his people. Again, in the opening verse, Ethan announces, "I will make your faithfulness known through all generations" (v. 1). Like the theme of love, the emphasis on God's faithfulness permeates the psalm. God establishes his faithfulness "in heaven itself" (v. 2); faithfulness "surrounds" him as one of his primary attributes (v. 8); God's faithfulness never ends (v. 33); and God's faithfulness is based on his promises to David. Even in this Lament, Ethan celebrates God's eternal love and faithfulness.

If God's love and faithfulness are not enough, Ethan mentions four more reasons why he praises Yahweh. He thanks God for the covenant he makes and keeps with his people. While the psalmist mentions various aspects of God's covenant in the psalm, he emphasizes especially God's promises to David, commenting particularly on his protection of David and his "faithful love" for him (vv. 20–24, 49–51). The fourth reason Ethan praises God in this Lament is his sovereign control over the nations (v. 10) and nature (vv. 5, 9, 11–13). As we noted earlier, God's sovereignty over everything guarantees that, when he says he will protect his people and be faithful to them, he will do so; if he were not sovereign, he could not fulfill his promises. The fifth reason for praise in this psalm is God's righteousness; Ethan states that God's throne is established in righteousness (v. 14) and that God's righteousness encourages God's people in their daily lives (v. 16). Finally, Ethan praises Yahweh for his holiness. Holiness is an important attribute of God, one that is often minimized today. However, Ethan makes it clear that God's rule as King over Israel is grounded in his holiness (v. 18) and that God's holiness guarantees that he will fulfill his promises to David (v. 35). We will find comfort in God's holiness many times in the Psalms.

Psalm 89, a Psalm of Lament, provides great encouragement to its readers. Though the psalmist feels as if God has deserted him, he fills the psalm with many reasons to praise God. If we are honest, we sometimes feel as if God has deserted us too. Perhaps an unexpected car accident that leaves a loved one seriously injured, the death of one of God's faithful servants, or even falling into sin can cause us to wonder "where" God is. Rather than indulging in self-pity as we are sometimes tempted to do, we should turn to the Psalms of Lament and, with the psalmists, work out an understanding of how much God loves us even when we do not feel as if he does.

Psalm 104 is one of a handful of Creation Psalms. These psalms offer praise to Yahweh specifically for what the creation teaches about the Creator. Because people (even Christians) take the creation for granted every day, it is easy for them to overlook the importance of praising God for his creation. Simply put, there is God and everything else (which we might call "non-God"). God is distinct from his creation, and everything that is not God is created. Even if Jesus Christ had not come to save us from our sins, we still would owe our lives to God because he made us. The Creation Psalms focus on these great truths.

Psalm 104 is an exalted psalm of praise to God for his work in creation and his sustaining power in the world. Consider just one of the truths the psalm teaches about God as Creator:

> He makes grass grow for the cattle,
>   and plants for man to cultivate—
> bringing forth food from the earth:
>   wine that gladdens the heart of man,
> oil to make his face shine,
>   and bread that sustains his heart.
>
> —verses 14–15

It is obvious that these verses celebrate God's provision of food for the people of the earth. However, these verses do more than this: they paint a picture of abundance. The psalmist states that God provides food for people, but then he adds two details to show how generous God is when he meets man's needs. These are the wine that "gladdens" man's heart and the oil that "makes his face shine." God meant for humans to enjoy the food he provides, and the great variety of foods and drink there are testifies to what we call God's "omnificence"—or his overflowing bounty in creation. One of the characteristics of God is that he teems with life, and he demonstrates this aspect of his character in the creation. When we bow our heads before a meal to thank the Lord for it, we give testimony to two of God's great characteristics—his omnificence and his faithfulness.

The brief references to these four psalms—18; 23; 89; and 104—give some idea of the many characteristics of God that the Psalms enumerate. It is true that we find our own emotions and thoughts expressed in the Psalms, and that the Psalms mirror an almost limitless variety of human experiences. Quite often, it is our human hurts and sorrows that send us to the Psalms for comfort. What we see of ourselves in the Psalms is important, for it is inspired by the Holy Spirit. However, it is equally true that the Psalms reveal much about God. If we wish to understand and appreciate the Psalms correctly, we will need to look for what they teach about God for, as we have seen in these few examples in this chapter, God meets the deepest needs of the human soul in every experience of life.

As we read the Psalms, we will find that all of these
attributes of Yahweh meet the deepest needs of our daily lives,
delight our souls, and satisfy us forever.

Chapter 5

The Heavens Declare His Glory: God as Creator

In the beginning God created the heavens and the earth.
—Genesis 1:1

FOR THE FIRST THEME IN THE PSALMS, we begin at the beginning. The opening chapters of Genesis boldly affirm that God created everything that exists; he created physical matter out of nothing and formed it into the orderly creation that we see around us every day. With these simple statements, we have the beginnings of a Christian worldview. The Christian view of things differs radically from the modern scientific view of the world. The modern secular opinion holds that physical matter always existed, and that matter is all that exists. This view of things is called "philosophical materialism." Materialism is essentially an atheistic view of things in that it discounts the existence of a deity outside of matter; in this sense it is a thoroughly secular view of the universe. Contrary to this materialist view, the Bible states explicitly in the opening chapters of Genesis that only God, not physical matter, has existed forever and that God created matter out of nothing. Of course the opening chapters of Genesis are not the only place the Bible speaks of God as Creator; the Bible ends in the book of Revelation with an account of God's creation of a new heaven and a new earth.

The Bible begins with the creation of this universe and concludes with a new creation. Between Genesis and Revelation, the Bible makes many references to creation. God's work as Creator is one of the most important and often-repeated themes of the whole Bible, Old and New Testaments alike.

> *If we have eyes to see and ears to hear,*
> *the whole cosmos gives testimony to the glory and splendor*
> *of Yahweh who created it all out of nothing.*

An example of an Old Testament reference to God as Creator can be found in the book of Job. After Job loses his children, his possessions, and his health, he suffers in silence while his friends tell him that his sin is the cause of his suffering. However, before the end of the book, Job breaks his silence; he criticizes God for dealing "unjustly" with him (chaps. 23; 24; 31), and he even asks for death (10:1). When God responds to Job to teach him what he needs to know, what does God say? He tells Job in four exalted chapters of Scripture (chaps. 38–41) that he—Yahweh—created everything and that he rules it all justly and righteously. Job is silenced. When God teaches Job how to handle his great suffering, he refers to his own creative act. Why? God begins with creation because, if God is sovereign over the whole of creation, he is surely sovereign over Job's life. Can we not trust such a God, who created and sustains all things, with our lives? If he controls all of the cosmos, and if he orders everything on this planet, does he not have our concerns under control? God does not teach Job an easy lesson. No doubt the most difficult time to trust God is when we are suffering and we do not know why. It is at these times, however, that we most need to remember that God is sovereign, and he controls all things.

In the New Testament, the apostle Paul stands before the intellectual elite of Athens and preaches creation and redemption. On the Areopagus, or Mars Hill, where the free citizens of Athens met daily to debate, Paul testifies to the gospel of Christ by asserting that God made the world and rules all the nations in it. Paul tells the Athenians that

God was now calling on them to repent (Acts 17:24–31). Paul begins with God as Creator to testify to the saving power of the gospel of Jesus Christ; Job needed to hear about God as Creator so he could bear his sufferings. The Bible reminds us frequently of this great truth.

The psalms make numerous references to God's creative work. The psalmists thought often about God's work as Creator. So did the pagans around them. Every ancient culture had its myth of the creation of things, and, in every ancient myth, one of the multiple gods was the creator. From the Babylonian *Gilgamesh,* to the Assyrian *Enuma Elish,* to the Greek Hesiod's account, all the nations surrounding Israel believed in a divine presence in creation; so did the ancient Oriental people. They were all polytheistic, and they all thought that there was a nature god who inhabited the nature he (or she, as the case may be) created. The psalmists, who were monotheistic, had good reason to write often of God's work as Creator; they had a testimony to the one true God of the universe, a witness to Yahweh, they had to maintain.

The Judeo-Christian belief differs from the pagan myths in many ways, but one of the most important distinctions is that, in Judeo-Christian belief, God does not inhabit nature. In the Bible, God is transcendent; that is, he is high above creation and not found within the creation he made. This is why Robert Alter can say there is no true "nature poetry" in the Psalms; for the Hebrews of old, there was no deity in nature to worship. They worshiped the Creator who stood apart from his creation. Alter captures the essence of the Hebrew Psalms that celebrate the Creator:

> There is no real nature poetry in the Psalms, because there is in the psalmist's view no independent realm of nature, but there is creation poetry, which is to say, evocations of the natural world as the embodiment of the Creator's ordering power and quickening presence.[1]

---

1. Robert Alter, *The Art of Biblical Poetry* (New York: Basic Books, 1985), 117.

The psalmists celebrate God, not nature. When they refer to natural things—and they do so frequently—they seek to glorify Yahweh who made nature, not nature itself. There are a few psalms that concentrate primarily on God as Creator, among them Psalms 8; 19 (the first six verses); 97; 104; and 148. Let us consider two of these psalms, beginning with Psalm 19.

The psalmists do not worship nature; rather,
they show nature to be a reason to worship Yahweh.

Psalm 19
GOD'S TWO BOOKS

In Psalm 19, David praises God for two of the ways he reveals himself to mankind. First, David rejoices in the self-revelation of God in creation (vv. 1–6); then he glorifies God for his self-revelation in the words of the Scripture (vv. 7–11). In the Middle Ages and Renaissance, Christians spoke of these two self-revelations of God as two "books." For these earlier Christians, the first book was nature, the second Scripture. Of course, the Bible is literally a book, God's Word, in which he tells the story of redemption in Jesus Christ. The idea of nature, or creation, being a "book" is a metaphor; it suggests that God communicates something of himself to us even in creation, something we can "read." The medieval image of nature as a book is similar to David's meditation in Psalm 19; it teaches that God reveals himself to us in nature as well as in the Bible.

> [1]The heavens declare the glory of God;
>   the skies proclaim the work of his hands.
> [2]Day after day they pour forth speech;
>   night after night they display knowledge.
> [3]There is no speech or language
>   where their voice is not heard.

⁴Their voice goes out into all the earth,
  their words to the ends of the world.

 In the heavens he has pitched a tent for the sun,
  ⁵which is like a bridegroom coming forth from his pavilion,
  like a champion rejoicing to run his course.
⁶It rises at one end of the heavens
  and makes its circuit to the other;
  nothing is hidden from its heat.

⁷The law of the LORD is perfect,
  reviving the soul.
The statutes of the LORD are trustworthy,
  making wise the simple.
⁸The precepts of the LORD are right,
  giving joy to the heart.
The commands of the LORD are radiant,
  giving light to the eyes.
⁹The fear of the LORD is pure,
  enduring forever.
The ordinances of the LORD are sure
  and altogether righteous.
¹⁰They are more precious than gold,
  than much pure gold;
  they are sweeter than honey,
  than honey from the comb.
¹¹By them is your servant warned;
  in keeping them there is great reward.

¹²Who can discern his errors?
  Forgive my hidden faults.
¹³Keep your servant also from willful sins;
  may they not rule over me.
Then will I be blameless,
  innocent of great transgression.

[14]May the words of my mouth and the meditation of my heart
  be pleasing in your sight,
O LORD, my Rock and my Redeemer.

What Is the Overall Effect of the Psalm?

The overall effect of Psalm 19 is tied very closely to its structure. The two are so closely related, in fact, that we will have to note the macrostructure of the psalm in order to comment on its general impression. The psalm contains three main sections: verses 1–6 speak of nature; verses 7–11 comment on the Word of God; and verses 12–14 provide a personal meditation on the part of the psalmist. All three sections emphasize the glory of God and invite us to acknowledge his majesty.

When we reflect on the cosmos, we should bow in adoration before God's great power. Consider a few facts. The sun has a diameter of 1,392,000 kilometers, or 865,000 miles.[2] The sun has "a volume over one million times that of Earth."[3] Its surface temperature is 5500 degrees Celsius,[4] and only one billionth of its energy reaches our planet.[5] As if this is not staggering enough, remember that the sun is only one of 100,000 million stars in the Milky Way, which in turn is only one of the many galaxies in space.[6] Consider a fact closer to home, a detail that makes the difference between life and death for us. If gravity were altered by "a mere one part in 10^{40}, stars like the sun would not exist, nor, one might argue, would any form of life that depends on solar-type stars for its sustenance."[7] Our very existence would cease if an arbitrary and infinitesimal change in the pull of gravity occurred. When

2. *The Scientific American Science Desk Reference* (New York: John Wiley & Sons, 1999), 174.

3. John Blanchard, *Does God Believe in Atheists?* (Auburn, Mass.: Evangelical Press, USA, 2000), 244.

4. *Scientific American Science Desk Reference,* 174.

5. Blanchard, *Does God Believe in Atheists?* 244.

6. Ibid., 245.

7. Paul Davies, *God and New Physics* (New York: Simon & Schuster Touchstone Books, 1984), 188.

David speaks of God's glory, he is speaking in an understatement. The world is filled with scientific books that cannot explain all of God's glory revealed in the heavens. By faith, however, we can accept that only God is capable of creating and sustaining such a marvelous universe and we can worship him for his wonderful creation.

John Milton saw the Creator's hand in the heavens. In book 5 of his great epic, *Paradise Lost,* he devotes a long section to God's creation of the world. Though Milton did not hold an orthodox view of creation in every respect, he did understand that God communicates something of his glory in his creation. When he begins to write of the creation of the heavens and earth, Milton states:

> These are thy glorious works, Parent of good,
> Almighty, thine this universal Frame,
> Thus wondrous fair; thyself how wondrous then!
> Unspeakable, who sit'st above these Heavens
> To us invisible or dimly seen
> In these thy lowest works, yet these declare
> Thy goodness beyond thought, and Power Divine.[8]
> —Lines 153–59

In this little doxology, Milton acknowledges that God is unutterably majestic, yet he chooses to reveal something of his glory in creation, his "lowest works." If we have eyes to see, we will recognize the Creator in his creation.

When we turn to inspired Scripture and think the way David and the other inspired psalmists of old thought, we should expect to see something of God's awesome power when we look toward the heavens. In the New Testament, Paul makes the same point David does in the Old Testament. Paul warns unbelievers about their lack of faith when he writes,

---

8. John Milton, "Paradise Lost," in *John Milton: Complete Poems and Major Prose* (New York: Odyssey, 1957), 306.

The wrath of God is being revealed from heaven against all the godlessness and wickedness of men who suppress the truth by their wickedness, since what may be known about God is plain to them, because God has made it plain to them. For since the creation of the world God's invisible qualities—his eternal power and divine nature—have been clearly seen, being understood from what has been made, so that men are without excuse.

—Romans 1:18–20

Paul makes two points here. The first is that God has indeed revealed himself in nature to everyone; he has shown us his "eternal power and divine nature" in creation. Paul and David both insist that God reveals something of himself in nature. Paul's second point in this passage is that, because God has revealed himself in nature, no one has an excuse for lack of faith. Paul's statement is a warning to unbelievers that they cannot say they did not know anything about God. The problem is not with God, who has revealed himself in nature. The problem lies with unbelievers who "suppress the truth" and choose not to see God in creation. Before we leave Paul's comments, we should understand them as Paul meant them. God's warning to unbelievers here is not harsh and unkind; it is an example of God's general grace that he gives witness to himself every time we open our eyes or ears. Simply by living in this world we should acknowledge God as the great Creator; nature shows us his glory.

When I read the opening verses of Psalm 19, I think of a poem by Gerard Manley Hopkins, "God's Grandeur." Hopkins begins:

> The world is charged with the grandeur of God.
>   It will flame out, like shining from shook foil;
>   It gathers to a greatness, like the ooze of oil
> Crushed.[9]

---

9. Gerard Manley Hopkins, "God's Grandeur," in *The Poems of Gerard Manley Hopkins,* 4th ed., ed. W. H. Gardner and N. H. MacKenzie (Oxford: Oxford University Press, 1967), 66.

Hopkins makes the same point that David and Paul do: nature communicates God's grandeur. Like electricity, Hopkins suggests in a simile, the world is powerfully charged with God's grandeur, ready to be expressed. Hopkins's second simile is that of aluminum foil shaken in the sunlight, reflecting the sun's rays in every direction. So it is with nature: everywhere you look you see God's glory reflected. The third simile compares God's grandeur to oil. When an olive is crushed, it is not destroyed in the sense that it simply produces oil. So too God's grandeur; it cannot be destroyed. Hopkins understands what David is saying in Psalm 19: no matter what we do, we cannot avoid God's self-revelation in nature. God reveals his grandeur everywhere. If we see things correctly, we will know that we were meant to glorify God even when we look at the world around us.

Turning from the cosmos to the Word of God, Psalm 19 extends God's glory by showing it to be reflected in the Bible as well as in nature. In rapid-fire in verses 7–9, David teaches us six truths about Scripture using brief statements of fact. Rather than using poetic imagery and figures of speech, David gives us propositional (or logical) statements about the Bible; he presents a series of six truths about the Bible in simple declarative sentences. The difference between verses 1–6, spoken almost entirely in figurative language, and verses 7–9, spoken in propositional statements, could not be more pronounced. We can learn something about God in nature, to be sure, but the Bible tells us explicitly about God. The Bible is the more complete and explicit revelation of the two. The psalm concludes with David's request of God that he might show God's glory in his thoughts and words.

Whether it speaks of nature or the Word of God, Psalm 19 declares the incomparable glory of Yahweh. God's glory is so far from being an academic subject for scholars and preachers alone that David applies it to himself personally by asking God to purify him and use him to his glory.

What Is the Structure of the Psalm?

As we suggested in the comments on overall effect, the structure of Psalm 19 is an important part of the way the psalm works. Psalm 19 is a Hymn, or a Psalm of Praise, to Yahweh. Hymns typically have three parts in their structure, but Psalm 19 does not follow the pattern of most Hymns exactly. Such slight variations in structure are not uncommon in the Psalms. Psalm 19 can be outlined in the following manner:

I. Verses 1–6:   Yahweh's Self-Revelation in Nature
II. Verses 7–11:   Yahweh's Self-Revelation in Scripture
III. Verses 12–14:   Concluding Resolution to Praise Yahweh

Most Hymns or Psalms of Praise begin with an introduction that contains a "Call to Praise"[10] or "An Imperative to Praise Yahweh."[11] This psalm, however, contains no such opening invitation to praise God, at least not explicitly. It may be, however, that verse 1 with its declaration of God's glory is an implicit call to those who hear the psalm to praise God too. If this is the case, the opening verse of the psalm serves as the invitation to praise the Lord. Whether the first verse serves this purpose or not, the three concluding verses certainly call on us to praise God. Though Psalm 19 does not fit the Hymn structure perfectly, it is still patterned in the typical three parts, all focused on God's praise.

What Are the Figures of Speech in the Psalm, and What Effects Do They Have?

As we saw in the structure of Psalm 19, David offers praise to God on two counts—God's majestic creation and the incomparable Scripture he inspired. In the four opening verses of the psalm, David personifies the heavens, depicting them as if they had a voice to speak God's praise. It is as if the heavens were like humans with an ability to speak and they used that ability to acknowledge the glory of God.

---

10. Leland Ryken, *Words of Delight: A Literary Introduction to the Bible* (Grand Rapids: Baker, 1992), 245.

11. Ronald Allen, *And I Will Praise Him: A Guide to Worship in the Psalms* (Grand Rapids: Kregel, 1999), 31.

Notice the different words in the opening verses that suggest nature speaks of God—*declaring, proclaiming,* and *voice.* The personification here suggests that the heavens were made with the express purpose of glorifying God, as if they could speak this truth as humans can (and should). Though the heavens do not literally speak God's praise, we should see God's glory when we ponder the cosmos. Even though the creation is silent, it still reveals God, if we only have the "eyes" to see it. If the heavens "speak" God's glory, how much more ought we, believers created in God's image and redeemed by his grace, give testimony to God's glory in our lives.

Notice David's careful patterning of these four verses. Verse 1 tells us that God's glory is everywhere and in all places; verse 2 tells us that God's glory is in nature at all times, or, as the psalmist pictures it in this verse, day and night. Today we might say that God's glory in nature is shown "24/7." Verses 3 and 4 form an antithetic parallelism, telling us the same truth negatively and then positively. Verse 3 tells us there is nothing that does not declare the glory of God (a "negative" statement), and verse 4 tells us that everything does declare the glory of God (a "positive" statement). The repetition of the same idea in negative and positive forms serves to emphasize the truth being taught; it is a technique employed in other psalms as well. Verses 1–4 make it abundantly clear that nature shows God's glory to those who will look for it. Implicit in these verses is the exhortation to us to praise God as nature does.

Finally, in the section of God's self-revelation in nature is a series of images in verses 4–6 that show God's beauty and power. David uses imagery in these three verses to communicate something about God in a way that we all can appreciate. The first image is the picture of God making the heavens a tent for the sun (v. 14). There are two important points about this poetic image. First, God is not to be identified with the sun, as many of the pagan nations surrounding Israel thought. Second, God is much greater than the sun. After all, he made the sun and its "tent," the heavens; he must be greater than the sun gods of the pagan nations. This image would have a particularly marked effect on the pagan nations of Old Testament times whose gods were sun gods, Egypt being among the most notable. Yahweh controls the sun, whereas the idols of the pagan nations cannot even speak or hear. What a contrast! The next two images of God are those of the bridegroom and champion. The image of the bridegroom, so well known to Christians from Paul's use of it in the fifth chapter of Ephesians, suggests the splendor and beauty of God, just as a bridegroom appears his best on his wedding day. The picture of God as a champion suggests his great strength and power. Taken together, the two images show that God's splendor is expressed in the heavens, yet God is much greater than his creation. As in all effective poetic language, the poet says much in a few words, showing us in these two images how glorious God is.

The opening section of Psalm 19 reminds us that we were created to glorify God. If even the silent creation around us speaks of God's glory, how much more ought we to do so, we who have been redeemed and can give testimony to God's saving grace in Jesus Christ? We alone of all creation can declare God's glory and grace; we alone can put words to his mercy. How quick are we to mention God's grace in our lives? How faithful are we? Are we effective ambassadors for Christ? Are our lives distinct enough from the unsaved around us that they notice Jesus Christ in our lives? Peter tells us we ought to live this way (1 Peter 2:9).

If the heavens "speak" God's glory, how much more ought we,
believers created in God's image and redeemed by his grace,
give testimony to God's glory in our lives?

Having shown how the silent creation tells of God's glory, David turns next to God's self-revelation in the words of Scripture. Whereas verses 1–6 turn the reader's attention to the skies, verses 7–11 focus on the Bible. The Bible reveals the glory of God in even greater detail than nature. Nature displays the divinity of its Creator and his great power. The Bible on the other hand teaches that God, who knew when he created Adam and Eve that they would sin, still provides forgiveness and reconciliation with himself through Jesus Christ. Nature teaches a little bit about God; the Bible teaches much more about God and, what is more, how human beings relate to him. The Bible tells us about ourselves as well as about God.

Avoiding images and other figures of speech in the second section of his poem, David makes six propositional statements about the Word of God in parallel form. Helpful in understanding what David is doing in these verses are Leland Ryken's comments in *Words of Delight*. Ryken states that David first ascribes a title to the Word of God, then he names a quality of the Word, and finally, he cites an effect of the Word of God. Following Ryken's lead, these verses can be understood according to the following chart.[12]

Verse	Title	Quality	Effect
7a	the law of the LORD	perfect	reviving the soul
7b	the statutes of the LORD	trustworthy	giving wisdom
8a	precepts of the LORD	right	giving joy to the heart
8b	commands of the LORD	radiant	enlightening the eyes
9a	fear of the LORD	pure	lasting eternally
9b	ordinances of the LORD	sure	making righteous

David makes six assertions, in each case using synthetic parallelism to state and expand the point. Taken together, these six points help us understand God's self-revelation in Scripture.

David's first point, stated in the first half of verse 7, goes right to the heart of what God reveals in the Bible but not in nature. He states

12. Ryken, *Words of Delight*, 195.

that the Bible ("the law of the LORD") is all that we need ("perfect") to understand salvation ("reviving the soul"). Only the Bible tells how people can be redeemed and restored to a right relationship with God. Nature cannot teach truths about redemption; only the Bible teaches about sin and salvation. With the first half of verse 7, David turns our attention from the glories of God in nature to his marvelous grace in our souls. In the parallel second half of the verse, David makes his second point about the Bible. He reiterates the spiritual dimension to the Bible, this time stating even more explicitly that the Bible gives us the spiritual wisdom that we cannot find in ourselves. With these two statements, the psalmist shows how God's glory is understood more completely in the Bible than it is in nature. Nature teaches of God's greatness, the Bible of his righteousness, love, and mercy. With this switch, the psalm moves from the heavens to a human soul, the macrocosmic to the microcosmic.

David's third and fourth points about the Bible, found in verse 8, extend his comments on the importance of the Bible even further. The third point is that the Word of God (here called "precepts") reflects the character of God, thereby bringing spiritual joy to the soul. The idea of "right" is that the Word of God is "straight" in that it accurately reflects its originator (God). It is therefore trustworthy. In the second half of the verse, David parallels this reference to the heart with the statement that the Bible "giv[es] light to the eyes" or mind. The Bible provides pure moral guidance; it speaks God's mind about what is right and wrong. Verse 8 teaches that the Bible encourages the heart in God's good will and helps the mind understand biblical morality.

By reemphasizing the purity and righteousness of God's character as revealed in Scripture, verse 9 teaches in yet another way that the Bible reveals God's character. We do not read the Bible simply to increase our knowledge (even if it is knowledge about God) for purely academic purposes. We read the Bible to apply its truths to our lives and thereby grow in grace. When we apply the teachings of the Word of God to our lives, we honor the Lord.

What does the Bible teach that nature does not? David's teaching, under the inspiration of the Holy Spirit, is unmistakable on this point.

The Bible teaches about salvation, sanctification, and glorification. Verse 7a teaches about salvation, or redemption; verse 7b teaches of sanctification, or spiritual growth; and verse 9a teaches about glorification, or our eternity with the Lord. Nature displays something of God's great glory, but the Bible teaches explicitly that we can know God in Jesus Christ and be reconciled to him by grace through faith. Nature shows that God has a witness of himself to all people; the Bible tells of God's grace in Jesus Christ.

In verses 10–12, David again uses figures of speech to show God's glory. David compares the Word of God to gold and honey, in both cases stating that he values the Word of God more than either of these precious things. Notice the climactic parallelisms in both verses. In verse 10, David states that the Word of God is "more precious than gold" and then extends his statement by adding the qualifier "much pure gold"; in the psalmist's view, gold—even a great deal of the best gold—cannot compare to the Word of God. In verse 11, the same type of climactic parallelism, this time using honey as the point of comparison, shows the incomparable value of the Word of God.

Carefully employing a series of personifications from nature in verses 1–6, David shows the glory of God in creation. God created everything, and he rules sovereignly over it all. Turning from personifications to propositional statements in parallel form, the psalmist speaks in verses 7–10 of how God shows his glory by providing his Word. To round out the section on the Word of God, David returns to the use of figures of speech to suggest how valuable the Word of God is for him: it is life to his soul. It is important that David shifts from figures of speech when he speaks of nature to propositional statements when he first speaks of the Word of God. With this shift, David suggests that, while nature displays something of God, the Bible teaches explicitly about God. The themes of the psalm focus on these ideas.

What Are the Themes and Theology in the Psalm?

The theology of Psalm 19 is so closely related to its structure and its figures of speech that we have already mentioned much of what the psalm teaches. The first two sections of the psalm focus intensely and exclusively on God's glory, praising God for who he is and what he has done. Specifically, Psalm 19 teaches that God created everything that exists and that he did so to show his glory to human beings. Think of it: all of nature is a testimony to the power of God. The stars in the night sky and the sun in the day sky are "books" that speak God's glory, for this is one reason they were made. The majesty of the heavens suggests the even greater majesty of the one who made them. The stars are not just beautiful in themselves; they are beautiful so they can demonstrate how glorious God, their Creator, is. In the second section of the psalm, David teaches three important aspects of what Yahweh has done in providing his Word. In Scripture we learn that God justifies, sanctifies, and glorifies. That is, God saves his people (justification), sets them aside as vessels fit for the Master's use (sanctification), and then takes them to heaven to live with him forever (glorification). Nature cannot teach these three truths; it takes the special revelation from God in the Bible to teach these spiritual truths. How could God do any more?

Isaac Watts, the great eighteenth-century English hymn writer, reflects on the truths of Psalm 19 in his hymn, "The Heavens Declare Your Glory, Lord." Meditating on Psalm 19, Watts writes:

> The heavens declare your glory, Lord;
> in every star your wisdom shines;
> but when our eyes behold your Word,
> we read your name in fairer lines.[13]

Watts knew that God's splendor and majesty were displayed in nature for all to see, but he also knew that God's provision of his Word was an even greater reason to praise him than nature.

Psalm 19 ends with a prayer that shows David's response to the glory of God in nature and Scripture. In verses 12 and 13, David prays

---

13. Isaac Watts, "The Heavens Declare Your Glory, Lord," in *Trinity Hymnal* (Philadelphia: Great Commission, 1990), 138.

that God would forgive and purify him. In a progressive series in these verses, he lists three types of sins. David first asks to be forgiven of his "hidden faults," or secret sins. These are the sins that no one else knows about; perhaps David has deceived his family and even himself into thinking he is not sinning. These are the personal sins that only the individual and God know about. David makes the same request of the Lord in Psalm 139:23, where he states, "Search me, O God, and know my heart." Guilty of adultery and murder, David knows all too well that sin begins in the heart. The second type of sin David mentions is "willful sins." These are the sins of pride, of knowing a thought or an action to be sin and indulging in it anyway. For David, these are the sins in which he willfully pits himself against God and deliberately says "No" to God. The third sin is the "great transgression." While we cannot be certain exactly what David means here, this much is clear: this is a sin of greater magnitude than the others. David lists sins in a progressive manner—from private sins, to sins of arrogance against God, to a great sin. As David meditates upon the glory of God revealed in nature and in the Bible, he is compelled to confess his sins and ask for God's mercy. So ought we.

C. S. Lewis calls pride "the complete anti-God state of mind" in that it puts ourselves above and against God (Mere Christianity).

With sins forgiven and the meditation on God's self-revelations in nature and the Bible complete, David turns to God in prayer. He asks that his words and his thoughts would honor the Lord. David offers both his public statements (his "words") and his private thoughts (his "meditation") to God. No doubt he means the psalm itself when he offers himself to God in this way, for the psalm began in his private meditation and became public when he wrote it down for others to hear and read. David's readers are doubly blessed, for they see David's reverence for the Lord in the words of Psalm 19 and can use the psalm themselves to honor the Lord in their lives. When we read this psalm, whether in private devotions or in corporate worship, we speak God's words after him and thereby honor him with our adoration. The psalm ends with David's final words of devotion to God, who is his Rock and Redeemer. These two references—the one a natural image (the Rock), the other a spiritual reference (Redeemer)—recall the two parts of the psalm: one that praises God as Creator and the other that praises God for the Bible. The psalm begins with the heavens' declaration of Yahweh's glory and ends with Yahweh himself. In the light of all that the psalm teaches about God, David asks that God would make him a fit spokesman for the Lord.

Applications

1. God has not remained silent. How can we? From our waking to our sleeping we receive daily reminders of God's goodness. The sun by day and stars by night remind us that God created everything and that he sustains it all by the word of his power. Psalm 19 encourages us to speak on God's behalf, giving a testimony to family and friends about God's goodness to us.

2. God has communicated his love and grace to us in the pages of the Bible. There we learn of Jesus Christ's willing sacrifice so that our sins might be forgiven and we might be declared righteous before God. Salvation is an even greater inducement to praise than creation. With David, we ought to love the Word of God more than anything else. Why? Because it shows us the way of eternal life.

3. These are the two "first principles" of our relationship with God. He made us and he offers to save us. He created us and he redeems us. Christians ought to give testimony to these two truths by the way they live and in the words they speak. May it be so of us.

Psalm 104
A CREATION HYMN

Our next Creation Psalm is Psalm 104, a great hymn of praise to God for his creation and his sustaining power over all things. Psalm 104 may well have been written as a companion poem to Psalm 103 in that both begin and end with the conventional admonition, "Praise the LORD, O my soul." Psalm 103 praises God for his special love for his people; Psalm 104 praises God for his more general acts of creation and his sovereignty over everything he created.

> ¹Praise the LORD, O my soul.
> O LORD my God, you are very great;
>   you are clothed with splendor and majesty.
> ²He wraps himself in light as with a garment;
>   he stretches out the heavens like a tent
> ³and lays the beams of his upper chambers on their waters.
> He makes the clouds his chariot
>   and rides on the wings of the wind.
> ⁴He makes winds his messengers,
>   flames of fire his servants.
>
> ⁵He set the earth on its foundations;
>   it can never be moved.
> ⁶You covered it with the deep as with a garment;
>   the waters stood above the mountains.
> ⁷But at your rebuke the waters fled,
>   at the sound of your thunder they took to flight;
> ⁸they flowed over the mountains,
>   they went down into the valleys,
>   to the place you assigned for them.
> ⁹You set a boundary they cannot cross;
>   never again will they cover the earth.

¹⁰He makes springs pour water into the ravines;
    it flows between the mountains.
¹¹They give water to all the beasts of the field;
    the wild donkeys quench their thirst.
¹²The birds of the air nest by the waters;
    they sing among the branches.
¹³He waters the mountains from his upper chambers;
    the earth is satisfied by the fruit of his work.
¹⁴He makes grass grow for the cattle,
    and plants for man to cultivate—
    bringing forth food from the earth:
¹⁵wine that gladdens the heart of man,
    oil to make his face shine,
    and bread that sustains his heart.
¹⁶The trees of the Lord are well watered,
    the cedars of Lebanon that he planted.
¹⁷There the birds make their nests;
    the stork has its home in the pine trees.
¹⁸The high mountains belong to the wild goats;
    the crags are a refuge for the coneys.

¹⁹The moon marks off the seasons,
    and the sun knows when to go down.
²⁰You bring darkness, it becomes night,
    and all the beasts of the forest prowl.
²¹The lions roar for their prey
    and seek their food from God.
²²The sun rises, and they steal away;
    they return and lie down in their dens.
²³Then man goes out to his work,
    to his labor until evening.

²⁴How many are your works, O Lord!
In wisdom you made them all;
    the earth is full of your creatures.

²⁵There is the sea, vast and spacious,
  teeming with creatures beyond number—
  living things both large and small.
²⁶There the ships go to and fro,
  and the leviathan, which you formed to frolic there.

²⁷These all look to you
  to give them their food at the proper time.
²⁸When you give it to them,
  they gather it up;
  when you open your hand,
  they are satisfied with good things.
²⁹When you hide your face,
  they are terrified;
  when you take away their breath,
  they die and return to the dust.
³⁰When you send your Spirit,
  they are created,
  and you renew the face of the earth.

³¹May the glory of the LORD endure forever;
  may the LORD rejoice in his works—
³²he who looks at the earth, and it trembles,
  who touches the mountains, and they smoke.

³³I will sing to the LORD all my life;
  I will sing praise to my God as long as I live.
³⁴May my meditation be pleasing to him,
  as I rejoice in the LORD.
³⁵But may sinners vanish from the earth
  and the wicked be no more.

Praise the LORD, O my soul.
Praise the LORD.

What Is the Overall Effect of the Psalm?

Poetry is meant to be experienced as well as understood. Poets typically appeal to the reader's senses with their images and to the emotions with the connotations of their words. Poems show as well as tell; they provide concrete pictures of what they are saying. Good poetry is like good teaching; it uses multiple methods to make a point. Effective teachers use analogies and appeal to the students' hearing and seeing to strengthen their understanding of the idea being taught. C. S. Lewis understood that readers need to see and hear as well as understand; consider any of his "apologetic" writings, such as *Mere Christianity,* and you will find numerous analogies and illustrations. Think of the many parables and object lessons the Lord himself used to teach those around him, and then think of the images and pictures in the book of Revelation. So it is in Psalm 104; the reader experiences the goodness of God in an accumulation of images that evoke our praise.

> *Psalm 104 is an invitation to praise Yahweh*
> *for his wonderful creation.*

Psalm 104 begins with the liturgical invitation, "Praise the LORD, O my soul" and ends with the psalmist's awe at God's great glory as he pours forth his praises in the last five verses. The contrast of the brief initial invitation to praise with the longer concluding expression of adoration indicates that the psalmist's meditation on God's glory overwhelms him with the majesty and splendor of the great Creator. Between the opening and closing exhortations to praise, the psalmist paints a series of concrete pictures of God's creating and sustaining power. The collective effect of these pictures encourages the reader to share the psalmist's joy, as a quick reading of the psalm for overall effect will demonstrate.

When we read a psalm for its overall effect, we read with the big picture in mind. We will come back to the details of the psalm when we read for figures of speech and parallelisms. When we read for the effect of Psalm 104, we are looking for the general pictures the psalmist paints and their overall impression on us. Fortunately, the writer identifies the themes of his praise to Yahweh in the opening verse: God's "splendor and majesty." The psalmist suggests God's greatness first in that he created the heavens for people to observe (vv. 2–4). Next the psalmist states that God created the foundations of the earth (vv. 5–9). Once the heavens and the earth were created, God filled the earth with animals and provided abundantly for them (vv. 10–18). God created and controls time, as well as geography. The psalmist shows God's power over time in his control of the seasons and the cycle of day and night (vv. 19–23).

The big picture of God's greatness as Creator is completed with the creation and sustenance of the sea and its creatures (vv. 24–26). God has made the heavens, the earth, land animals, time, and the sea. As if this were not enough, the psalmist goes on in the next verses to meditate on the fact that Yahweh sustains it all. The implications of this simple statement are staggering. Think of what the psalmist has just written about God. God has created the heavens and controls them as a warrior does his chariot. He set the limits to the earth and sea and keeps their boundaries in check. He provides abundantly for animals and humans alike, rejoicing our hearts in the overflowing variety of food. He marks the seasons, keeping them in fine balance to provide for us. He created the myriad of sea creatures and delights in the play of the leviathan (a large sea creature). And now the psalmist states that this God sustains everything by the word of his power. How can we respond with any emotion other than awe? How can we not praise Yahweh for his splendor and majesty in creation?

After he meditates about so many of God's wonderful works in creation and his care for human beings, the psalmist then makes his encouragement to praise God explicit. Up to this point in the psalm, the writer has let God's works speak for themselves. Only the opening verse calls explicitly for praise; the rest of the psalm makes an implicit invitation to praise God by its celebration of his splendor and majesty. Now, however, the psalmist calls explicitly for praise. These verses (31 and 32) extend a twofold call for prayer. In the first part of verse

31, the psalmist prays that humans might praise God; it is in human understanding of God's great work that his glory "endures." In the second part of the verse, the psalmist prays that God might be pleased in his creation. That is, the psalmist knows that all of nature proclaims God's splendor and majesty to mankind. In effect, humans are the only ones who can interpret the message in nature, the only ones who can give words to the characteristics and great acts of God that nature demonstrates. If nature is to praise God, then, people (i.e., believers) must state explicitly what nature demonstrates about God. And this is exactly what Psalm 104 does. It gives voice to God's glory by interpreting nature as an expression of God's splendor and majesty. The psalmist does what he calls his readers to do: he models his praise in the words of the psalm.

What Is the Structure of the Psalm?

Psalm 104 is a Hymn and follows the typical tripartite structure of the Hymn, only with a magnificent long middle section.

I. Verse 1:   The Invitation to Praise Yahweh
II. Verses 2–30:   Yahweh's Great Work of Creation
III. Verses 31–35: Concluding Resolution to Praise Yahweh

The psalmist articulates the two themes of the psalm in verse 1, which is also the opening section of the psalm. He encourages his readers to praise the Lord and declares that God is splendid and majestic. These two themes run throughout the psalm, the call to praise always being present as the attitude the psalmist wishes his readers to have and the splendor and majesty of God being the subjects of the long middle section. In the opening verse even the names of God that the psalmist uses, "O LORD my God" (Yahweh Elohim), underscore the power and sovereignty of God. The name *Yahweh* indicates variously God's eternal existence and his special love for his people; *Elohim* speaks of God's supreme power over all things, or his sovereignty. Taken together, the names of God referenced at the beginning of Psalm 104 emphasize God's omnipotence and sovereignty. This is the God the psalmist praises in the opening invitation.

The long middle section of the psalm provides five detailed pictures of God's power as Creator and Sustainer of all things. As Robert Alter notes, there are no nature poems among the Psalms;[14] rather, the psalmists write "Creation Poems," which use nature to show the glory of the Creator. So it is in Psalm 104. The "snapshots" in the middle section of the psalm do not glorify nature; rather, they point to the splendor and majesty of the one who created and sustains nature. Each of the pictures presented in the middle section of the psalm points to the greatness of God. In the first picture, that of the heavens, we see that God is greater than his creation. The psalmist declares that, no matter how awe inspiring the heavens are, Yahweh is greater, for the heavens merely point to his greatness (vv. 2–4). Again, in the picture of the earth's foundations, the power of the oceans is transcended by the great power of Yahweh, who controls the seas and does not let them flood the land (vv. 5–9). When the psalmist pictures God's provision for land animals, his account focuses on God's greatness again, for he provides everything that man and beasts alike need (vv. 10–18). When the psalmist moves from God's provision to the cycles of seasons and days, he shows God's control over time, providing times for work and rest for all of his creatures (vv. 19–23). As God provides for the land animals, so he does for the creatures in the sea, even the leviathan, that great sea creature no one but God can control (vv. 24–26). God is so great, the psalmist tells us in the next picture, that all animals live and die under his sovereignty (vv. 27–30). In every picture of God's power as Creator and Sustainer, the psalmist draws the reader's attention to God himself. The details of the natural phenomena all point to the greatness of their Creator. As the psalmist states in verse 1, God is "great."

In the final section of the psalm, the concluding resolution to praise Yahweh (vv. 31–35), the psalmist calls for the people to worship Yahweh. After having read about the glory of God in creation, how can we

---

14. Alter, *Art of Biblical Poetry,* 117.

respond in any way other than praise? The psalm's multiple reminders in the middle section that God is the one who created everything
and that we owe our lives to him alone should encourage us to worship the one who is so glorious and great. That is certainly the way the
psalmist responds, singing to the Lord and rejoicing in him as he calls
on his readers to do the same.

Psalm 104 is structured in a "picture frame" manner. The picture is
the five images of God's work as Creator and Sustainer (vv. 2–30); the
frame to the picture is the opening invitation (v. 1) and concluding
exhortation (vv. 31–35) to praise God. This particular structure to the
psalm does at least two things. First, by referencing God's great works
in creation, it shows the glory of God. Second, it focuses all of God's
glory as Creator as a reason for people to praise him. This psalm is no
academic exercise in creation science on the one hand, nor a fanciful
picture of an animate universe filled with a divine nature on the other
hand. Rather, all of nature calls on us to praise Yahweh, and the psalmist
sees God's glory as Creator as an incentive to devotion. So should we.

What Are the Figures of Speech in the Psalm, and What Effects Do They Have?

Because Psalm 104 is a Hymn that celebrates creation, we can expect to see frequent figures of speech that show God's glory revealed
in the natural creation he has made. The psalmist attempts to capture
something of the transcendent character of God through the finite
resources of the physical universe, using the inferior physical world to
suggest the superior character of Yahweh. To do so, he must "figure
forth" God in physical comparisons. C. S. Lewis calls the attempt to
capture the superior (here, God) with imagery from the inferior (in
this case, the natural creation) *transposition* and suggests that we can
find it everywhere in literature when writers try to depict the transcendent.[15] The physical world is simply too limited to be compared

---

15. C. S. Lewis, "Transposition," in *The Weight of Glory* (New York: Simon & Schuster, 1996), 72–89.

on a one-to-one basis with the spiritual world. Tremper Longman suggests that, because God is incomprehensible, it may be that figures of speech like images and metaphors are one way we can approximate his glory.[16] In the terms of Psalm 104, nature cannot be compared directly to Yahweh; it can only suggest something about him. Throughout the psalm, the writer attempts to express God's glory by what he has made in nature. When we see how glorious creation is, and when we remember that all the psalmist can do with the images from nature is approximate the glory of God, we can appreciate something of the psalmist's awe and praise for God.

Writing economically and wasting no time, the psalmist uses parallelism with great effect in verse 1. The second half of the verse expands the first by ascribing two particular attributes to God to define his greatness, and it is these two characteristics of God that the psalm in its entirety develops. The first verse uses the image of clothing— God "wears" splendor and majesty. This image does more than paint a nice picture of God; it suggests that all of nature can only hint at God's greatness, just as a person's clothing can only give a suggestion of what the person is really like. The psalmist expands on God's splendor in the image of light and the simile of a tent (vv. 2–3). Light is often an image of God in the Bible. For example, there is the Shekinah glory of the temple, the fire that leads the Israelites in the wilderness, the light in the prologue to John's gospel (vv. 4–5), and the great pictures of Jesus Christ at the beginning and ending of Revelation (1:13–16; 21:23–24). They all suggest something of God's splendor. In Psalm 104:2, light is compared to God's "garment" and implies that God, who is a spirit, reveals himself to us as a light shines in the darkness. In the second half of verse 2 and the first half of verse 3, the psalmist compares God to a great Oriental potentate living in a magnificent tent. God's "tent," however, is like no earthly potentate's tent; his tent is the heavens, and the waters of the heavens form the foundation for the tent. The effect of this simile is to emphasize God's

---

16. Tremper Longman, *How to Read the Psalms* (Downers Grove, Ill.: InterVarsity, 1988), 121.

splendor; no earthly king can boast such magnificence as God can. In two concise and intense images, the psalmist provides a glimpse of God's splendor.

While the domestic pictures of garments and tents suggest God's splendor, the military imagery that follows suggests his majesty, the other attribute of God mentioned in verse 1. The psalmist presents an image of Yahweh as a great warrior, riding a chariot of clouds on the wind. These details show God's majesty to be like that of a great king going forth in all his glory to war. Completing the picture, the winds become "messengers," warning of the approach of the great warrior, and fire becomes a servant. Perhaps the reference to fire in verse 4 parallels the imagery of light in verse 2; if so, light/fire forms a frame of God's great power around the images of the tent and warrior. In any event, the picture of God in these verses hints at his great power and majesty. Verses 2–4 present a high view of God as the one who controls the heavens.

> *Because words cannot fully express the splendor and*
> *majesty of God, the psalmist uses images to hint at God's glory.*
> *This is why he compares the heavens to a tent and*
> *God to a great warrior who lives in the tent. Language*
> *cannot do justice to God's glory.*

When the psalmist turns his eyes from the heavens to the earth, there too he sees God's glory reflected in his creation. Again he uses images and parallelisms to approximate the glory of God. The psalmist suggests the permanence of the dry land in two ways in verse 5. Using the image of a "foundation," the psalmist emphasizes the stability of the dry land; he echoes the same idea in the synthetic parallelism that begins with a "foundation" and ends with the fact that it can "never be moved" (v. 5). In verses 6–8, the psalmist impresses the reader with God's power by showing his command over the seas. In an extended simile, the writer says that the water covers the whole earth, even the mountains, as a garment does a person. This simile repeats the clothing imagery in verse 1 and serves to maintain a singular focus on God throughout this part of the psalm. No doubt this passage references the Noahic flood, in which the waters covered the earth to a depth of twenty feet over the tallest mountain (Gen. 7:20). Mountains rose and valleys fell under the tremendous water pressure. It would be easy to read this comparison too quickly and not appreciate the magnitude of what the psalmist is saying by reminding us of the Noahic flood. We should pause and think of God's great power, for he alone can bring a universal flood and then take the waters away again.

Perhaps we can put it in perspective with a few comparisons. Have you ever carried ten gallons of water? How far could you carry it? Or think of it this way: forty million gallons of water a minute go over the Canadian Niagara Horseshoe Falls, forty-five million gallons a minute over the two falls at Niagara taken together. Could you stop this flow? Or again, think of the effects of a thirty-foot-high tsunami on a city like New York City, San Francisco, or New Orleans; the damage would be incalculable. The four largest tsunamis of the twentieth century had catastrophic effects: 100,000 people died in the 1911 tsunami in China; 57,000 died in China in 1949; 10,000 perished in Bangladesh in 1960; and 15,000 lost their lives in the Indian tsunami of 1979.[17] When we realize that the oceans cover 70 percent of the earth's surface and that God sets limits to the oceans, we catch just a glimpse of his great power. If we reflect on God's promise to Noah that the water will never again cover the whole earth (Gen. 8:21), we should be filled with awe at God's omnipotence. The psalmist brings the picture of the earth's stability to closure with the antithetic parallelism of verse 9. Stated positively in the first half of the verse, God set boundaries for the oceans; stated negatively in the second half of the verse, the waters will never again cover the earth. Whichever way we look at it, God is sovereign over the oceans and the land.

After demonstrating God's power over the heavens and the earth, the psalmist turns attention next to God's provision for living things on the earth (vv. 10–18). In these verses, the psalmist presents both

---

17. *Scientific American Science Desk Reference,* 285.

the big picture and the small picture. In the big picture are all of the land creatures that are fed by God's provision; in the small picture are humans for whom God provides abundantly. This psalm reflects the opening chapters of Genesis in two ways. First, God is omnificent; that is, he is all-creative. He overflows with creativity; he is abundant in his creativity. Second, this psalm, like the opening two chapters of Genesis, presents both the big picture of all creation (Gen. 1), followed by the small picture of mankind (Gen. 2). God created everything and delights in it all.

In these verses, the psalmist changes his poetic technique slightly. He does not use many figures of speech to describe God's omnificence; rather, he uses multiple parallelisms to emphasize his points. The synonymous parallelism of verse 10 emphasizes God's provision of water, flowing abundantly "into the ravines" and "between the mountains." There is no lack of water for living creatures. Verse 14 contains a triple synthetic parallelism of grass for animals and plants for humans, both of which are summarized in the final colon of "food from the earth." The triple repetition serves to emphasize God's provision for his creation. The next verse focuses specifically on God's provision for humans and uses the same triple parallelism to emphasize God's goodness to us. God provides wine, oil, and bread for man, but notice that these are more than the mere necessities of life, for wine "gladdens," oil makes the face "shine," and bread sustains the "heart." The triple parallelism shows that God's provision is not niggardly but generous to overflowing. He is omnificent and good.

In the brief section on God's control of time, the psalmist again uses parallelisms to reflect the orderliness of God's creation (vv. 19–23). The synthetic parallelism of verse 20 suggests the process of night falling. Verse 22 uses another synthetic parallelism to suggest the activity of the animals returning to their dens at the break of day. The psalmist uses the same technique in verse 23 to show man's daytime activity and its cessation at evening. In these effective parallelisms, the writer shows the orderliness of the day and night cycle of time and captures the process of human activity during the day and animal activity at night; the parallelisms echo the passing of time, underscoring the activity that is described. God orders all of this activity within his providence.

So far, the cumulative effect of the psalm—God created the heavens, the earth, the seasons, day and night, the sea—is intended to overwhelm the reader with God's splendor and majesty (v. 1). Just meditate on any one of these awesome deeds apart from their cumulative effect, and you will praise God. Who is like him? Put all of his deeds in creation together, and we cannot help but bow in adoration and worship. The entire psalm up to this point is designed to encourage the reader to acknowledge that there is none like God; he alone is Lord. Then, in verses 27–30, the psalmist states in a simple, factual manner that God sustains everything that he has made. The factual tone and simple language in these verses comes as a sharp contrast to the earlier descriptions in the psalm. The change from figurative language and multiple parallelisms to a simple statement emphasizes the point being made: God sustains everything he creates. The psalmist does use two personifications in these verses, both of which speak of God. God is pictured as "open[ing]" his "hand" to give food, showing his generous provision (v. 28), but when he "hide[s his] face," the animals perish (v. 29). The first personification shows God to be beneficent, the second that he is sovereign over death. The long middle section of the Hymn ends with an image of God who creates life and takes it away. With that, the psalmist turns to the final section of the psalm, the concluding resolution to praise Yahweh.

In the final section of the psalm, the writer presents God's majesty in two quite different ways and calls on people to praise Yahweh. The first way the psalmist shows God's majesty is by using the literary device of hyperbole, or exaggeration. To demonstrate God's authority over the earth itself, the psalmist writes of the earth trembling and the mountains smoking. This hyperbole is intended to communicate the great power and awesome strength God possesses. While it is true that God could literally make the earth tremble and the mountains smoke, and did so at Mount Sinai (Exod. 19), it is likely that the psalmist uses these pictures as a hyperbole to encourage readers to stand in awe of

God's majesty. The second way the psalmist shows God's majesty is the call for judgment on sinners (v. 35). This call for judgment likely strikes many modern readers as vengeful and out of place in Psalm 104. However, there is no mistake here: with the call for God's judgment on sinful people, the psalmist shows God's glory. How? When the reader realizes how clearly and majestically God has revealed himself in nature, it is arrogant not to praise him. If one were to read this psalm and not praise God, it would be a grievous sin. This verse is not vengeful; rather, it shows the responsibility—and privilege—we all have to praise God when we see his glory so wonderfully portrayed. Paul reminds us in the first chapter of Romans that God's self-revelation in nature makes it inexcusable for people to say they did not know God had revealed himself to them. Psalm 104 does much the same as the passage in Romans and underscores the point by this imprecatory note at the end of the psalm. With the reading of Scripture comes responsibility and choice; readers are put in the position of choosing to praise God with the psalmist or reject him as so many people do. The psalmist wants his readers to be certain that they understand God's glory so that they may choose to praise him freely.

These are not all of the poetic devices the psalmist uses. The important point is, however, that the psalmist uses these devices to demonstrate God's splendor and majesty in images that approximate the reality of Yahweh. The psalmist knows that he cannot describe God's glory completely, and so he uses poetic devices as transpositions (to use C. S. Lewis's term) to show his readers something of what he wants to communicate. It is particularly important in Psalm 104 that the psalmist uses fewer figures of speech toward the end of the long middle section and more frequent statements of simple fact. He does so because he has made his point over and over again with his imagery, and now he wishes to make the point factually. The switch from figurative language to simple description makes it clear to the readers that they should praise the Lord with the psalmist. Indeed, the writer invites his readers to do just that in the last colon of the psalm: "Praise the LORD." "Hallelujah."

What Are the Themes and Theology in the Psalm?

Psalm 104 is one of the Hymns of Creation that reveal nature as a reason to praise God. It has three primary themes. First God is splendid and majestic. From the beginning of the psalm to its final call to worship God, the psalmist demonstrates in numerous ways that God's creation shows his splendor and majesty. Yahweh's majesty is shown in his great power over creation, for he created it, sustains it, and orders it. The reader is to reflect on what kind of a God could create and then rule over such a world. Yahweh's splendor is shown in the wondrous provision he makes for all of his creatures. He demonstrates his omnificence in the abundant provision he makes for animals and humans alike, for he gives more than the essentials for survival.

A second theme in Psalm 104 is that God is superior to everything he has made. When we reflect on the many images the psalmist uses, we are reminded that nature is inadequate to describe Yahweh. The psalmist can only approximate God's glory, for he is greater than the words the psalmist can use to describe him. Think of how pathetic—literally—it is for people to make something in nature or even something man-made into a god! When we realize how infinitely superior Yahweh is to his creation, all other gods pale in comparison.

A third theme in the psalm is that we are to make praise personal. The psalm begins and ends in the psalmist's personal praise. Between the two frames of the psalm, the writer demonstrates five ways that God is great. When we examine the structure of the psalm, it is clear that the psalmist means for the frame and the picture to fit together, for the praise at the conclusion of the poem overwhelms the psalmist. We are not to praise nature; rather, we are to see nature as itself a source of praise to Yahweh. Psalm 104 does not simply teach that God created a wonderful world; it calls the reader to respond by praising Yahweh, the God who created the universe.

Robert Grant echoes the praise of Psalm 104 in his well-known hymn, "O Worship the King." Grant begins the hymn with a doxology to God who is "all glorious above"; he is "the Ancient of Days, pavilioned in splendor and girded with praise." God alone is worthy of Grant's praise. In a later stanza, Grant meditates on God's provision for his people:

> Your bountiful care what tongue can recite?
> It breathes in the air; it shines in the light;
> It streams from the hills; it descends to the plain;
> And sweetly distils in the dew and the rain.[18]

Taken in its context, this stanza is startling, for it declares that the omnipotent, transcendent God who created the universe graciously provides for the daily needs of his children. When we remember the doxology of the opening stanza, these words can only add to our praise.

Applications

1. What is your vision of God? Is he as majestic and splendid as the psalmist indicates he is?
2. Do we ever think of the natural creation as a source of meditation upon God? We need to be careful not to adopt the New Age and extreme environmentalist idea of pantheism (or, to coin a word, "ecotheism"), seeing God in nature. God does not inhabit nature; he created it out of nothing. When we think of how magnificent nature is and remember that God is superior to it, we should realize again how majestic he is.
3. Do we think humanistically, even though we are Christians? For example, what do you think of the Human Genome Project, the mapping of the human DNA for scientific research? While it has great promise, do you think we will abuse it? Do we remember that we are simply recording what only God can do? God alone can create something out of nothing. No human has made a chromosome or a gene. We must be careful to use the research and technologies that come from the Human Genome Project for God's glory, not our own.

---

18. Robert Grant, "O Worship the King," in *Trinity Hymnal* (Philadelphia: Great Commission, 1990), 2.

4. Christ tells us in the New Testament to ask God for our "daily bread." When we pray before our meals, do we reflect on the truth that God sustains everything he makes and pours it abundantly into our storehouses, even in this fallen world of ours?
5. As the seasons change, do we remember the Noahic covenant in which God promised the seasons in their cycles until he creates a new heaven and a new earth? Do the changing seasons remind us to praise God for his faithfulness?
6. Do we praise God for what we see, taste, touch, smell, and hear?

Encountering God as Creator

With the psalmists of old, we should have a high view of God as the Creator and Sustainer of all things. If we hold a low view of God as Creator and underestimate his direct creation of the universe, we will have difficulty accepting the promises he makes to his people—for we will have denied the truth of the Word of God in its beginnings in Genesis. We cannot hold the position of the eighteenth-century deists, who believed that God created the world and then did not involve himself actively in the cosmos. Nor can we hold the view of the modern secular scientist, who thinks that there is no God in creation at all. Such views are at odds with the God of the Bible, who created everything out of nothing and who sustains it all. If we wish to appreciate the promises of the Psalms, we must have the same high view of Yahweh that the psalmists have. With them and the other writers of Scripture, we must understand that God is personally involved with his creation; he is immanent as well as transcendent. Only then will we be able to rest confidently on the promises made in the Psalms, for the promises of God depend on his ability to rule the nations and control the creation.

A high view of God and a high view of Scripture
go hand in hand; both are necessary if we are to appreciate
the promises of God in the Psalms.

If Yahweh were not sovereign over the universe and the affairs of men, he could not manage our personal lives to answer our prayers and sustain us in distress. Even more important, if God does not rule sovereignly over nature and the nations, he could not fulfill the promises of redemption he makes in the Psalms. The Messianic Psalms would make no sense without the Creation Psalms. Knowing God as Creator and Sustainer, then, is necessary for a rich devotional life.

The first and foundational truth in the Creation Psalms is that Yahweh has taken the initiative to communicate with us in every way possible. He has given himself a constant witness in the creation around us, and every time we open our eyes or ears we are reminded of the great Creator of all things. At least, the writer of Psalm 19 thinks so, and so does Paul in the New Testament (Rom. 1:18–20). God has not remained silent.

The second lesson in the Creation Psalms is that Yahweh is superior to everything he has made. When we encounter atheists and secular materialists who hold that matter is all that exists, we can suggest to them that matter only hints at the majesty and splendor of God. "If you think nature is majestic," we can say to them, "God is more majestic yet." When we meet New Age people who, at the other extreme, think that the divine spirit inhabits nature and us alike, we can tell them that nature does indeed teach us something about God, but God is infinitely more majestic and splendid than nature. Knowing God as Creator and Sustainer will help us bear witness to our faith.

The third lesson in the Creation Psalms is that human beings are to make praise personal. That is, we need to meditate on God's great power demonstrated so clearly in creation and be thankful that he invites us to know him personally in Jesus Christ. It is certainly true that the greatest story of all is free redemption in Christ's finished work at Calvary; however, God affirms his redemptive power in the very act of creation. When we pray according to God's will, he looses the same power that raised Christ from the dead to accomplish his sovereign purposes. We should be filled with praise when we meditate on this truth.

These Creation Psalms look in two directions. They acknowledge

Yahweh as the sovereign Lord of the universe, on whose grace our very breath depends. At the same time, the Creation Psalms invite us to participate with God in a "borrowed glory," to be responsible for all of the earth. When we realize the "glory" that God bestows upon us, we will worship him.

Chapter 6

Abounding in Love:
God as Covenant Maker

May your unfailing love come to me, O LORD,
your salvation according to your promise.
—Psalm 119:41

THE PSALMS CELEBRATE GOD'S LOVE for his people. The Hymns, or Psalms of Praise, worship God for who he is as Yahweh and for all he does for his people. Laments ask God for help in present difficulties. Royal Psalms meditate on the kingly reign of God (and often his earthly representative, David). Thanksgiving Psalms express gratitude directly to God for his many blessings in this life. Wisdom Psalms teach us to apply what God has shown us about himself to our own lives. All of the Psalms focus on Yahweh in one way or another, and many of them express his unfailing love for his people.

God demonstrates his unfailing love for his people in many ways. To begin, he forgives their sins. "As far as the east is from the west, so far has he removed our transgressions from us," David exclaims under the inspiration of the Holy Spirit (Ps. 103:12). To be sure, God's mercy is the beginning of his love for his people, at least from a human perspective, because forgiveness initiates the life of faith. The New Testament teaches clearly that no one is righteous enough on his or her own to stand before Yahweh (Rom. 3:23). Had Christ not taken the punishment of his people's sins on the cross and set them free from judgment for their sin, they could not know God at all (Rom. 4:6–8, 23–25; 5:17). Surely, God's loving mercy in forgiving sins by grace through faith in Jesus Christ is the beginning of his love for his people.

A second way God shows his love to us is his everyday goodness. Think of the many blessings we enjoy each day, all of which come from God (James 1:17). Whatever measure of health we enjoy is God's gift— even the health that allows us to go to work every day to earn food for our families is from God. Family and friends who share our joys and sorrows are God's gracious provision in our lives. Christian friends, some close to home and some scattered around the globe, with whom we share our love of Christ and a wish to see others converted, all come from God. Not to mention the material blessings God showers on us every day. God provides abundantly for us, both temporally and spiritually. And all of these gifts are manifestations of his unfailing love.

A third way God demonstrates his love for us is his daily provision of grace to live the Christian life he has called us to live. We are to glorify God in all that we do (1 Cor. 10:31). However, we cannot glorify God except by his grace. We cannot enjoy fellowship with God apart from his grace, nor can we serve him without grace. Indeed, all of the Christian life is learning to live by God's grace. The psalmists celebrate this daily provision in a variety of ways. In fact, all of the ways God showers his grace upon us are designed to encourage us to praise him and acknowledge his blessings. Grace is an expression of God's unfailing love.

The Hebrew word used in the Psalms for God's unfailing love is *ḥesed.* It means variously forgiveness, goodness, and love. In his comments on the perfections of God, Willem VanGemeren states, "The love of Yahweh is his commitment to those who love him to be unceasingly generous in his forgiveness, compassion, and blessings."[1] *ḥesed* involves both spiritual and temporal blessings. Spiritually, God's

---

1. Willem VanGemeren, *Psalms,* vol. 5 of *The Expositor's Bible Commentary,* ed. Frank E. Gaebelein (Grand Rapids: Zondervan, 1991), 236.

unfailing love begins in forgiveness of sin, continues in grace and peace for the Christian in this life, and is perfected in the Christian's glorification in heaven. Temporally, it involves God's goodness in providing the necessities of this life for his children. God's people are forever the objects of his unfailing love, his *ḥesed,* both spiritually and temporally. No wonder the psalmists celebrate Yahweh's unfailing love for them. Christians should do no less.

In this chapter, we will meditate on two psalms that emphasize God's unfailing love for his people. We begin with Psalm 33, an exuberant call to worship God and an exalted study of the character of God all in one.

> *"The quality of God's love guarantees the continual operation of all his benefits (perfections) toward his people, including righteousness, uprightness, justice, forgiveness, patience, and compassion." (VanGemeren)*

Psalm 33
God's Unfailing Love

¹Sing joyfully to the Lord, you righteous;
  it is fitting for the upright to praise him.
²Praise the Lord with the harp;
  make music to him on the ten-stringed lyre.
³Sing to him a new song;
  play skillfully, and shout for joy.

⁴For the word of the Lord is right and true;
  he is faithful in all he does.
⁵The Lord loves righteousness and justice;
  the earth is full of his unfailing love.

⁶By the word of the Lord were the heavens made,
  their starry host by the breath of his mouth.

[7]He gathers the waters of the sea into jars;
    he puts the deep into storehouses.
[8]Let all the earth fear the LORD;
    let all the people of the world revere him.
[9]For he spoke, and it came to be;
    he commanded, and it stood firm.
[10]The LORD foils the plans of the nations;
    he thwarts the purposes of the peoples.
[11]But the plans of the LORD stand firm forever,
    the purposes of his heart through all generations.

[12]Blessed is the nation whose God is the LORD,
    the people he chose for his inheritance.
[13]From heaven the LORD looks down
    and sees all mankind;
[14]from his dwelling place he watches
    all who live on earth—
[15]he who forms the hearts of all,
    who considers everything they do.
[16]No king is saved by the size of his army;
    no warrior escapes by his great strength.
[17]A horse is a vain hope for deliverance;
    despite all its great strength it cannot save.
[18]But the eyes of the LORD are on those who fear him,
    on those whose hope is in his unfailing love,
[19]to deliver them from death
    and keep them alive in famine.

[20]We wait in hope for the LORD;
    he is our help and our shield.
[21]In him our hearts rejoice,
    for we trust in his holy name.
[22]May your unfailing love rest upon us, O LORD,
    even as we put our hope in you.

What Is the Overall Effect of the Psalm?

One of the great psalms of praise in the Psalter, Psalm 33 focuses our attention on Yahweh and encourages us to exalt and glorify him. From beginning to end, the subject of the psalm is God. The psalmist writes of God's character, his rule over creation and the nations, and his unfailing love for his people. Throughout, Psalm 33 is an invitation to public praise of God, as the enthusiastic opening call to praise and the final statement of confidence in God's unfailing love attest. We may be able to conclude from the closing verses of the psalm that God's covenant people needed his protection in some way, for the psalmist calls Yahweh "our help and our shield" (v. 20), though we do not know what particular circumstance prompted the writing of this psalm. Whatever the situation behind the psalm, the psalmist understands the truth that the Lord is the only one who can meet his needs. Psalm 33 is a hymn of public praise, and it is fitting that we should turn to this psalm in times of public tragedy and fear. Psalm 33 reminds us that, no matter what our circumstances, God is sovereign and, because he knows and controls all things, we can trust him. This psalm pours forth praise to God, even in the face of the difficulties that prompt the psalmist to call Yahweh a "help" and "shield" (v. 20).

*Though the psalmist is in distress, he focuses his
attention entirely on Yahweh. It is not until the closing verses
of the psalm that we discover the psalmist's adversity.
May we turn first to God in our moments of affliction.*

What Is the Structure of the Psalm?

Psalm 33 is a Hymn of Public Praise to Yahweh. It is designed to encourage believers in corporate gatherings to take comfort in the sovereignty and love of God as their help in times of trouble. This was one of the first psalms I turned to on September 11, 2001, when the terrorists attacked the World Trade Center and the Pentagon. This was the psalm our church read at a prayer meeting the next day. When trouble strikes, there is no adequate refuge apart from Yahweh, "our help and our shield" (v. 20). It is fitting to praise Yahweh at all times, perhaps especially in times of national crisis, for God alone is sovereign over all the nations (cf. vv. 10–11).

Like most Hymns, Psalm 33 follows a three-part structure that helps encourage readers and listeners to praise God. The psalm has a frame-and-picture structure as follows:

I. Verses 1–3:   The Public Call to Praise Yahweh
II. Verses 4–19:   Yahweh's Praiseworthy Acts and Attributes
III. Verses 20–22: Exhortation to Trust Yahweh

The opening and concluding verses form a frame in which the psalmist calls for public praise of God. The long middle section, verses 4–19, provides the picture of God's character and actions that warrant our praise.

In the opening call to praise, the writer offers a threefold invitation to praise Yahweh. In its turn, each of the parts of the invitation repeats the call to praise. The result is that Psalm 33 begins with a sixfold call to praise God, encouraging everyone in the congregation to turn their attention toward God.

The middle section of the psalm, which runs from verse 4 to verse 19, recounts the various praiseworthy acts and attributes of God. In this section, Psalm 33 provides a host of God's perfections, any one of which would be reason enough to praise Yahweh forever. Taken together, God's perfections should move us to overwhelming and spontaneous praise. When the psalmist meditates on Yahweh's perfections, he is overcome with his majesty and splendor.

In its turn, the middle section of Psalm 33 can be divided into three subsections, each focusing on a particular cluster of God's attributes or actions. Note how the psalmist structures his praise of God in this section. He begins with acknowledging God's truthfulness and goodness (vv. 4–5), initiating his praise of God in the very character of God himself and in his self-revelation in Scripture. In the second subsection of this part of the psalm, the writer praises God that he is sovereign over all things, both creation and the nations (vv. 6–11). The psalmist ends this long middle section with his gratitude for God's unfailing love for his people (vv. 12–19). It is as if the psalmist is designing the architecture of a great building in this psalm. He lays the foundation in God's character (vv. 4–5). He constructs the first floors in God's sovereignty over the nations, which is necessary if he is to turn events in this life to bless his people. Finally, he finishes the upper stories of the building with God's special care for his own people. The three subsections of the middle portion of Psalm 33 articulate the glorious theme of Yahweh's greatness.

The concluding exhortation in Psalm 33 (vv. 20–22) takes its cue from the final portion of the middle section. The psalmist closes the psalm by focusing directly on God's unfailing love for his people, as both provider and protector. The psalm begins in an invitation to God's people to praise him, provides three overarching aspects of God's character as motives to praise him in the middle section, and concludes with the sure hope that God will turn all of his perfections to his people's good and his own glory. It is not until the concluding exhortation to praise Yahweh that the reader learns that God's people were in distress when this psalm was written. The psalmist turns the attention of God's people to God first, even in times of peril, for only the sovereign Lord of the universe, Yahweh, can meet the deepest needs of the people he has created and especially of those he has redeemed.

What Are the Figures of Speech in the Psalm, and What Effects Do They Have?

The opening call to praise Yahweh in Psalm 33 uses no figures of speech; it is written in simple declarative sentences. It provokes the hearers and readers of the psalm to praise by its parallel repetitions that vary the exhortation to praise God in three ways. In the opening verse, the psalmist begins by encouraging us to "sing joyfully" to God and to "praise him." Perhaps even more important in this opening verse is the fact that the writer addresses his call to praise to God's people. Only God's people recognize that their blessings come from Yahweh, and not themselves. Here, the psalmist identifies God's people in two ways, thus providing the first instance of parallelism in the psalm (in this case, a synonymous parallelism). He calls them "righteous" and "upright."

In his second introductory invitation to praise (v. 2), the psalmist calls on the people to praise God with musical instruments, specifically stringed instruments. In verse 1, he invites singing; in verse 2, he asks for musical instrumentation. We are to use both voice and instruments to praise Yahweh. The synonymous parallelism in this verse augments the invitation to praise by using the two types of musical instruments (the harp and the lyre) as metonymies to represent all types of musical instruments. The parallelism of instruments has the effect of suggesting that music is fitting in our praise to God.

In the third invitation to praise (v. 3), the psalmist combines voice and instrument to give a harmonious musical crescendo of praise to Yahweh. Verse 3 forms a climactic parallelism to verses 1 and 2, combining voices with instruments to complete the call to praise Yahweh. The opening section of Psalm 33 gains its effect by its crescendo-like structure that builds toward a climax of praise to God.

Unlike the short introductory section, the long middle section of the psalm is rich in figures of speech and parallelisms. With the figures of speech in much of this section, the psalmist demonstrates God's character and encourages our active reading of the psalm. Verses 4 and 5 provide the foundation for the middle section by establishing God's character as the basis for all he does. These verses are simple statements of fact, devoid of all figures of speech. They are, however, carefully organized in that the word *right* (v. 4) is the same idea as *upright* (v. 1). The use of the same word in these verses—in one case to characterize God's people, and in the other to speak of God's Word—is an example of the literary device we call "stitching" or "stitch words." The effect of using the same word is to join the second section of the Hymn to the first, thereby uniting the two parts.

Verses 6–11 further emphasize Yahweh's sovereignty over everything in nature and over all the nations. These verses do more than state that God is sovereign; they demonstrate his sovereignty in the orderly way they are written. In the English text, verse 6 begins with the statement "By the word of the LORD" and ends with "by the breath of his mouth." These two statements point to God's works as Creator, and they frame the verse with an A-A pattern. In the middle of the verse, the psalmist declares that God makes the "heavens" and "their starry hosts." These are the objects that God has created, providing a B-B pattern. The patterning in the English text (A-B-B-A) reflects God's care in creating the heavens. Further suggesting God's infinite power is the image that he "breathes" all of the stars and planets ("starry hosts") into existence—no difficult task for him! Think of what the psalmist is saying here. We think now that there are twenty galaxies within 2.5 million light-years of the earth, several thousand within 50 million light-years, and "more than 100 million can be photographed with modern telescopes."[2] When we think of how vast the heavens that Yahweh created actually are, we should indeed "sing joyfully to the LORD" (v. 1).

The psalmist does not just tell us that God is sovereign over everything; rather, he demonstrates God's power over the sky and the seas in the images he uses. These reflections of God's power invite us to praise him.

Verse 7 adds the seas to the mix. It begins with an image that suggests God's immense power over the oceans, for it is as if he gathers the oceans in "jars" (LXX), or perhaps "heaps" (Masoretic Text; cf. Exod. 15:8). The word for "jars" is related to the way in which Yahweh stopped the flow of the waters for his people to cross the Red Sea (Exod. 15:8) and reminds the reader of God's omnipotence. The verse ends with a synthetic parallelism in the image of God placing the deep in "storehouses." God is so majestic that the psalmist depicts him as able

---

2. *The Scientific American Science Desk Reference* (New York: John Wiley & Sons, 1999), 173.

to "pocket" the 140 million square miles of ocean that constitute 70 percent of the earth's surface.[3] It staggers the imagination to think of a being that has that kind of power. Like the sky, the seas provide life-giving sustenance, and like the sky, they can turn violent and kill. But God controls both the sea and sky; indeed, he sustains all of nature (Col. 1:17). And the psalmist offers God's creative power as a reason to praise him.

Just as Yahweh has power over nature, so he controls the nations (vv. 8–11). The nations surrounding ancient Israel were polytheistic; they believed in many gods, each with his or her own sphere of influence. The Philistine grain god, Dagon, comes to mind because of the Philistines' praise of him when they captured Samson (Judg. 16). The Philistines would have found it difficult to think that there was only one God and that he was sovereign over everything, nature and nations alike. In the early twenty-first century, we can take comfort in knowing that God is sovereign over the nations (and the terrorists for whom some nations may provide refuge), and that he rules over all human affairs. In a synthetic parallelism, verse 9 states emphatically why all the peoples of the earth should worship Yahweh, not the gods of the pagan nations. The psalmist states that God spoke everything into existence, and he continues to support everything he has made. This is one reason why the nations should revere the Lord; he is omnipotent and sovereign.

Notice that the psalmist declares God's sovereignty over the nations both negatively and positively. This technique serves to emphasize Yahweh's power. Negatively, in verse 10, the writer states that God frustrates the "plans" and "purposes" of the nations, "thwarting" the plots of the nations. Positively, in verse 11, the psalmist declares that Yahweh does what he wishes; his "plans" and "purposes" are always carried out. God is sovereign in that he can stop the nations from their evil plans, and he is sovereign in that he does what he wills to be done. We may feel vulnerable to the attacks of godless men, but Yahweh will ultimately bring them to justice.

---

3. Ibid., 278.

In verses 12–19, the psalmist writes some of the most encouraging words to people who feel weak and vulnerable. He tells us that this same God—the one who rules nature and the nations—loves his people. The encouragement the psalmist offers in these verses (and through to the end of the psalm, for that matter) rests in God's unfailing love for his people. Once he has chosen his people (v. 12), God works sovereignly on their behalf. In verses 13 and 14, the psalmist paints an image of God in heaven, almost like an ancient landowner, watching mankind (like a landowner's servants) on earth. We should not think that this image suggests a complacent God who sits in his rocking chair observing what goes on in the earth from a comfortable and disinterested distance. Rather, the psalmist uses this image, repeated for emphasis in a synonymous parallelism, to underscore Yahweh's absolute rule over everything that happens among the nations of the earth. He has such control of human affairs that he "looks down" (v. 13) and "watches" (v. 14) his will unfolding. In case we are not convinced that God is in absolute control of the actions of the nations, verses 16 and 17 assure us in pointed terms that God is more powerful than any nation's army or weapons of destruction. Yahweh is sovereign, even over the armies and weaponry of man. When we are confronted by a "faceless enemy," we should take heart in the knowledge that God knows the face of the enemy, and he has him on a tether.

Even more encouraging are the words of verses 18 and 19. The writer personifies God in verse 18, depicting him as having "eyes" to watch his people. In opposition to the title of the Zora Neal Hurston book, *Their Eyes Were Watching God*,[4] the psalmist states that God watches his people. The picture of God's eye looking over his people is a common one in the Bible, underscoring God's personal knowledge of and care for his people. As a father watches his children so that they come to no harm, so Yahweh's eye is on his children. Fear is turned to hope (v. 18), for God directs his unfailing love providentially toward his people, rescuing them from death and providing for them in famine

---

4. Zora Neal Hurston, *Their Eyes Were Watching God* (New York: Perennial Classics, 1998).

(v. 19). Notice the double statement in verse 19, which states God's love negatively (protecting from harm) and positively (providing food during famines). It is as if the psalmist organizes the verse to reflect the care of God's providential rule over the earth for the good of his people—protecting and providing. No enemy has the power to withstand him.

We should note here how God's providence is different from the ancient idea of fate and the modern idea of determinism. Both fate and determinism teach that an impersonal force rules over all human activity with no regard to people's welfare. The Christian idea of providence, however, teaches that God is not impersonal in his dealings with his creation. He is keenly interested in each individual person, and he performs his will for his glory and the good of his people. Providence is the polar opposite of fate and determinism, for in his sovereignty God shows his unfailing love for his people, even when he demonstrates his absolute power over nature and the nations. He can do what he purposes to do, as no human being can. With such a God as our defender and provider, with such a loving providence, how can we fear?

In the concluding exhortation to trust Yahweh (vv. 20–22), the psalmist once again invites God's people to praise him. The only figure of speech in this short section is the metaphor of Yahweh as a shield in the reference to him as "our help and our shield" (v. 20). As a "shield," God protects from the attacks of the enemy, just as the full-length shield of the psalmist's day protected the warrior from head to foot. Stating the same idea in a positive, rather than a negative, sense, the psalmist also calls God our "help," emphasizing God's provision for us. He protects and provides. When we remember the sovereignty of God that the psalmist has repeated and emphasized in the middle section of the psalm, the fact that he provides for and protects his people gives great encouragement. In the final verse of the psalm, the writer returns to his primary theme of Yahweh's *hesed*, his unfailing love, as the source of all of the goodness of God toward his people. The psalm begins and ends in simple declarative statements calling on us to praise the Lord; in the middle section, the psalmist uses a number of figures of speech to demonstrate God's goodness on behalf of his people.

What Are the Themes and Theology in the Psalm?

As is true with other psalms, the themes and theology of Psalm 33 are expressed in the details of the psalm, particularly through the figures of speech and parallelisms we have already noted. The primary theme of the psalm is the admonition to God's people to praise him for his unfailing love; the theology of the poem relates to what we learn about Yahweh in the psalm. Framed at the beginning and end with the call to praise Yahweh, Psalm 33 gives us many reasons why we should wish to praise him at all times, even in distress. First, God is righteous and true (vv. 4–5), and his unfailing love is based on these two important characteristics. If God were not righteous and true in all he says, we could not trust him when he promises his *ḥesed* to us.

Second, God is sovereign (vv. 6–11). In this psalm, the writer emphasizes God's sovereignty over nature and the nations; God created and rules the natural world, and he overrules the plans and purposes of the nations. If God were not sovereign, he could not carry out his purposes of *ḥesed* for his people. Think of the combination of God's characteristics the psalmist has listed in these few verses. We can trust God to do what he says because he is righteous (and therefore truthful in what he promises) and sovereign (and therefore able to fulfill his purposes).

Third, God turns all of his goodness upon his people (vv. 12–19), ruling over nature and the nations to establish his loving providence in his people's lives.

> *Absolute power and unconditional love—*
> *these are the comforts of Psalm 33.*

Applications

1. Like the Israelites of old, Christians are "the apple of [God's] eye" (Deut. 32:10). He will never leave us nor forsake us. Even when we do not *feel* as if he is close to us, we know he is always there (Matt. 28:20).

2. Psalm 33 testifies to God's unfailing love toward his people of all the ages. As Christians, we can turn to this psalm in times of discouragement and fear. It reminds us that we can trust him in the face of the unknown. He is sovereign, righteous, and loving.

3. No one ever catches God by surprise; no circumstance ever nullifies his unfailing love for his people. Remember that the one who says he loves us is also the one who rules nature and the nations for our good.

4. Finally, the better we know Yahweh, the more we will be able to appreciate what he does for us. How can we get to know him? Study the Scriptures. It is important for us to study the Bible to see God as he reveals himself to us. Reread Psalm 33 and review the characteristics of God that the writer emphasizes. Know God.

Psalm 103
Bless the Lord for His Unfailing Love

Are you weary in well doing? Does it seem that others, even Christians sometimes, are doing evil and not being punished? Are you discouraged at work, or even at home? Is a loved one seriously ill? Does unconfessed sin weigh you down? If you are troubled in any of these ways (and who of us is not from time to time?), this psalm is for you. It takes all of these difficulties, and more, into account and still calls on us to praise Yahweh with our whole being. How can the psalmist expect us to praise God when we are troubled, and God appears not to care? In this psalm, David praises God for his unfailing love *(ḥesed)* and the blessings that issue from that love.

¹Praise the LORD, O my soul;
   all my inmost being, praise his holy name.
²Praise the LORD, O my soul,
   and forget not all his benefits—
³who forgives all your sins
   and heals all your diseases,
⁴who redeems your life from the pit
   and crowns you with love and compassion,
⁵who satisfies your desires with good things
   so that your youth is renewed like the eagle's.

⁶The LORD works righteousness
   and justice for all the oppressed.

⁷He made known his ways to Moses,
   his deeds to the people of Israel:
⁸The LORD is compassionate and gracious,
   slow to anger, abounding in love.
⁹He will not always accuse,
   nor will he harbor his anger forever;
¹⁰he does not treat us as our sins deserve
   or repay us according to our iniquities.
¹¹For as high as the heavens are above the earth,
   so great is his love for those who fear him;
¹²as far as the east is from the west,
   so far has he removed our transgressions from us.
¹³As a father has compassion on his children,
   so the LORD has compassion on those who fear him;
¹⁴for he knows how we are formed,
   he remembers that we are dust.
¹⁵As for man, his days are like grass,
   he flourishes like a flower of the field;
¹⁶the wind blows over it and it is gone,
   and its place remembers it no more.
¹⁷But from everlasting to everlasting

the LORD's love is with those who fear him,
and his righteousness with their children's children—
[18]with those who keep his covenant
and remember to obey his precepts.

[19]The LORD has established his throne in heaven,
and his kingdom rules over all.

[20]Praise the LORD, you his angels,
you mighty ones who do his bidding,
who obey his word.
[21]Praise the LORD, all his heavenly hosts,
you his servants who do his will.
[22]Praise the LORD, all his works
everywhere in his dominion.

Praise the LORD, O my soul.

What Is the Overall Effect of the Psalm?

In Psalm 103 David expresses enthusiastic, even lavish, praise to Yahweh for who he is and what he has done. There is not a verse in the psalm that does not look toward God and honor him. From beginning to end, Psalm 103 exalts God as the one who is worthy of the writer's praise and adoration. David's praise is lavish because he knows how much God has done for him; when he meditates on his sinful condition, David realizes afresh how profound God's love for him is. In turn, this realization prompts overflowing praise to God.

Behind all of the exhortations in the psalm to praise God lies an implicit sense of the difficulties from which God has rescued the psalmist. Sin, disease, oppression, and frailty—these form the backdrop against which David praises God. In every situation, God has expressed his *hesed,* or his abounding love, to David and to his people; in every situation, God's love has rescued his people and met their needs. So it is for us today.

As we read Psalm 103, we need to think in two directions at the same time. With David, we need to come to the psalm keenly aware of our needs, frailties, and sins. And with David, we need to look for God's grace that forgives our sins and provides for our needs. If we will approach the psalm this way—the way David wrote it and the Holy Spirit inspired it—we will reap many blessings from our reading.

What Is the Structure of the Psalm?

Psalm 103 is a Hymn, or a Psalm of Praise, to Yahweh in which David celebrates God's goodness to him personally and to God's people as a whole. Like most Hymns, Psalm 103 has a tripartite structure. It begins and ends with the liturgical statement, "Praise the LORD, O my soul" and is patterned as follows:

I. Verse 1:   The Call to Praise Yahweh
II. Verses 2–19:   Reasons to Praise Yahweh
III. Verses 20–22: Concluding Call to Praise Yahweh

The opening invitation to praise Yahweh in verse 1 strikes the note of praise at the outset of the psalm. In this verse, David speaks to himself, encouraging his "soul" to praise the Lord. This self-dialogue may strike the modern reader as odd, but the opening dialogue establishes a dramatic note that involves the reader actively and personally in the praise to Yahweh. It is as if the psalmist is speaking to the reader or listener, as well as to himself. The effect of this opening call to praise is to engage the reader in the praise of Yahweh. The psalm ends as it begins, with the repetition of the self-dialogue. At both the beginning and ending of Psalm 103, David personalizes the praise to Yahweh and encourages our wholehearted participation in the psalm.

In the middle section of Psalm 103, David lists the various reasons why we should praise Yahweh. In this part of the psalm, David moves in an ever-expanding circle from personal to universal blessings, always inviting the reader to share his praise of Yahweh. David begins with the blessings God gives to him personally, specifically mentioning forgiveness, healing, deliverance, and provision (vv. 2–5). It is likely that this list is not intended to be comprehensive; rather, with it David wants his readers to know that God provides for him both temporally and spiritually in every way. Next, David lists the gifts God gives to his people—"national blessings," we might call them (vv. 6–18). David begins this part of the psalm with an allusion to God's faithfulness to Moses and the people of Israel. We should not skip over this reference to Moses, for this mention of God's protection of his people in the Exodus from Egypt and through the wilderness reminds those who heard David's psalm—and us—that God is sovereign. He is able to do what he promises. Against the backdrop of God's faithfulness to his people even in times of great trouble and adversity, David repeats one particular characteristic of Yahweh, namely, his compassion (see especially vv. 6, 8, 13). We need God's fatherly kindness even in times of trouble, perhaps most urgently in such times. Finally, in the middle section of the psalm, David emphasizes God's sovereignty and providence over all things (v. 19), thereby ending the section with a reference to God's care and control of the universe at large. Throughout this middle part of the psalm, David continually invites his readers to praise Yahweh with him, for praise is the proper response to the divine perfections that David mentions in the psalm.

In the concluding call to praise Yahweh, David extends his invitation to praise infinitely by inviting every created being to join him. Angels, "heavenly hosts" (v. 21), servants, and "all his works" (v. 22) are not enough to offer adequate praise to the sovereign Lord. The psalm begins in personal praise, offers more and more reasons to praise God in its middle section, and finally calls on everything everywhere to praise. Then David concludes the psalm by repeating the opening phrase, "Praise the Lord, O my soul." In so doing, he accomplishes two goals. He maintains the personal focus of praise, and he makes the doxology (or hymn of praise) of the middle section his own. In fact, Psalm 103 is one of David's doxologies, for in it he offers his personal praise to God for all he has done for him. Psalm 103 is designed to increase our praise to Yahweh.

What Are the Figures of Speech in the Psalm, and What Effects Do They Have?

Between the opening call to praise (v. 1) and the concluding invitation to praise (vv. 20–22), David writes a carefully designed Hymn in which he alternates reasons to praise God with images that encourage us to praise God. He alternates logical explanations with concrete illustrations. Here is David's design:

I.	Verses 2–4a:	Personal reasons to praise God
II.	Verse 4b:	An image that encourages praise
III.	Verses 5–10:	Blessings that God bestows on his people
IV.	Verses 11–13:	Images of God's blessings
V.	Verse 14:	A reminder of why we need God's blessings
VI.	Verses 15–16:	An image of man's condition
VII.	Verses 17–19:	A statement of God's character

This pattern that makes use of explanations and illustrations appeals to our minds and our imaginations, convincing us logically and encouraging us emotionally to praise God.

David begins the middle section by citing reasons to praise God. He does so in two antithetic parallelisms by alternating negative and positive arguments. First, he states positively that we are to praise God (v. 2a); then he states negatively that we are not to forget his blessings (v. 2b). Next, he states negatively that God does not hold our sin against us (v. 3a); then he states positively that God heals our diseases (v. 3b). Whether we think of what evil God spares us on the one hand or what blessings he gives us on the other, we are to praise him.

David follows these reasons to praise God with the image of a crown (v. 4b), representing God's love and compassion for the believer. The image suggests that God's grace is our glory. Just as a crown signifies a monarch's position and power, so God's love and compassion are the highest ornament we can lay claim to. We cannot boast in ourselves but only in the Lord (1 Cor. 1:31). The image of God's love and compassion as the believer's crown is a fine example of how poetic imagery conveys theology in the Psalms. Coming after the reasons to praise God (vv. 2–3), the indication that God crowns us with love and compassion should inspire our praise. Indeed, this is the response the psalmist and the Holy Spirit wish to evoke.

> *The very best we can boast of (our "crown") is nothing we*
> *have done ourselves but God's grace alone.*

In verses 5–10, David briefly lists several blessings God bestows on his people. All of these blessings are based on the attributes he mentions in verse 8, where he states that God is "compassionate and gracious," patient and loving. In one way or another, all of these characteristics of God reflect his loving-kindness, or *hesed*. They provide the basis of God's kindness toward his people. Leading up to this list of God's attributes, David states that God provides good things for us (v. 5); he upholds the cause of the downtrodden (v. 6); and in earlier times he showed his great power to his people, as in Moses' day (v. 7). Following the characteristics of God, David states that God forgives sin and treats us mercifully (vv. 9–10). Any one of the reasons listed in this section is enough to encourage us to praise Yahweh, for without these blessings, we would be lost. Taken together in the rapid-fire manner David presents them, they should prompt our enthusiastic praise.

Following these reasons to praise God, David paints two images of God's blessings to his people. Surely among the most beautiful verses in all Scripture, verses 11 and 12 demonstrate how great God's love for his people is. First, David states that God's love is as "high as the heavens are above the earth." How high is that? Where do the heavens begin? Even with all of our modern scientific knowledge, we cannot answer such questions, for the heavens are too huge. This image implies that the "height" of God's love is infinite and inexhaustible. David's second image relates to God's forgiveness of our sins and is expressed in the distance between east and west. How far east do you have to travel to find the west? How far west to find the east? The point is that you can never find the west by traveling east, nor the east by going west; you are always traveling in one direction or the other. How far is the east from the west? The distance is infinite. So far does God remove our sins from us in his mercy. Rudyard Kipling suggests something of the scope of what the psalmist is saying in his famous lines, "Oh, East is East, and West is West, and never the twain shall meet."[5] In Psalm 103, we are reminded that it is God's character, not our confession, which confirms his mercy. It is clear now why David spent so much of the early part of the psalm naming God's characteristics; it is because they point to his forgiveness that is greater than our sins. Our assurance is God's character, not ours. This is why God's holiness is mentioned in verse 1; it is the only sure foundation for his mercy.

In verse 14, David states that one reason God is so compassionate toward us is that he knows how frail we are. This simple statement of fact introduces another image (vv. 15–16) that demonstrates the brevity of human life and our vulnerability in the face of death. We are so familiar with the images of these verses that we do not even think of them as poetic. Like grass or flowers that rise up and then are gone quickly, we live and die. In our turn, we are forgotten. In our garden at home, we have a Hibiscus plant that has one of the most beautiful flowers imaginable. Its blossoms are six inches across and dazzle the eye with their beauty and color. But they last only one day; the blossom that opened yesterday is dead today. Our lives are like those flowers, brief and vulnerable. Forgotten by God (v. 16); think of it! Such a simple image, such a sobering reality!

In case we despair, David follows this image of our human frailty with the glorious truth that God's love for his people is eternal (vv. 17–19). David uses no figures of speech in these verses; rather, he states explicitly that God's unfailing love rescues his people from the grave. Because Christ has overcome the grave, we can say with John Donne, "One short sleep past, we wake eternally / And death shall be no more;

---

5. Rudyard Kipling, "The Ballad of East and West," in *Works of Rudyard Kipling* (New York: National Library, 1909), 10:1.

Death, thou shalt die."[6] More confidently than this, with Hosea (13:14) and Paul, we can say,

> Where, O death, is your victory?
> Where, O death, is your sting?
> —1 Corinthians 15:55

With David, we can trust in the Lord's unfailing love that rescues us from the grave.

In the middle section of Psalm 103, David provides an exalted expression of his praise for God. The section begins with David's gratitude to God for the blessings he gives to him personally (vv. 2–5); it expands to include God's blessings for the nation at large (vv. 6–18); and it concludes in a glorious statement of God's sovereign rule over everything in the universe (v. 19). Any one of the blessings David cites is reason enough to praise God eternally; taken together, they build to a crescendo of praise that we are intended to share.

David concludes his poem with a repeated call to praise God. Note that the final section of the psalm begins the same way the middle section does with the statement, "Praise the LORD" (vv. 2, 20), thus unifying the two parts of the Hymn. Such an exhortation to praise is typical of Hymns, but in Psalm 103 David concludes with the same words with which he began, "Praise the LORD, O my soul" (v. 22). In this way, he frames the psalm with a personal call to praise God. We call this device a bookend, for the psalm is brought full circle. The end reminds us of the beginning—with one important difference. By the end of the psalm we have seen a host of motivations to praise Yahweh, and for that reason our concluding praise is greater than our opening praise. In the words of T. S. Eliot, "to make an end is to make a beginning. / The end is where we start from."[7] When we come to the end of

---

6. John Donne, "Holy Sonnet 10," in *Donne Poetical Works*, ed. Sir Herbert Grierson (London: Oxford University Press, 1933), 297.

7. T. S. Eliot, "Little Gidding," in *T. S. Eliot: The Complete Poems and Plays, 1909–1950* (New York: Harcourt Brace, 1980), 144.

the psalm, we should begin to praise God. By repeating the beginning in the ending, David brings all that the psalm has stated about God's character and actions—his unfailing love, mercy, and sovereignty—home to us and encourages us to praise God in our lives.

Along with David, we praise God at the end of Psalm 103.

What Are the Themes and Theology in the Psalm?

Psalm 103 looks in two directions at the same time: toward ourselves and toward God. Verses 2 to 5 admonish us early in the psalm to remember our frailties and sins; we need God. At the same time that we recognize our needs, the psalm turns our attention toward Yahweh and shows him to be the only one who can meet our needs. David mentions three primary reasons why we should praise God, and they each reflect the character and work of God. First, God treats David with compassion and love (vv. 2–5); second, he is faithful to his people (vv. 6–18); and finally, he reigns in sovereignty over the universe (v. 19). If we think of these three themes in reverse order, we may feel the effect of the psalm more forcefully, for the final idea (God's sovereignty) is what remains in our minds when we finish reading the psalm. Because God rules the universe, nothing can ultimately thwart his will; his will includes his faithfulness toward his people to manifest his goodness and glory; and he is compassionate to each one of us (David being the representative in the early part of the psalm of the individual believer). Our comfort and encouragement do not come from ourselves; they come from the character of God and his love toward us. Psalm 103 is a practical psalm, for it teaches us that Yahweh protects and provides for his people.

Henry Lyte praises God for his protection and provision in his hymn, "Praise, My Soul, the King of Heaven." In the well-known opening stanza, Lyte summarizes his reasons for writing the hymn:

> Praise, my soul, the King of heaven,
> To his feet your tribute bring;
> Ransomed, healed, restored, forgiven,
> Who, like me, his praise should sing?
> Praise him praise, praise him,
> Praise the everlasting King.[8]

Yahweh has ransomed us from the penalty of sin, healed us, restored us to fellowship with him, and forgiven our sins—all in Jesus Christ. We could do none of these things for ourselves. It took God's Son becoming our Savior to do what we could not do. Lyte's hymn, based on Psalm 103, goes on in the remaining stanzas to offer more reasons why we should praise Yahweh.

In a similar vein, the seventeenth-century hymn writer, Joachim Neander, offers praise to Yahweh in the familiar hymn, "Praise to the Lord, the Almighty." In his second stanza, Neander yokes God's sovereignty over the universe with his grace toward his children:

> Praise to the Lord, who o'er all things so wondrously reigneth,
> Shelters thee under his wings, yea, so gently sustaineth!
> Hast thou not seen how thy desires e'er have been
> Granted in what he ordaineth.[9]

If Yahweh does not reign over the universe—if he is not sovereign—he could not shelter his children from danger or sustain them in times of adversity. We should be quick to acknowledge God's sovereignty, for his grace toward us depends on it.

---

8. Henry F. Lyte, "Praise, My Soul, the King of Heaven," in *Trinity Hymnal* (Philadelphia: Great Commission, 1990), 76.
9. Joachim Neander, "Praise to the Lord, the Almighty," in *Trinity Hymnal* (Philadelphia: Great Commission, 1990), 53.

Applications

1. Whenever we tire of the responsibilities and trials of life, we can remember that God gives us strength like an eagle's. He heals us according to his will and gives us daily grace with our daily bread.
2. When we sin—and it is not "if" we sin but when—we can be certain that God will forgive us if we are in Christ. As we confess our sins, he forgives them and removes them from us so far that they cannot be seen or remembered against us again. If you are a Christian, keep "short sin accounts" with God and enjoy the peace he gives. If you are not a Christian, the only way to participate in God's peace is to trust Christ.
3. Let us never think that we have earned God's blessings, for, if we have, we can lose them as well. Rather, it is God who has blessed, not we who have earned the blessing. David reminds us in Psalm 103 that all of God's blessings are based on his own character of righteousness and love; they are guaranteed by his sovereignty. We can add nothing to divinity; we only receive gratefully what he promises us.
4. How can we respond to this kind of unfailing love? Trust and praise.

Encountering God as Covenant Maker

We can only begin to meditate on some of the lessons from these psalms that praise God for his unfailing love. These psalms show us the deep, deep love God has for his people throughout the ages. He forgives our sins when we do not deserve to be forgiven; he remembers them no more. He protects us and provides for our daily needs; he is the only one who can move heaven and earth to do so on our behalf. He gives us grace to live the kind of lives that honor him and bring blessings upon us. When the psalmists meditate on who God is and what he does for his people, they burst out spontaneously into joyous praise. We ought to do the same.

But how? To begin, we need to know God as he is revealed in Scripture. We need to read and meditate upon the words of the Bible with an eye to what they teach, not only about us but also, and more importantly, about the Lord. How can we honor him, or enjoy him for that matter, if we do not know what he is like? Of course, implicit in this encouragement to read the Scriptures to learn about God is the fact that we must have a high view of Scripture—that it is inerrant and inspired—if we are to trust what it says about anything, including God.

Apart from knowing about God by reading the Scriptures, we need to know him personally in Jesus Christ, his Son. Jesus said, "Anyone who has seen me has seen the Father" (John 14:9). We need to know Jesus Christ as Savior if we are to be freed from our sin, if we are to know the peace of God in this life, and if we are to have eternal life in heaven. How do we come to know Jesus Christ as Savior? By faith. We must acknowledge that we are sinners, that we can do nothing to solve the separation from God that our sin has created, and ask Christ to save us. We must know Jesus.

Beyond faith in Jesus Christ and studying the Bible to see what it says about God, we ought to praise God. The psalmists do; we have seen them break forth into praise repeatedly, even in the two psalms we have studied in this chapter. How can we praise God? We praise God with our words and in our actions. When we delight in God, his Son, and the Bible, that delight will find expression in our speech. We will want to acknowledge in the hearing of others all that God has done for us. We praise God when we testify to his grace. With our words, however, must go our actions. If we are to please God, we must do acts of mercy and kindness in his name. Helping the orphans and widows (James 1:27), contributing time and financial resources to a local church, loving family members even when it costs us: these are some of the ways we can show, as well as say, our love for the Lord. Paul summarizes the idea when he says, "so whether you eat or drink or whatever you do, do it all for the glory of God" (1 Cor. 10:31). We must witness Christ's saving grace, and we must do good deeds to corroborate our testimony.

As we study Scripture, as we witness to God's grace in Jesus Christ, and as we do good deeds in his name, we must always remember that we are not earning merit and praise for ourselves. It is Christ in us who, by grace, enables us to honor the Lord. Read the words of Paul the apostle on this matter:

> I have been crucified with Christ and I no longer live, but Christ lives in me. The life I live in the body, I live by faith in the Son of God, who loved me and gave himself for me.
> —Galatians 2:20

Do you see why we must know right doctrine if we are to live right lives? God reveals himself in Scripture, which he, in turn, inspired (2 Tim. 3:16–17). If we do not have a high view of the Bible, we will put little trust in what it says about the Lord. We need to know God so that we can learn to be like him. Paul encourages us to become increasingly Christlike when he writes:

> Therefore, I urge you, brothers, in view of God's mercy, to offer your bodies as living sacrifices, holy and pleasing to God— this is your spiritual act of worship. Do not conform any longer to the pattern of this world, but be transformed by the renewing of your mind. Then you will be able to test and approve what God's will is—his good, pleasing and perfect will.
> —Romans 12:1–2

I wonder how often we look back to the closing verses of chapter 11 of Romans to see why it is that we should present ourselves to God in this way? Read Romans 11:33–36, and you will get some idea of why we should wish God to make us increasingly like Christ. In those verses, Paul tells us something about God the Father: that he is transcendent and supreme (v. 33), that he upholds all creation by his power (v. 36), and that he is the only true God (vv. 34–35). This is why we should become more like Christ—because we were created and redeemed for this purpose. May our meditations on these psalms of God's unfailing love make us more like Christ.

Chapter 7

Who Is This King of Glory?

Your kingdom is an everlasting kingdom,
and your dominion endures through all generations.
—Psalm 145:13

AMERICANS DO NOT OFTEN THINK about kings, for the founding fathers worked hard not to have a king in the new country at all. The abuses of the English Crown toward the colonies warned the framers of the United States Constitution not to enshrine a monarchy. The result was the separation of powers in the United States among the executive, legislative, and judicial branches of government. Americans elect their president; he is one of their own and cannot remain in power forever. Even so, many of us would wait hours to see the president, would we not?

In such a culture it is difficult to imagine how important the idea of kingship and a kingdom is to many other peoples. British people continue to hold on to their monarchy, and many Britons openly celebrate royalty. But not Americans. Kings are ordinary people to Americans, whereas for others they are qualitatively distinct from ordinary people.

If in our modern context we are to understand the many references to kings in the Psalms, we will have to think of kings as people set apart from ordinary people, called (even "anointed") to a particular role as sovereign leader of a people. This is the way it was for many nations until the sixteenth or seventeenth century; people believed in the divine right of kings as justification for the monarchy. This is the way it was for the Old Testament Israelites when they asked for a king; they wanted a ruler who would protect and provide for them. Seen this way, something of David's significance to his people becomes more evident. How much more significant are the references in the Psalms that depict Yahweh as the great King over his people!

> *If we would wait hours to see a king or a president,*
> *how should we attend Yahweh, the King of Kings*
> *and Lord of Lords?*

Both Old and New Testaments call Yahweh the great King who rules over the earth. When the Israelites asked for a human king, God reprimanded them and said to them, "the LORD your God was your king" (1 Sam. 12:12). From the time he called the nation of Israel into existence at Mount Sinai, God was the King over his people. So important is God's reign as King, the New Testament begins with a reference to the reign of Jesus Christ in the words, "A record of the genealogy of Jesus Christ the son of David, the son of Abraham" (Matt. 1:1), placing Christ in the royal lineage of David. When we speak of some of Christ's parables as "Kingdom Parables," we are tacitly acknowledging the truth that Jesus Christ is the King. And the Bible concludes in the Apocalypse with the picture of Jesus Christ reigning forever as King of Kings and Lord of Lords:

> The kingdom of the world has become the kingdom of our
> Lord and of his Christ, and he will reign for ever and ever.
>   —Revelation 11:15

Christ will reign in future glory as our great King, and he reigns now in sovereign power over the universe. From the beginning of

Genesis to the end of Revelation, God's sovereignty declares his king-ship over all things.

The psalmists frequently speak of Yahweh as the King in references scattered throughout the Psalms. We call the Psalms that concentrate on Yahweh as King the "Royal" or "Kingship" Psalms. Psalms 2; 20; and 24 depict Yahweh as King, as the great chorus of Psalm 24 that Handel wrote into his oratorio, *The Messiah*, attests. Psalm 72 speaks of Solomon, the son and heir of King David. Psalms 84; 96; and 132 all speak of King David's heirs; the last of these is the divine King who will rule forever—Jesus Christ himself. In this chapter, we will look at two Royal Psalms to see what they have to say to us about our great God as King.

The context of the king in the Old Testament is important to our understanding of the Royal Psalms (and of Christ's role as King, for that matter). From the time of Moses and Joshua through the period of the Judges, Yahweh was the King of Israel. While the nations sur-rounding Israel all had kings, Israel had no human king through this period. The lack of a human king made it clear to the Israelites that Yahweh was their provider and protector; what is more, it was a testi-mony to the nations that Yahweh was the only true God. It is notewor-thy that Gideon declined to rule over Israel in his day, stating, "The LORD will rule over you" (Judg. 8:23). God's ideal for Israel was that he would be their King.

In Samuel's day, however, the Israelites feared for their future if the prophet's sons should become rulers, and before he died, they asked Samuel to appoint a human king. It is clear in the Old Testament ac-count of this event that the Israelites' desire for a king was sin and a rejection of Yahweh (1 Sam. 8:7); nonetheless, God granted his people's wish and appointed Saul as their king (1 Sam. 9:17–10:25). In his mercy, God appointed a human king over Israel while still maintaining his covenant with them. Writing of this incident, Tremper Longman states, "The conclusion comes in 1 Samuel 11:14–12:25, which is a covenant renewal ceremony reaffirming the nation's trust in the Lord while es-tablishing the monarchy."[1] With the anointing of Saul as king, a new

---

1. Tremper Longman, *How to Read the Psalms* (Downers Grove, Ill.: InterVarsity, 1988), 69.

chapter in the history of Israel begins, one that climaxes in the rule of King David: Israel had both a human king and Yahweh as their King.

> *"And the LORD told him [Samuel]: 'Listen to all that the people are saying to you; it is not you they have rejected, but they have rejected me as their king.'" (1 Sam. 8:7)*

With David's rule, Yahweh establishes a covenant with his people and makes an explicit pledge that leads to the birth of Messiah, Jesus Christ. Yahweh promises David that his descendants will sit on the throne in perpetuity and that he will love him forever (2 Sam. 7:5–16). This covenant forms the basis for the Royal Psalms, for it provides the various types of kings the Psalms mention: the human king who is David or his descendants, Yahweh the King, and the anticipation of Messiah as King. In this chapter, we will look at Psalms 84 and 96. Psalm 84 emphasizes Yahweh's rule over his people Israel, and Psalm 96 extends Yahweh's rule as King over all the nations. In Psalm 84, the psalmist displays his overwhelming longing for the Lord and the protection and peace the Lord provides for him; in Psalm 96, the psalmist extends a jubilant invitation to the "nations," or those outside the community of faith, to embrace Yahweh as their King.

Psalm 84
A LONGING FOR YAHWEH IN HIS SANCTUARY

Psalm 84 reflects the royal reign of Yahweh over his people. It is simultaneously a joyous psalm of praise to God for his righteous reign over his people and an expression of the psalmist's deep longing to be with the Lord and away from the wicked. The only explicit reference to God as King is in verse 3, where the psalmist calls Yahweh his King and his God. However, the image of Yahweh as King runs throughout the psalm, from the reference to the "courts of the LORD" (v. 2), to the "house" of God (v. 10), and even the "altar" (v. 3) of the tabernacle. All of these references evoke the presence of God, "the Great King, whose name is 'LORD Almighty' (Yahweh Sabaoth), and who is worshiped as [the psalmist's] God."[2] We will study the psalm as an example of the reign of God as King over his own people.

It is worth noting before we turn to the psalm itself that the psalmist does not ask anywhere in the psalm for temporal or personal material blessings. His attention is altogether riveted on God, his King. When we find it difficult to pray for even a few minutes without asking for something from the Lord, Psalm 84 will help us recover the right emphasis of prayer. All the psalmist wishes is to share the kingly reign of Yahweh and "dwell" with him forever (v. 4).

> [1]How lovely is your dwelling place,
>   O LORD Almighty!
> [2]My soul yearns, even faints,
>   for the courts of the LORD;
>   my heart and my flesh cry out
>   for the living God.
>
> [3]Even the sparrow has found a home,
>   and the swallow a nest for herself,
>   where she may have her young—
>   a place near your altar,
> O LORD Almighty, my King and my God.
> [4]Blessed are those who dwell in your house;
>   they are ever praising you. *Selah*
>
> [5]Blessed are those whose strength is in you,
>   who have set their hearts on pilgrimage.
> [6]As they pass through the Valley of Baca,
>   they make it a place of springs;
>   the autumn rains also cover it with pools.

---

2. Willem VanGemeren, *Psalms*, vol. 5 of *The Expositor's Bible Commentary*, ed. Frank E. Gaebelein (Grand Rapids: Zondervan, 1991), 543.

[7]They go from strength to strength,
    till each appears before God in Zion.

[8]Hear my prayer, O LORD God Almighty;
    listen to me, O God of Jacob. *Selah*
[9]Look upon our shield, O God;
    look with favor on your anointed one.

[10]Better is one day in your courts
    than a thousand elsewhere;
I would rather be a doorkeeper in the house of my God
    than dwell in the tents of the wicked.
[11]For the LORD God is a sun and shield;
    the LORD bestows favor and honor;
    no good thing does he withhold
    from those whose walk is blameless.

[12]O LORD Almighty,
    blessed is the man who trusts in you.

What Is the Overall Effect of the Psalm?

If I may coin a word, Psalm 84 is "theotropic": *theos,* meaning "God," and *tropic,* meaning "inclined to." That is, Psalm 84 focuses entirely on God. The psalm is inclined toward God, with every word reflecting the psalmist's overwhelming and singular desire for God. Unable to attend the temple worship in Jerusalem, the psalmist envies the birds whose nests lie in sight of the sanctuary (v. 3). Cut off from the worship of his God and King, he thinks of himself as a pilgrim in the most arid and difficult part of the pilgrimage to Jerusalem (vv. 5–7). Offered wealth with wickedness, he would rather have one day with Yahweh than life with ill-gotten gain (v. 10). Everything the psalmist writes inclines toward God and draws the reader to worship God.

Just as green plants are "heliotropic" (that is, they grow toward the sun—"helios"), so too Christians ought to be "theotropic," or focused on God ("theos").

What is it that draws the psalmist's singular attention? He is attracted to the righteous reign of the peace of Yahweh over his people. The calm picture the psalmist paints of dwelling with the Lord in his sanctuary implies that God has established his people in Zion (v. 7) in peace with the surrounding nations. Domestic tranquility is predicated on national security. In the same way, spiritual peace is based on God's blessing. In his profound longing to be in the presence of the Lord at his sanctuary, the writer of Psalm 84 gives testimony to the righteous reign of Yahweh over his people. The psalm invites us to enjoy the blessings of the Great King's rule.

What Is the Structure of the Psalm?

Psalm 84 is a mixture of different psalmic genres. It has elements of the Hymn, the Lament, and the Royal or Kingship Psalm.[3] As such, it is difficult to insist too rigidly on any one structure for the psalm. Still, the overall effect of the psalm is unquestionably one of praise to Yahweh. In this hybrid psalm, the structure is more implicit than explicit:

  I. Verses 1–4:   Blessings of God's Presence
 II. Verses 5–10:   The Psalmist's Desire to Dwell with God
III. Verses 11–12:   Closing Statement of Confidence in God

At the least, this structure captures the tone of the psalm. Whether the psalmist is thinking of sparrows close to the altar of God or of the pilgrims making their way through the dry land to Jerusalem to be

---

3. VanGemeren states, "This psalm contains a collage of diverse genres: hymn, prayer, lament, and a song of Zion" (ibid., 541).

near the temple for a few days, he always longs for the presence of God. As I suggested in chapter 2, the Royal or Kingship Psalms do not have a set structure; they are characterized by their emphasis on the King, rather than their structure. Psalm 84 fits in the "group of kingship psalms [that] proclaim that God is king."[4]

What Are the Figures of Speech in the Psalm, and What Effects Do They Have?

The psalmist opens his psalm with a metonymy. Metonymy establishes meaning by association. Here, the psalmist references Yahweh when he speaks of his "dwelling place." The dwelling place—the temple—is beautiful not only because of its artistry but more important because of the presence of God there. In other words, the beauty of the temple, which the psalmist will emphasize later in the psalm, comes from God, not the building itself. By extension, when he longs to be in the temple, the psalmist is stating that he longs to be in the presence of God. This is the keynote for the psalm.

Verse 2 makes the metonymy of verse 1 even more explicit. In a synthetic parallelism, the psalmist first states that he longs for the "*courts* of the LORD" (emphasis added), and then adds that he longs for "the living God" (v. 2). Here the psalmist establishes the fact that it is the presence of God for which his whole being yearns. Notice the way in which the psalmist intensifies his longing for God by building toward a climax. First, he states that his soul "yearns, even faints" for the temple of the Lord; then he adds that his whole being (as imaged in his "heart" and "flesh") cries out for the living God (v. 2). Everything about him—body and soul—longs for Yahweh. There is no secular/sacred dichotomy here.

With the imagery of the birds' nests (v. 3), the psalmist deepens his longing to be in the Lord's presence in at least three ways. First, the fact that even the humble sparrow and swallow live close to the temple makes the psalmist's absence from the temple all the more intense for

---

4. Longman, *How to Read the Psalms,* 34.

him. As a man created in the image of God, he loves Yahweh as no bird can; yet he cannot be close to Yahweh's temple as these birds are. Second, the domestic imagery of birds' nests suggests the peace and tranquility that reign at the Jerusalem temple; the simple picture underscores the peace that comes with God's reign over his people. Third, the psalmist envies the birds their proximity to Yahweh's temple. What a moving picture of the depth of the psalmist's love for the Lord, that he should notice the birds' nests in the temple and reflect on his desire to "dwell" there too! In all these ways, the psalmist transforms the simple imagery of birds' nests in the temple of God into his intense longing to be with God.

The psalmist's three references to Yahweh at the end of verse 3 deepen his longing even further. He begins by calling on God as his covenant Lord ("LORD Almighty"), the one who loves his people with his unfailing love, or *ḥesed.* He then calls on God as his "King," the first explicit reference in the psalm to the theme of the royal rule of God. Finally, he calls Yahweh "God," underscoring his sovereign power over all things. Echoing verse 2, where he states that everything about him longs for God, here the psalmist establishes that God is everything to him. The focus of these verses is singular and theotropic.

In verses 5–10, the writer extends his description of his longing for God yet further. In verses 5–7, he turns to the pilgrims who traveled to Jerusalem for the important holy days of the year. These are the Israelites who lived outside of Jerusalem and had to make a special effort to come to the temple and worship God. The psalmist calls these pilgrims "blessed" because they have chosen to set their hearts on pilgrimage. That is, God and his worship are so important to them that they willingly undergo the difficulties of the journey to Jerusalem to worship God as he deserves. In fact, they are more than willing to travel; they desire to do so. It is "set" in their "hearts" (v. 5). The Songs of Ascent, Psalms 120–34, come to mind as the best examples in the Psalms of the love the pilgrims held for their annual temple worship in Jerusalem. These fifteen psalms were likely sung on the way to Jerusalem and at the temple when the pilgrims arrived. The psalmist says that, despite the difficulties along the way, these pilgrims are "blessed" (v. 5).

Often those who made the pilgrimage to Jerusalem had to travel through dry wastelands. With few places to stop, and with the danger of robbers and highwaymen always present, the pilgrims had enough concerns. Adding to their difficulties was the arid landscape through which they often had to travel. Note what blessings the psalmist observes, however. God turns the arid lands into "springs" (v. 6) for the travelers and refreshes the pilgrims in the dry places. In regard to verse 6, Spurgeon suggests that the pilgrims dug trenches to catch springwater and the dew; Spurgeon goes on to state that we should extend outstretched hands to receive God's blessing when we come to worship.[5] Spurgeon's allegory may be stretched, but what is clear here is that God refreshes us in the difficult places. We should not miss the subtle implication of verse 6 that God will sometimes allow us to go through difficult circumstances; he will not always lead us in easy and prosperous paths. The important point is that God refreshes us when he does allow us to undergo trials and difficulties, not that he will remove us from them.

In the next section of the psalm, the writer imagines himself already in the courts (temple) of the Lord. In verse 8, the psalmist references two of God's names and uses them to call upon God for blessing. First is the reference to the "LORD God Almighty," the sovereign one who rules over all nations. Second, the writer calls God the "God of Jacob." The psalmist uses another literary device here, this time a synecdoche, in which a part represents the whole—Jacob representing all of Israel. Jacob is often used in the Psalms to represent all of Israel, for he is the progenitor of the twelve tribes and recipient of the covenant promises made to Abraham and Isaac. The important point is that the reference to Yahweh as the God of Jacob expresses God's unfailing love for his people. The two names of God, one emphasizing God's sovereignty over everything and the other God's unfailing love for his people, frame a repeated call to God to hear the psalmist's prayer. A modern parallel might be calling upon God in prayer as "almighty

---

5. Charles Haddon Spurgeon, *The Treasury of David* (Grand Rapids: Baker, 1983), 4:74.

God and our heavenly Father," suggesting our worship of him as the sovereign Lord and our personal relationship with him as our heavenly Father. We need to appreciate God's sovereignty and his unfailing love if we are to understand God as he represents himself in this psalm.

In verse 9, the writer asks God to prosper the human king of Israel. In a synonymous parallelism, the psalmist parallels the "shield" (or alternately "sovereign") with the "anointed one." The "shield" here and the "anointed one" are references to the king on the throne of David at the time the psalm was written. VanGemeren's comments are helpful here:

> The king is the Lord's "anointed" "shield" for his people. Since he too is dependent on the Lord's blessing, the psalmist prays that the Great King may extend his goodness to the earthly ruler.[6]

In turn, God's protection of the king of Israel extends to all of Israel. The blessings God gives to the king belong also to the people. When the psalmist asks God to bless the earthly king, he is asking God to bless the nation, himself included.

As the psalmist begins verse 10, he returns to the temple imagery of the opening verses and contrasts the courts of the Lord with the dwellings of the wicked. He tells us he would rather have a relatively minor responsibility, such as that of "doorkeeper" (or temple guard), in God's temple than receive great honor in the tents of those who do not love the Lord. The image is uncertain, but it may depict a person standing or resting at the threshold of the Lord's house. Here too the poet uses a literary device, this time hyperbole—deliberate exaggeration to make a point. He states that one day in God's house is better for him than a thousand days in the tents of the wicked. In effect, the poet says that serving as a temple guard for one day (or perhaps worshiping for one day) is better than the equivalent of three years of luxurious living with the wicked. If we read this statement carefully, we will see that

---

6. VanGemeren, *Psalms*, 5:545.

implicit in it is the fact that the ungodly will perish if they do not turn to Christ. Though we may think a thousand days is a long time and perhaps even be tempted to think them a good trade for one day, they too inevitably must end; so will the wicked. Even if all he had were one day with God, the psalmist is saying, it would be better than many days of sinful living with the wicked.

> *When one day of righteous living for the Lord is more important to us than five days' transactions on the stock exchange, we will understand what the psalmist is saying.*

Why is the psalmist willing to trade a thousand days with those who are wicked for one day in the courts of the Lord? He tells us in verse 11, listing some of the blessings God gives to his people. The psalmist arranges these blessings both positively and negatively. By now we have seen this to be a regular technique the psalmists use to emphasize God's blessings. First, stated positively, God is a "sun," providing life-giving material sustenance and "favor and honor" for us (v. 11). God provides for both our temporal and spiritual needs, giving good gifts for this life and showering spiritual abundance upon us (John 10:10). Stated negatively, the psalmist tells us that God is a "shield" to protect us from attack and that he will not withhold any good thing from us (v. 11). Understood positively, this statement asserts that God will shower good gifts upon us for his glory and our good (James 1:17). A smart trade, don't you think? A lowly place with God forever in exchange for ill-gotten wealth for a short time? Peace for worry? Righteousness for sin? The positive/negative pattern to the psalmist's words here underscores the fact that, no matter which way we look at it, God is gracious and loving.

What Are the Themes and Theology in the Psalm?

Everything about Psalm 84 turns on Yahweh's rule as King over Israel. Within this general subject, the psalmist develops four themes, all of them related. The first theme is the recognition of the reign of a human king over Israel. The only explicit reference in the psalm to an earthly king is the psalmist's request that God might bless the king in Israel (v. 9). As we suggested earlier, the psalmist's appeal that God might prosper the king of Israel is also a petition that he might prosper all of Israel, for the nation is personified in its king.

A second theme in Psalm 84 is the righteous reign of Yahweh as the Great King over Israel. Though this psalm makes no explicit mention of it, God's reign extends to all his people of all time and ultimately to Jesus Christ's eschatological reign over the whole earth. Here in Psalm 84, however, the reign of Yahweh relates specifically to the nation of Israel, God's chosen people. The references to "courts" (vv. 1, 10), "altar" (v. 3), and of course to the "King" (v. 3) all attest to God's role as King over his people. When Christians read of God's rule over Israel, they should think of Christ's reign as the heir of David's throne, a reign that will be "established forever" (2 Sam. 7:14). Christ is our great Prophet, Priest, and King who reigns in majesty over us. Christ's reign as David's heir is so important that the very first words of the New Testament affirm it. Matthew writes, "The record of the genealogy of Jesus Christ, the Son of David, the Son of Abraham" (Matt. 1:1). Matthew assures us at the beginning of his gospel that Jesus Christ will fulfill God's covenant with David and one day reign in righteousness forever. Psalm 84 begins with a reference to God as the sovereign Ruler of the universe and continues with this reference to God as the covenant King over his people. The effect is to put both God's sovereignty and his goodness together to demonstrate that God loves us and is able to fulfill his plans for us.

As King over Israel, Yahweh demonstrates his unfailing love to his people in a variety of ways. In Psalm 84, the writer specifically emphasizes God's goodness and his protection. The psalmist references God's goodness to his people implicitly and explicitly. In the reference to the birds nesting near the temple, the writer creates an image that implies the peaceful reign that Yahweh brings to his people. Toward the end of the psalm, he emphasizes God's goodness explicitly in the statement, "no good thing does he withhold from those whose walk is blameless"

(v. 11). The psalmist mentions the protection God gives his people in a variety of ways. God protects the pilgrims who are on their way to Jerusalem to participate in temple worship (vv. 5–7). He provides water for them and leads them safely through a journey fraught with dangers from thieves and murderers. In regard to the picture of the pilgrims, VanGemeren states:

> The strength and joy of the godly stems from their hope in God. Faith in God is ultimate and transforms weak people into those who "go from strength to strength."[7]

The psalmist also implies God's protection of his people in the image of the "shield" (v. 11), a common image of God in the Psalms as he defends his people against evildoers. Though we are not certain of the historical context that prompted the psalmist to write Psalm 84, it may well be that he was under military threat and could not travel to the temple in Jerusalem as he wished. Whatever the situation, he emphasizes God's protection of his people as one of his roles as their King.

The third theme of Psalm 84 relates to the blessings that Yahweh's righteous reign brings to his people. "Blessing" means the happy state in which God's people live. As Christians, we enjoy many blessings that this psalm may call to our minds. First, we have peace with God (Rom. 5:1) because our sins are forgiven. Second, we have the "peace of God, which transcends all understanding" (Phil. 4:7) in all our affairs in this life. Finally, we have a stability that non-Christians can only envy. In this regard, Isaiah writes, "The steadfast of mind You will keep in perfect peace, because he trusts in You" (Isa. 26:3 NASB), no matter what difficulties he may encounter. Surely we are blessed!

The final theme of Psalm 84 shifts our attention from God to ourselves. When we consider all that God does for us, our response ought to be one of praise and longing. These are the responses of the psalmist. "Blessed are those who dwell in your house," he writes, "they are

---

7. Ibid., 544.

ever praising you" (v. 4). C. S. Lewis understood something of how important praise is for the Christian. Lewis writes that praise for God, like admiration for a painting, "is the correct, adequate or appropriate, response"; if we do not praise God, Lewis goes on to say, "we shall have missed something."[8] When we meditate on God's reign over us, we should be moved to praise—just as the writer of Psalm 84 was. Our second response to God's goodness should be one of longing. Rather than asking for temporal and material blessings, the psalmist simply longs to be with God in his temple. Though he may be facing military threat, he only wishes to be in the presence of God, serving as a simple temple guard. In another psalm, the writer expresses his longing with the words, "As the deer pants for streams of water, so my soul pants for you, O God" (Ps. 42:1). In Psalm 84, the writer longs to be in the "dwelling places" of the "LORD Almighty" (v. 1); he would give up everything else for the presence of Yahweh. Do we long for Jesus Christ this way? "O LORD Almighty," the psalmist concludes, "blessed is the man who trusts in you" (v. 12).

Applications

1. As we read this psalm, we should note how much it speaks of God and how little it speaks of us. We would do well to follow the psalmist's lead and see God at the center of our lives, not ourselves.

2. Do we return God's love to him so much that we long to come to church? Does the prospect of hearing God's Word preached make us eager to attend corporate worship services? Or do we find ways to avoid attending church? Our attitude toward church attendance is one marker of our love for God.

3. Do we know God's blessings in the hard times, the wilderness paths of our lives, in a way that allows him to refresh us even in the midst of difficulties? Oftentimes, when we are in difficult

---

8. C. S. Lewis, *Reflections on the Psalms* (New York: Harcourt, Brace, Jovanovich, 1958), 92.

circumstances, we begin to think quickly how to extricate ourselves. With the psalmist, our first thought in such circumstances should be of God, not ourselves.

4. Do we long to find a place of service, no matter how apparently insignificant, in the church and let God use us in his kingdom work? Spiritual gifts fall into two categories: speaking and serving (Rom. 12:3–8; Eph. 4:7–16). With our spiritual gifts we either speak to God's glory, or we can minister to others' needs to God's glory. We would do well to know our spiritual gifts and use them in the local church to his glory, even if we think our gifts insignificant. The psalmist wishes to be a temple guard; we might be an usher or a Sunday school worker.

5. Can we pray without asking for material blessings? The only direct request the psalmist makes of God is to be with him in his temple—to worship him. He repeats this request in verses 2 and 10. Between these two requests, the psalmist notes that God blesses those he loves in multiple ways. The psalmist ends with the confidence that God, the sovereign Lord of the universe, has his eye on his own.

This psalm should encourage most Christians to do some soul-searching. We are admonished to place God at the center of our lives and live accordingly. The difficulty lies in the fact that human nature tends to place self at the center. We must reverse our thinking. We are further encouraged to pray without always asking for personal needs to be met.

We should pray simply to glorify God.

Psalm 96
LET ALL THE NATIONS PRAISE YAHWEH

When we turn from Psalm 84 to Psalm 96, we turn from God's righteous reign over his people to his sovereign rule over all nations. Psalm

96 invites all people to bow before Yahweh, the only true King, and to share in the blessings of his righteous rule. Like Psalm 84, there is only one explicit reference to God as King in Psalm 96, and that is the confident proclamation, "The LORD reigns" (v. 10). As in Psalm 84, God's reign as King hovers implicitly behind much of the rest of the psalm, from references to God's "splendor and majesty" (v. 10), to "his courts" (v. 11), and finally to his role as judge of the nations (v. 13). Yahweh is King over all the nations, Psalm 96 announces, and all nations are invited to acknowledge his reign and participate in its blessings.

> [1]Sing to the LORD a new song;
>> sing to the LORD, all the earth.
> [2]Sing to the LORD, praise his name;
>> proclaim his salvation day after day.
> [3]Declare his glory among the nations,
>> his marvelous deeds among all peoples.
>
> [4]For great is the LORD and most worthy of praise;
>> he is to be feared above all gods.
> [5]For the gods of the nations are idols,
>> but the LORD made the heavens.
> [6]Splendor and majesty are before him;
>> strength and glory are in his sanctuary.
>
> [7]Ascribe to the LORD, O families of nations,
>> ascribe to the LORD glory and strength.
> [8]Ascribe to the LORD the glory due his name;
>> bring an offering and come into his courts.
> [9]Worship the LORD in the splendor of his holiness;
>> tremble before him, all the earth.
>
> [10]Say among the nations,
> "The LORD reigns."
> The world is firmly established, it cannot be moved;
>> he will judge the peoples with equity.

[11]Let the heavens rejoice, let the earth be glad;
   let the sea resound, and all that is in it;
[12]let the fields be jubilant, and everything in them.
Then all the trees of the forest will sing for joy;
   [13]they will sing before the Lord, for he comes,
   he comes to judge the earth.
He will judge the world in righteousness
   and the peoples in his truth.

What Is the Overall Effect of the Psalm?

Psalm 96 is a majestic, jubilant statement that Yahweh excels all human kings and all the imaginary gods of the nations. At the same time, Psalm 96 invites all the nations to participate in the blessings of Yahweh's righteous reign over the earth. Psalm 96 simultaneously declares God's royal authority over everything in the universe and offers peace to all who will bow the knee to his throne. With Charles Wesley, the psalmist proclaims, "Rejoice, the Lord is King,"[9] and with Frances Havergal, the psalmist asks:

Who is on the Lord's side? Who will serve the King?
Who will be his helpers, other lives to bring?
Who will leave the world's side? Who will face the foe?
Who is on the Lord's side? Who for him will go?[10]

Psalm 96 is suitable for public worship of Yahweh, our Great King and God, for it lists many reasons why Yahweh is worthy of our praise. However, the psalm is also appropriate for evangelism of the lost. In regard to this aspect of the psalm, Charles Haddon Spurgeon says that it is "a grand Missionary Hymn"[11] because of its open and compelling

---

9. Charles Wesley, "Rejoice, the Lord Is King," in *Trinity Hymnal* (Philadelphia: Great Commission, 1990), 309.
10. Frances R. Havergal, "Who Is on the Lord's Side?" in *Trinity Hymnal* (Philadelphia: Great Commission, 1990), 587.
11. Spurgeon, *Treasury of David*, 4:336.

invitation to all people to join in the praise of Yahweh. Spurgeon is responding in part to the opening threefold invitation to everyone to praise God and its ending in joy for those who join the song of praise. Psalm 96 does indeed communicate the great joy that comes from having peace with the King of the universe and joining in his praise.

What Is the Structure of the Psalm?

Psalm 96 is another Hymn, a Psalm of Praise to Yahweh as the King of the nations. Throughout, its emphasis is the public praise of Yahweh, suggesting its classification as a Sabbath Psalm. Notice that the invitation is universal, for it is extended to "all the earth." In his opening invitation to praise God, the psalmist reflects Yahweh's covenant with Abraham, for when he called Abraham, Yahweh proclaimed, "all peoples on earth will be blessed through you" (Gen. 12:3b). In Psalm 96, the writer expresses this part of God's covenant with Abraham.

Like most Hymns, Psalm 96 has a tripartite structure. Because the praise rendered to God in this psalm is multidimensional, the patterning of the psalm does not reflect directly the theme of God as the Great King. Rather, Psalm 96 follows the typical structure of most Hymns:

I. Verses 1–3:   An Invitation to Praise Yahweh
II. Verses 4–9:   Yahweh's Great Attributes Worthy of Praise
III. Verses 10–13: The Righteous Reign of Yahweh

As this division implies, Yahweh's role as King is reflected most explicitly in the concluding four verses, where again the call to praise is universal ("Say among the nations" and again "Let the earth be glad"). Coming at the end of the psalm, the universal scope of the call to praise is the final impression the reader has. The idea of God as King of the nations, however, permeates the entire psalm.

What Are the Figures of Speech in the Psalm, and What Effects Do They Have?

Psalm 96 begins with three invitations to praise God and three commands to proclaim his glory to the unbelievers.

Psalm 96 immediately strikes the listener and the reader (perhaps the listener even more emphatically than the reader) with its opening threefold repetition of "Sing to the LORD" (vv. 1–2). The psalmist writes this triple invitation in a climactic parallelism, and each time he calls for song, he focuses his invitation differently. The effect of the climactic parallelism is to amplify the call to praise with each repetition. The first call to sing to the Lord answers the question, "What are we to sing?" We are to sing a "new song" of praise for the "salvation" God gives us (v. 1). The second time the psalmist calls on the congregation to sing to the Lord, he answers the question, "Who is to sing to the Lord?" Everyone—"all the earth" (v. 1)—is to praise Yahweh. The third call answers the question, "Why are we to sing to the Lord?" We are to sing to the Lord to offer him the praise he rightly deserves. Our song, then, is to be one of praise to the Lord for the blessings of salvation, and we are to invite the nations to join in this praise. It is as if the earth is God's temple, and the nations are the congregation. It is easy to see why Spurgeon thought of this psalm as a great Missionary Hymn, for it extends the invitation of salvation to "whosoever will."

Paralleling the threefold call to sing to the Lord are the three imperatives of the opening verses. We are instructed to "praise his name," "proclaim his salvation day after day," and "declare his glory among the nations" (vv. 2–3). Note that all three imperatives require us to speak a word on God's behalf, for it is the spoken testimony that explains God's glory to those who do not acknowledge him. Note too that we are told when and where we are to speak God's praises. In verse 2, we are to speak a word of praise all the time ("day after day"). And in verse 3, we are to praise God everywhere ("among the nations"). What could be clearer? Only two verses into the psalm, and the psalmist has invited everyone to sing to the Lord and instructed believers to declare God's salvation and "his marvelous deeds" to all who will hear (v. 3). The triple call to praise, paralleled by the triple imperatives to give testimony to the glory of the Lord, establishes the double focus of the psalm in its opening verses: God's people are to praise him and to represent him as his ambassadors to the nations.

In the middle section of the psalm (vv. 4–9), the psalmist provides concrete expressions of why we should praise the Lord and give testimony to his glory. First, the psalmist dismisses the "gods of the nations" as mere idols, unable to speak on their own, let alone do anything for their people (vv. 4–5). The declaration that God created the multitude of stars and planets in the heavens (v. 5) crushes any pretensions of the pagan idols to true deity, for Yahweh alone made the heavens. The psalmist offers no argument against the pagan idols, and he enters into no debate with the pagans about their feeble claims concerning their deaf and dumb idols. Yahweh's claim to divinity is exclusive, and it is proven by his sovereignty over the heavens. In this claim to sovereign control over the universe, the pagans surrounding ancient Israel would have understood immediately that the psalmist was stating that there is only one true God.

In verse 6, the writer paints a concrete picture of God's grandeur by personifying his attributes as if they were attendants before his throne. "Splendor" and "majesty," two qualities associated closely with a king, stand "before him" in his court. The splendor and majesty the psalmist ascribes to God have a double effect in this verse and form an image of God as a Great King, for we naturally associate majesty with royalty. Likewise, the psalmist paints a picture of "strength and glory" as if they were attendants in the sanctuary, showing God's mighty acts as royal servants ready to do the bidding of the monarch. The two pairs of attendants fit together because the glorious acts testify to the majesty of the King. The psalmist uses these personifications deliberately, for they encourage readers to put themselves in the position of one of God's attendants, recognizing the splendor and majesty of the King and the strength and glory of his mighty deeds. King David reminds us in another psalm that he is not the great King; Yahweh is:

> I will exalt you, my God the King;
> I will praise your name for ever and ever.
>
> —Psalm 145:1

It is as if we are in the royal throne room with David, adding our voices to the hymn that honors Yahweh as the Great King of the earth.

Balancing the triple exhortations at the beginning of the psalm to sing to the Lord (vv. 1–2) are the three commands roughly at the midpoint of the psalm to "ascribe to the LORD" (vv. 7–8a) the "glory and strength" (v. 7) he deserves. As in the opening invitations, the psalmist uses a climactic parallelism in these verses, with the effect of graduating the ascription of glory to Yahweh in each command. Willem VanGemeren captures the feeling of the psalmist in these verses when he writes, "The psalmist has a renewed urgency in proclaiming the divine name."[12] The repeated call at this point in the psalm to proclaim glory to Yahweh intensifies the importance of the command for the reader as well. "Ascribe to the LORD," the psalmist begins, only to stop in midsentence and add "O families of nations" (v. 7). What are we to ascribe to the Lord, we ask? We must read on to find out. "Ascribe to the LORD glory and strength," the writer adds in response to our rhetorical question. The climactic parallelism in this verse engages the readers actively by forcing them to ask the psalmist to finish his command. To increase the urgency even more, the psalmist finishes his command with "Ascribe to the LORD the glory due his name" (v. 8). Now we see that the glory and strength of Yahweh's actions attest to the glory of his person, and we join in attributing glory to God by the way the psalmist composes his verse, answering his unanswered question only when we read on.

Completing the middle section of the psalm, the psalmist balances his opening statement of the middle section that God is "worthy of praise" (v. 4). At the end of this section, the writer paints another picture of God's glory, this time the familiar image of nations "trembling" before his holiness (v. 9). God's reign as King includes his

---

12. VanGemeren, *Psalms,* 5:622.

righteousness and justice. Those who have not bowed the knee to the King would do well to tremble, for Yahweh is the judge; those who have bowed to the King rejoice in his righteous reign. Between the two assertions that God is worthy to be praised, the psalmist has shown us his royal glory and commanded us to acknowledge Yahweh as King.

The final section of the psalm assures us that the righteous reign of Yahweh will last forever (vv. 10–13). God will "judge the peoples with equity" (v. 10) and the nations with righteousness and truth (v. 13); we will rejoice under our King. The psalm opens with a triple invitation to praise God followed by a triple imperative to speak his praise, and it ends with a triple statement that the whole world will praise God. With the images of the heavens, the earth, the sea, the fields, and the trees (vv. 11–12), the psalmist declares that the whole of God's creation is a source of praise for him. The writer personifies all of these aspects of God's creation, as if they could worship God. All of nature, the psalmist states, "will sing before the LORD" (v. 13), the maker of everything. With a rapid succession of images, one aspect of nature after another bringing praise to its Creator, the psalmist creates a sense of expectancy that implicitly invites the reader to join in the praise. This sense of anticipation is increased in the final verse of the psalm with a double climactic parallelism. The first phrase of verse 13 ends with the statement, "for he comes"; the second phrase of the verse begins with the same statement, "he comes." This repetition underscores the assurance of God's sovereignty as expressed in his certain return. In the second parallelism of the verse, the writer states at the end of the second phrase that Yahweh comes "to judge the earth," a phrase he repeats and elaborates in the third phrase of the verse, "He will judge the world in righteousness and the peoples in his truth." Here too the writer emphasizes Yahweh's righteous judgment that will cover all the nations of the earth. Between the images of nature rejoicing in its Creator and the emphatic repetitions of God's future reign in righteousness over the whole earth, the psalmist writes a fitting conclusion to the psalm, for it concentrates on Yahweh and invites the reader to participate in Yahweh's praise.

Rounding out the careful patterning of Psalm 96 is the tight organization of the whole psalm in the form of the "three threes" that unify the psalm. Three times the psalmist calls for praise. The writer begins the psalm with three exhortations and three imperatives to praise Yahweh. At the midpoint of the psalm, he calls on his readers three times to ascribe praise to God. At the conclusion of the psalm, he states three times that all of nature praises God. The "nations," for whom this psalm is written, cannot miss the point that God will reign as King over the earth, and they are invited to participate in his majestic and righteous rule.

What Are the Themes and Theology in the Psalm?

Though there are numerous topics that a thorough commentary on Psalm 96 might illuminate, two great themes in the psalm stand out. First, Psalm 96 voices corporate worship to Yahweh as the King of the nations. The psalmist addresses the opening invitations to sing praise to God to the congregation of the faithful. These are the Old Testament Jews in the temple and us as New Testament Christians. Christians recognize that the kingdom spoken of in this psalm began in Israel and is ultimately fulfilled in the future reign of Jesus Christ as KING OF KINGS AND LORD OF LORDS. Speaking of Christ in the Apocalypse, John states, "On his robe and on his thigh he has this name written: King of Kings and Lord of Lords" (Rev. 19:16). Jesus Christ will rule the nations, and we are his people. The first theme of Psalm 96 is the future righteous rule of Jesus Christ that the faithful of all ages will acknowledge forever.

The second great theme of Psalm 96 is the invitation to the nations—those outside of the community of faith—to share in the blessings of the kingdom. No less than seven times in the psalm, the psalmist instructs believers to tell the nations of Yahweh their King and invite them to join in his praise (vv. 1, 2, 3, 7, 8, 9, 10). This is a jubilant psalm intended to communicate the joy of covenant faith to those who need it most. We might think of Psalm 96 as an Old Testament expansion of the blessing pronounced to the faithful in the parable of the ten virgins, "Come and share your master's happiness" (Matt. 25:21).

With Handel, we can sing the "Hallelujah Chorus" of the book of Revelation to God's glory, for all believers will share in the wedding of the Lamb (Rev. 19:6b–8).

Applications

1. The two great themes of Psalm 96 give us one emphatic application. As believers we are to communicate the joy that comes from being members of the community of faith, and we are to do so in our worship services and in our evangelism. Worship is the act of ascribing glory to Yahweh; evangelism is the declaration of Yahweh to the unbeliever. There is a place for jubilant praise in church and evangelism.

2. Do our church services reflect the spiritual joy that comes from knowing Jesus Christ? We should not sing superficial, upbeat songs and worship choruses to try to manufacture an emotional praise in the congregation. Rather, we should focus our singing of hymns, our prayers, and our preaching on Jesus Christ. No matter how difficult the section of the Word of God we may be studying on any given Sunday, we should come away encouraged that we belong to Christ, who is the King of the universe.

3. Does our evangelism reflect our gratitude and joy at being God's children by grace through faith in Jesus Christ? Do our everyday lives communicate something of our status as citizens of God's kingdom to those who do not know Christ by faith? We should not be always superficially happy. Rather, the overall tone of our lives should reflect our kingdom status.

Encountering God as King of Kings and Lord of Lords

The psalmists of ancient Israel understood what Christians of today need to know: God reigns as King over the affairs of men and superintends everything for his glory and the good of his people. In a word, Yahweh is sovereign. While as Christians we would not disagree with such a statement, we sometimes do not appreciate its underlying truth and its practical implications. If God is absolutely sovereign (and that is what his kingship promises us), he must have authority and control over everything. Sovereignty means that God controls the microscopic details necessary to the sustenance of life and the greatest natural wonders; he directs the events of each human life and the affairs of great nations. The practical implication of God's sovereignty is that no event in our lives is an accident. God knows everything that will happen to us and promises to provide for and protect us in those circumstances according to his will. God's sovereignty means our peace.

Yahweh's reign as King relates to every aspect of our lives. Kings in ancient times held absolute sway over their subjects; they had the power of life and death over their citizens. In the case of Yahweh's reign over us, we have a King who rules for our good as well as his glory. Yahweh's reign is righteous. As King he provides for our needs and protects us from harm. Yahweh's absolute power assures us that nothing escapes him; nothing happens to us without his foreknowledge and permission. How are we to respond to such a King? Like the psalmists of old—with praise.

The seventeenth-century English poet George Herbert renders his praise to God in his volume of poetry, *The Temple.* Favored at the court of the king for advancement, Herbert forsook worldly glory and accepted the call to a small rural church, where he ministered for three years and then died. In one way or another, all of Herbert's poems attest to his faith in Christ. One of his poems, "Antiphon I," has been adapted as a hymn, "Let All the World in Every Corner Sing." Here is Herbert's full poem:

> Let all the world in every corner sing,
> My God and King.
>
> The heavens are not too high,
> His praise may thither fly:
> The earth is not too low,

His praise there may grow.
Let all the world in every corner sing,
My God and King.

The church with psalms must shout,
No door can keep them out:
But above all, the heart
Must bear the longest part.
Let all the world in every corner sing,
My God and King.[13]

Herbert recognizes that everything that lives owes praise to God. Most of all, however, Christians owe praise to God in their public assemblies and in their private hearts. Herbert lived a godly life that verified the witness of his poems. He praised God in his poetry and his ministry.

How do we praise God? The answer of course is that everything we do or think should praise God. Paul's admonition in Romans 12:1–2 is that we honor the Lord with all of our lives. In the two psalms we have studied in this chapter, however, the psalmists emphasize four specific ways we can praise God. Psalm 84 provides the first two ways we can praise God when the psalmist encourages us first to meditate on God and second to serve him in the congregation of the faithful (or the church). We meditate on God by reading his Word and allowing the Holy Spirit to illuminate our reading. We honor the Lord when we read the Scriptures to learn what they say about him. We praise God by our service at church, whether it is teaching, ushering, serving in the nursery, or cleaning the sanctuary. Such service praises the Lord; it is part of our worship. We might say that Psalm 84 encourages us to praise God "silently"—by studying the Scriptures and serving him in church (though of course such service may involve speaking). Psalm 96 provides the other two ways we can praise God when the writer of

---

13. George Herbert, "Antiphon I," in *The English Poems of George Herbert,* ed. C. A. Patrides (Totowa, N.J.: Rowman & Littlefield, 1974), 72–73.

the psalm invites us to praise God with our lips. We can praise God with our words in two ways: among believers, we are to ascribe glory to God and sing his praises, and among unbelievers, we are to declare God's name and invite the non-Christian to faith in Christ. How are we to praise God? By what we say and what we do.

> *We can praise God silently and orally—by what we do and what we say. We were created to "glorify God and enjoy him forever" (Westminster Catechism).*

Chapter 8

You Are My Son: Messianic Psalms

Lift up your heads, O you gates;
   be lifted up, you ancient doors,
      that the King of glory may come in.
Who is this King of glory?
   The LORD strong and mighty,
      the LORD mighty in battle.
Lift up your heads, O you gates;
   lift them up, you ancient doors,
      that the King of glory may come in.
Who is he, this King of glory?
   The LORD Almighty—
      he is the King of glory.

                     —Psalm 24:7–10

THE GREATEST NEWS OF HISTORY IS THE incarnation, crucifixion, and resurrection of Jesus Christ, the Son of God. Jesus is the Christ, or the Messiah, to use the Hebrew equivalent of *Christ,* for both *Messiah* and *Christ* mean the "Anointed One." Messiah is present in both the Old and New Testaments. The Old Testament anticipates the Incarnation, and the New Testament records the Incarnation and looks forward to the return of Christ in glory. The psalms that refer to Jesus Christ (or Messiah) are called "Messianic Psalms." While the Psalms are not prophecies in the same way as the prophetic books of the Old Testament, they do at times anticipate the coming Messiah. It is only natural that they should do so, for the expectation of Messiah was one of the key elements of Old Testament life. Under the old covenant the Psalms formed an important part of congregational worship; when the Messianic Psalms were read (or sung, as the case may be), the congregation was reminded of their coming Messiah. In fact, the Old Testament Jew was to live his whole life expecting the Messiah, just as New Testament Christians are to live anticipating the second coming of Jesus Christ in glory (1 Thess. 5:6; 2 Peter 3:11–14). Living with such expectancy changes the way we live this life—or at least it should.

> *Jesus shall reign where'er the sun*
> *Does his successive journeys run;*
> *His kingdom stretch from shore to shore,*
> *Till moons shall wax and wane no more.*
> —Isaac Watts, 1719

The term *Messianic Psalms* has a double reference. In the first place, it refers to the Psalms that mention the royal household of King David and his descendants. Of this first aspect of the Messianic Psalms, Willem VanGemeren writes, "The 'messianic psalms' celebrate the divine promises granted to the Davidic dynasty."[1] God first made these promises to King David after David had brought the ark of the Lord to Jerusalem, the city of David (2 Sam. 6–7). God promised David then that he would bless him and his descendants with an everlasting kingdom. "Your house and your kingdom will endure forever before me," God tells David, "your throne will be established forever" (2 Sam. 7:16). This is the first type of messianic reference in the Psalms—the men-

---

1. Willem VanGemeren, *Psalms*, vol. 5 of *The Expositor's Bible Commentary*, ed. Frank E. Gaebelein (Grand Rapids: Zondervan, 1991), 586.

tion of King David and his descendants on the throne of ancient Israel. Many psalms either mention the king of Israel or take the kingdom for granted. Of course, the ultimate fulfillment of the promise of an eternal throne is found in Jesus Christ.

The second use of the term *Messianic Psalm* is more limited; it is to those psalms that anticipate the reign of David's "greater Son," Jesus Christ. Explicit references to Jesus Christ are perhaps what most Christians think of when they mention the Messianic Psalms, and with good reason, for the New Testament applies quotations from these psalms directly to the life and death of Jesus of Nazareth (e.g., Acts 13:33; Heb. 1:8–9; 2:6; 10:5–18). The messianic applications that the New Testament writers make of Old Testament passages—and they are many—provide the clearest indication that certain passages in the Psalms are to be seen as having messianic meaning. However, as New Testament Christians we need to be careful that we do not think of the Psalms that reference Jesus Christ as applying only to us and not to the Old Testament Jews; they had Old Testament applications as well. Writing of the balance we need to maintain when we interpret messianic passages in the Psalms, Willem VanGemeren states, "Yet whatever is attributed to the Davidic king also applies to God's son, our Messiah!"[2] The Messianic Psalms have a double orientation—King David and his descendants on the one hand, and Jesus Christ on the other. Tremper Longman emphasizes the same point when he writes of an "ultimate fulfillment" of messianic passages in Jesus Christ (such as Ps. 16:10 in Christ's resurrection). Longman states, "However, to say that the ultimate fulfillment of Psalm 16:10 is found in Jesus' resurrection is different from arguing that the passage has no Old Testament application."[3] The point that VanGemeren and Longman both make is that the Messianic Psalms that anticipate Jesus Christ also refer to King David or his descendants; that is, these psalms have a double reference—an Old Testament function and a New Testament application.

---

2. Ibid.
3. Tremper Longman, *How to Read the Psalms* (Downers Grove, Ill.: InterVarsity, 1988), 68.

When we read the Messianic Psalms, we need to keep both David and Jesus in mind. The suffering expressed in Psalm 22, for example, is in the first instance David's suffering at the hands of his enemies, but it is also in the second case the suffering of Jesus Christ on the cross. David suffers in his own life, and God deepens David's trust in him through the trial. Jesus Christ suffered in our place as our substitute on the cross; through his death and resurrection, God offers salvation to all who believe. Psalm 22 is about David and Christ. On the opposite end of the spectrum of Messianic Psalms is Psalm 45. The glorious king of the psalm is a Davidic king, for he marries a bride who is described in some detail. At the same time, the bridegroom/warrior of Psalm 45 is Jesus Christ himself as the writer of Hebrews makes clear (Heb. 1:8–9). As we read these psalms, then, we will pay attention to both the human king and the divine king; this way, we will not misunderstand these psalms.

We read the Messianic Psalms in a "binocular" way—
keeping both David and Jesus Christ in full view.

Psalm 22
THE SUFFERING KING

The opening words of Psalm 22 are the words Christ cried out in his great anguish on the cross. It may be that by referencing Psalm 22 with its opening words, Christ was indicating that the whole psalm applied to his passion on the cross. With this allusion to Psalm 22, Christ agonized over the Father's judgment for sin poured out on the Son and his turning away from his Son for those moments on the cross. There is no greater cry of desolation anywhere in the world's great literatures, nor is there any greater indication of divine grace; for in Christ's desolation is our salvation.

¹My God, my God, why have you forsaken me?
  Why are you so far from saving me,
    so far from the words of my groaning?
²O my God, I cry out by day, but you do not answer,
  by night, and am not silent.

³Yet you are enthroned as the Holy One;
  you are the praise of Israel.
⁴In you our fathers put their trust;
  they trusted and you delivered them.
⁵They cried to you and were saved;
  in you they trusted and were not disappointed.

⁶But I am a worm and not a man,
  scorned by men and despised by the people.
⁷All who see me mock me;
  they hurl insults, shaking their heads:
⁸"He trusts in the LORD;
  let the LORD rescue him.
Let him deliver him,
  since he delights in him."

⁹Yet you brought me out of the womb;
  you made me trust in you
    even at my mother's breast.
¹⁰From birth I was cast upon you;
  From my mother's womb you have been my God.
¹¹Do not be far from me,
  for trouble is near
    and there is no one to help.

¹²Many bulls surround me;
  strong bulls of Bashan encircle me.
¹³Roaring lions tearing their prey
  open their mouths wide against me.

[14]I am poured out like water,
    and all my bones are out of joint.
My heart has turned to wax;
    it has melted away within me.
[15]My strength is dried up like a potsherd,
    and my tongue sticks to the roof of my mouth;
    you lay me in the dust of death.
[16]Dogs have surrounded me;
    a band of evil men has encircled me,
    they have pierced my hands and my feet.
[17]I can count all my bones;
    people stare and gloat over me.
[18]They divide my garments among them
    and cast lots for my clothing.

[19]But you, O LORD, be not far off;
    O my Strength, come quickly to help me.
[20]Deliver my life from the sword,
    my precious life from the power of the dogs.
[21]Rescue me from the mouth of the lions;
    save me from the horns of the wild oxen.

[22]I will declare your name to my brothers;
    in the congregation I will praise you.
[23]You who fear the LORD, praise him!
    All you descendants of Jacob, honor him!
    Revere him, all you descendants of Israel!
[24]For he has not despised or disdained
    the suffering of the afflicted one;
he has not hidden his face from him
    but has listened to his cry for help.

[25]From you comes the theme of my praise in the great assembly;
    before those who fear you will I fulfill my vows.
[26]The poor will eat and be satisfied;

they who seek the LORD will praise him—
  may your hearts live forever!
²⁷All the ends of the earth will remember and turn to the LORD,
  and the families of the nations will bow down before him,
²⁸for dominion belongs to the LORD
  and he rules over the nations.

²⁹All the rich of the earth will feast and worship;
  all who go down to the dust will kneel before him—
  those who cannot keep themselves alive.
³⁰Posterity will serve him;
  future generations will be told about the Lord D.
³¹They will proclaim his righteousness
  to a people yet unborn—
  for he has done it.

What Is the Overall Effect of the Psalm?

Psalm 22 runs the gamut of emotions, from extreme desolation to profound joy. It begins with God's desertion of the King and ends with the King praising God for the blessings he gives so generously. In messianic terms, Psalm 22 expresses Christ's agonized separation from God when the Father pours the sin of the world on him at his crucifixion and the profound joy that comes to us from Christ's sacrifice. How can one psalm express such extremities of emotion? For King David, the author of the psalm, the answer lies in the fact that he is under attack from his enemies (vv. 6–8), yet he is encouraged by God's past faithfulness to trust him again (vv. 3–5). For Jesus Christ, the greatest agony of all is his separation from God on the cross (vv. 1–2, 14–18), and his greatest joy is the eternal kingdom the Father provides believers through his death (vv. 22–31). Messiah is both the suffering servant (vv. 1–21) and the Great King of an eternal kingdom (vv. 22–31). Psalm 22 begins in the depths of despair and ends in the greatest hope ever offered.

What Is the Structure of the Psalm?

Psalm 22 is an individual Lament Psalm, for its primary emphasis is petition to Yahweh for blessings only he can bestow (rescue from enemies and salvation for the lost). As with so many other Lament Psalms, however, Psalm 22 does not follow a rigid structure; it omits some sections of typical Laments (such as the curses and the confessions of some Laments) and modifies the order of the remaining sections. Rather than moving from complaint to petition to a statement of confidence in Yahweh as do many Lament Psalms, Psalm 22 alternates the confidence and petition sections and then concludes with an extended vow to praise God that is much longer than the conclusions in many Lament Psalms. We might diagram the structure of Psalm 22 in the following manner:

Verses 1–2	Lament #1:	The Speaker's Desolation
Verses 3–5	Confidence #1:	Yahweh's Faithfulness in the Past
Verses 6–8	Lament #2:	The Enemies' Attacks
Verses 9–10	Confidence #2:	Yahweh's Care for the Speaker
Verse 11	Petition #1:	A Plea for Deliverance
Verses 12–18	Lament #3:	Attackers on All Sides
Verses 19–21	Petition #2:	A Second Plea for Deliverance
Verses 22–31	Vow to Praise Yahweh:	Yahweh's Gracious Salvation

The structure in verses 1–21, alternating Laments with statements of confidence and then with petitions, serves two purposes. First, it intensifies the extremity of David's vulnerable position because he keeps returning to the overwhelming fear his enemies evoke in him. Second, it serves to keep a double perspective before the reader. That is, at the same time we experience David's fear, we are reminded of Yahweh's faithfulness and sovereignty; the alternating pattern keeps Yahweh, as well as David, in the front of the psalm. This way, the psalm constantly assures us of God's providential care for David and, in messianic terms, for Christ (and through him, all believers). Finally, the concluding vow to praise Yahweh (vv. 22–31) begins in praise from the Israelites of old and ends in praise from believers of all the ages, Jew and Gentile alike. Psalm 22 begins in abject rejection and isolation, progresses through the suffering of Messiah for his people on the cross, and ends in a glorious doxology (hymn of praise) from those who by faith enter the kingdom of God.

What Are the Figures of Speech in the Psalm, and What Effects Do They Have?

David uses a combination of effective figures of speech and carefully placed parallelisms to express the extremes of intense desolation and joy in Psalm 22. The speaker emphasizes his profound anguish by opening his Lament with the repeated call upon almighty God. He further intensifies the effect of isolation in the opening verse with the climactic parallelism, "Why are you so far from saving me, so far from the words of my groaning?" The repetition of "so far" and the omission (ellipsis) of "Why are you . . . ?" in the last phrase of the verse show how deeply the speaker feels God's desertion of him in his hour of need. David demonstrates how completely he feels God's distance from him by stating that he calls on God day and night, but to no avail (v. 2). The opening verses express the isolation and anguish that only those deserted by God would feel.

Following the fear of the opening Lament, David expresses his absolute trust in God's providence. Still speaking to God, David announces his confidence in God's sovereign rule as the "Holy One" (v. 3) on the throne of Israel. The double reference to God's rule as the Great King of Israel in this verse communicates trust in the sovereign acts of God. Here, of course, the writer acknowledges that God's sovereignty includes the enemies surrounding David and the agony of Christ's passion on the cross. In the context of these difficulties, David uses an antithetic parallelism to affirm his trust in God's care and love (v. 4). Stated positively, all those who trusted in God's love in the past "were saved" (v. 5); stated negatively, they "were not disappointed" (v. 5). David answers the double cry of anguish in the opening verses with a double statement that God is in absolute control. Even the opening address to God in the first statement of confidence in God turns the reader's attention away from self to God. "Yet you," David begins verse 3, as he does verse 9 in his second statement of confidence in God's sovereignty.

The alternating pattern of the psalm, moving from David's Lament to consolation in Yahweh's protection and love, emphasizes Yahweh's sovereignty as the answer to human problems. If Yahweh is in control, what can we fear?

Returning to his second Lament, David signals a sharp contrast with the words, "But I" (v. 6). In the graphic image of a worm trodden underfoot and disregarded by all (v. 6), David demonstrates how absolutely rejected by God he feels. His enemies mock him and "hurl insults" at him (v. 7), laughing him to scorn for trusting in God when God apparently is not answering his pleas. When applied to Jesus Christ on the cross, the image of the worm underscores the irony of the crucifixion; it is hard to think that the Creator of the universe should be compared to a worm, one of the lowliest of his creations! The psalm underscores the irony of those who mock David and Jesus Christ, for they taunt them by jeering at their trust in God, which their enemies take to be vain. Notice the chiasm of verse 8, however, in which the mocker is mocked:

(A)   confidence in the LORD;
(B)   let the LORD rescue him;
(B)   let the LORD deliver him;
(A)   for he delights in him.

The speaker's trust in God (A), followed by the vain taunts of the mockers (B and B), is proven to be well founded, for God loves the speaker (A). David implies the vanity of the mockers by showing how foolish they are to challenge God's love for his chosen ones.

In the third Lament (vv. 12–18) the writer combines David's fear of death with Christ's mortal suffering on the cross. David depicts the enemies who attack him first as bulls of Bashan (v. 12) surrounding him and cutting off his escape.[4] David then turns the threat of circling bulls into the aggressive attack of lions with open mouths ready to devour (v. 13). David's next image for his enemies is that of dogs (v. 16a). Finally, he speaks of the attack on him in military terms with the image of the sword (v. 16b). The effect of these threatening enemies is to paralyze David with fear (vv. 14–15). The image of the melting wax suggests that David's courage fails him; the picture of his tongue sticking to his mouth depicts the abject fear he feels. Seen in the light of the Messiah's suffering on the cross, verses 14 and 15 are even more profound. They demonstrate the cruelty of the cross that pulls limbs out of joint (v. 14), the thirst that the slow death causes (v. 15), and the excruciating suffering as the victim has hours (and sometimes days) to contemplate his death (v. 15). Even more intense than these visual images of suffering and fear is the simply stated account of Christ's crucifixion in verses 16b–18. In simple declarative statements, the writer describes the pierced hands and feet, the body contorted on the tree, and the despicable gambling going on at the foot of the cross. The effect of this understated and "minimalist" account is profound. Like Luke's account of the Crucifixion (Luke 23:33–46), there is no attempt to play on readers' emotions by describing in detail Christ's physical sufferings; rather, the writer gives a simple statement of the

---

4. The bulls of Bashan were particularly well fed and posed a serious threat.

facts, thereby showing their horror all the more. The third Lament shows the deep suffering David and Christ experience.

Following the extended third Lament, David asks the Lord a second time to rescue him (the first petition being in v. 11). He makes his petition by reversing the threats listed in the earlier Lament. First, he asks to be delivered from the sword (v. 20), perhaps an image to parallel the pierced hands and feet of Christ on the cross. Then he asks for deliverance from dogs (v. 20), lions, and wild oxen (v. 21), reminiscent of the bulls of Bashan. Repeating the list of threats in reverse order serves to emphasize the Lord's power over his enemies and the enemies of his people. The petition presumes God's sovereign power over everything and therefore ends implicitly on a note of confidence and faith.

The concluding vow to praise Yahweh (vv. 22–31) amounts to a doxology or hymn of praise to Yahweh for his love and protection. David introduces the theme of praise in this concluding section by another chiasm (v. 22):

(A) I will declare your name
(B) to my brothers;
(B) in the congregation
(A) I will praise you.

Beset by enemies, David still knows he can trust Yahweh and will therefore praise him publicly for his love. Immediately he calls on those in the covenant community to praise Yahweh with a threefold announcement (v. 23). Like a musical crescendo, David builds toward the climax of the psalm. These verses demonstrate the "call-and-answer" motif so common in the Scriptures. Yahweh promises Jeremiah, "Call to me and I will answer you and tell you great and unsearchable things you do not know" (Jer. 33:3). Yahweh gives Isaiah the same promise: "Then you will call, and the LORD will answer; you will cry for help, and he will say: Here am I" (Isa. 58:9). The psalmists record the same promise from Yahweh: that he would hear their cry and answer their distress (e.g. Pss. 91:15; 102:1–2). David is encouraged in the knowledge that Yahweh will answer his call and relieve him in his distress.

In the remaining verses of the psalm, David shows the extent of Christ's kingdom, beginning with the needy (v. 24), and extending to the poor (v. 26), all nations (vv. 27b–28), the rich (v. 29), and all those yet to be born who will believe (v. 30). Christ's kingdom extends to the Jew and Gentile, to the rich and the poor, to people living now and those yet to be born—in short, to everyone everywhere who believes in Jesus Christ by faith. Simeon understood the messianic hope, for when Mary and Joseph brought the infant Jesus to him to be dedicated, he sang that the Christ child was "A light for revelation to the Gentiles and for glory to [his] people Israel" (Luke 2:32). We should not miss the irony of the concluding vow to praise Yahweh for the kingdom of his son. David was threatened by enemies and Jesus Christ was nailed to the tree, but the Holy Spirit inspires the psalmist to sing of a posterity for David and an eternal kingdom for Jew and Gentile who believe on Jesus Christ. Death is not the end.

What Are the Themes and Theology in the Psalm?

The theology of Psalm 22 is rooted in the situations in which David and Jesus Christ are depicted in the psalm. David saw no escape from his enemies, and Jesus Christ was nailed to a cross, forsaken by God. It looked hopeless. Even in the face of such apparent disaster and defeat, however, Psalm 22 brings hope out of despair, and it does so by proclaiming God's sovereignty over even the darkest moment of all history—the crucifixion of his Son. David develops at least three themes about God in the psalm.

The first theme in Psalm 22 is that Jesus Christ had to suffer and die to pay the price of sin. Centuries before Calvary, Isaiah prophesied that the Messiah would suffer to redeem his people (Isa. 53). God did not dispense with his justice and sidestep the punishment for sin when Christ died on the cross. Rather, he poured out his wrath against sin on his own Son so that the price would be paid in full. In the second letter to the Corinthians, Paul speaks of the doctrine of imputation, or what we might call "the great transaction," namely, that in his grace God declares us righteous and pours our sin on Jesus Christ:

> God made him who had no sin to be sin for us, so that in him we might become the righteousness of God.
> —2 Corinthians 5:21

The salvation that God offers by grace, though free to us, cost the Father everything—his Son, Jesus Christ. Though Christ quotes Psalm 22 in his crucifixion agony, we hear in the words the most gracious news of all: Christ died that we might live.

The second theme of the psalm is that God is faithful to his promises. David takes his first comfort in Psalm 22 from God's faithfulness to his forefathers (vv. 3–5). God's past love for his people is a guarantee of his present love for his people today. Psalm 22 reminds us of the Davidic covenant in which God promised David a kingdom forever and ruler on his throne forever (2 Sam. 7). While the nation of Israel disappeared in A.D. 70 with the fall of Jerusalem, God has fulfilled his promise of a Davidic king in Jesus Christ ruling over all who believe in him. In one sense, all Christians live in the kingdom of God because they are children of God by faith and citizens of a heavenly kingdom in which Jesus Christ is King.

The third theme of Psalm 22 relates to Christ's future kingdom. There will come a time when "at the name of Jesus every knee should bow" and "every tongue confess that Jesus Christ is Lord, to the glory of God the Father" (Phil. 2:10–11). Until that time, we await the future kingdom. So did David, as the concluding verses of Psalm 22 show (vv. 27–31). With David, we can be assured, however, that God's past love guarantees his future love. Writing the last book of the Bible, John heard the song of the Lamb, promising that

> All nations will come
> and worship before you [Christ],
> for your righteous acts have been revealed.
> —Revelation 15:4

This is the ultimate hope of Psalm 22, a psalm that begins in God's forsaking his Son as he becomes sin for us. How gracious God is!

Based on Psalm 22, the hymn "All You That Fear Jehovah's Name" offers a musical rendition of David's Messianic Psalm for use in public worship today. Just as David calls on all who fear Yahweh to praise him (Ps. 22:23), the hymn opens with an invitation to worship:

> All you that fear Jehovah's name,
> His glory tell, his praise proclaim;
> You children of his chosen race,
> Stand in awe before his face,
> Stand in awe before his face.

The invitation is universal, and it calls on all believers to praise and adore God. In the second stanza, the hymn writer goes to the heart of Psalm 22 and expresses Messiah's confidence in God's love:

> The suffering One he has not spurned,
> Who unto him for help has turned;
> From him he has not hid his face,
> But answered his request in grace,
> But answered his request in grace.[5]

Separated from God when the punishment of our sin was poured on him at Calvary, Jesus Christ died that God's grace might be ours. Psalm 22 reminds us that God planned Calvary before the worlds began. Its witness to the atoning death of Jesus Christ penned nine hundred years before the Crucifixion reminds us how expensive God's free grace to believers is.

---

5. "All You That Fear Jehovah's Name," in *Trinity Hymnal* (Philadelphia: Great Commission, 1990), 9.

Applications

1. As we contemplate Psalm 22, we should be amazed again at the grace of God that Jesus Christ would die for us. When we consider that Christ went to the cross willingly (John 10:15), knowing that he would become sin for us and be separated from God on that tree, we should be moved to praise for our Savior. It would be good for us to contemplate the words of Christ, "My God, my God, why have you forsaken me?" and remember that we are the reason he was forsaken by God. He did for us what we could not do for ourselves. Shakespeare's Macbeth comes to mind here. When everything he wanted had turned to dust and his wife had died, Macbeth evaluated his life with the words, "It is a tale/Told by an idiot, full of sound and fury, /Signifying nothing" (5.5.26–28).[6] Whenever we are discouraged and think that our lives are insignificant, we should remember that Jesus Christ took our sin upon himself on the cross and that his death shows that our lives are worth much to God. Though an individual Lament Psalm, Psalm 22 praises God for his grace in Jesus Christ.

2. When we suffer through no fault of our own, such as when someone slanders us in the workplace, we can take comfort in David's realization that God knows our suffering and, in his providence, will care for us as he has since our birth (Ps. 22:9–10). David's confidence in God's faithfulness during his time of trial assures Christians of God's love. We can turn to Lament Psalms like Psalm 22 when we suffer difficulties and be encouraged by the words we read. Psalm 22 is an individual Lament, and while we cannot apply its messianic meanings to ourselves, we can be certain that God is faithful to his people in the dark providences of life.

Christ died that we might live.

---

6. William Shakespeare, *Macbeth*, in *The Riverside Shakespeare* (Boston: Houghton Mifflin, 1974), 1385.

Psalm 45
THE ROYAL BRIDEGROOM

When we turn from Psalm 22 to Psalm 45, we turn from suffering and rejection to celebration and community. Like other Messianic Psalms, Psalm 45 refers to the Old Testament king in David's line and to the New Testament fulfillment of the promise of an eternal King in Jesus Christ. Psalm 45 is an ancient wedding song of a son of David. It celebrates the noble qualities of the groom (vv. 2–9) and the beauty of the bride (vv. 10–15); it concludes with the promise of heirs to the throne (vv. 16–17). At the same time, the psalm refers to Jesus Christ's future reign in glory. The writer of Hebrews quotes verses 6–7 in reference to Jesus Christ (Heb. 1:8–9), and the psalm's concluding verse can only be understood to have its final fulfillment in Jesus Christ, the son of David. Like Psalm 22, Psalm 45 has both an Old and a New Testament point of reference.

Psalm 45 has proven difficult for commentators to classify, though most modern scholars see it as a Royal Psalm. Richard D. Patterson sees it as "a Royal Psalm celebrating the marrying of a king in the line of David."[7] Willem VanGemeren sees the psalm as a Royal Psalm that "In a special way . . . also applies to our Lord, who rules as the Son of David."[8] Among earlier commentators, John Calvin recognizes the messianic references in the psalm.[9] Charles Haddon Spurgeon goes so far as to say that Psalm 45 does not refer to David's sons at all but only to Jesus Christ in a messianic way.[10] While most readers would disagree with Spurgeon, almost all scholars now affirm that Psalm 45 is a Royal Psalm with messianic allusions. In this commentary, we will emphasize the messianic references in the psalm without diminishing the obvious applications to the Old Testament son of David.

---

7. Richard D. Patterson, "A Multiplex Approach to Psalm 45," *Grace Theological Journal* 6, no. 1 (1985): 33.
8. VanGemeren, *Psalms,* 5:343.
9. John Calvin, *Commentary on the Book of Psalms,* vol. 1, trans. James Anderson (Grand Rapids: Baker, 1998).
10. Charles Haddon Spurgeon, *The Treasury of David* (Grand Rapids: Baker, 1983), 2:351.

¹My heart is stirred by a noble theme
    as I recite my verses for the king;
    my tongue is the pen of a skillful writer.

²You are the most excellent of men
    and your lips have been anointed with grace,
    since God has blessed you forever.
³Gird your sword upon your side, O mighty one;
    clothe yourself with splendor and majesty.
⁴In your majesty ride forth victoriously
    in behalf of truth, humility and righteousness;
    let your right hand display awesome deeds.
⁵Let your sharp arrows pierce the hearts of the king's enemies;
    let the nations fall beneath your feet.
⁶Your throne, O God, will last for ever and ever;
    a scepter of justice will be the scepter of your kingdom.
⁷You love righteousness and hate wickedness;
    therefore God, your God, has set you above your companions
    by anointing you with the oil of joy.
⁸All your robes are fragrant with myrrh and aloes and cassia;
    from palaces adorned with ivory
    the music of the strings makes you glad.
⁹Daughters of kings are among your honored women;
    at your right hand is the royal bride in gold of Ophir.

¹⁰Listen, O daughter, consider and give ear:
    Forget your people and your father's house.
¹¹The king is enthralled by your beauty;
    honor him, for he is your lord.
¹²The Daughter of Tyre will come with a gift,
    men of wealth will seek your favor.

¹³All glorious is the princess within her chamber;
    her gown is interwoven with gold.

¹⁴In embroidered garments she is led to the king;
  her virgin companions follow her and are brought to you.
¹⁵They are led in with joy and gladness;
  they enter the palace of the king.

¹⁶Your sons will take the place of your fathers;
  you will make them princes throughout the land.
¹⁷I will perpetuate your memory through all generations;
  therefore the nations will praise you for ever and ever.

What Is the Overall Effect of the Psalm?

Like any important wedding, the marriage celebrated in Psalm 45 evokes awe and majesty. This is no mere society wedding, however; this is the wedding of the King's son, the heir to the throne. We might get a small glimpse of the aura of majesty and beauty surrounding such a wedding if we were to think of the wedding ceremony of Prince Charles of England to Diana, flawed though the marriage sadly proved to be. Millions of people around the world watched the ceremony, some rising in the middle of the night to view the wedding on television, and were moved by its dignity and splendor. So too in ancient Israel, the wedding of the King's son would have been a national occasion, bringing thousands of people to Jerusalem for the ceremony. Psalm 45 is at one and the same time an exuberant celebration of one of the happiest events in Israelite life and the most blessed event of Jesus Christ's union with his church. With the psalmist in the opening verse, we are to be overcome with the beauty and importance of the occasion.

If we transpose these earthly (and flawed) marriages to the perfect
marriage of Messiah with his bride, the church (Eph. 5:25–30;
Rev. 19:6–9), we will have a small idea of the splendor and
rejoicing involved in this psalm.

What Is the Structure of the Psalm?

Royal and Messianic Psalms do not follow a rigid structure, and Psalm 45 is no exception; it develops its own pattern. The psalm begins with the speaker's announcement of how much he delights in celebrating the marriage of the King. He is moved to awe and praise. Following the opening "trumpet call" to praise the King and his bride, the psalm falls into three sections. These might be outlined in simplest terms in the following manner:

I. Verses 2–9:   The Majesty and Splendor of the King
II. Verses 10–15: The Beauty of the Bride and Her Attendants
III. Verses 16–17: The Promise of a Posterity

Psalm 45 celebrates the King/Messiah. It begins by presenting the King in two primary images: as a brave warrior (vv. 3–5) and as the bridegroom (vv. 8–9). These two images dominate the psalm and, in contrast to modern weddings, focus our attention on the King/bridegroom more than the bride. The picture the psalmist presents of the bride draws attention to the King, for she is brought in her beautiful gown and with her attendants to the King (v. 14). Even so, the bride is beautiful and dressed gorgeously in her royal robes. The bride represents believers in Jesus Christ, and it is appropriate that the psalm praises her as well as the groom.

What Are the Figures of Speech in the Psalm, and What Effects Do They Have?

As a wedding song, Psalm 45 is full of marriage imagery and celebration. It begins, however, with a picture of the King as a great warrior (vv. 3–5). Calling the King the "mighty one" and urging him to take his sword with him, the psalmist advises the King to "clothe [himself] with splendor and majesty" (v. 3). Of course, "splendor and majesty" are two characteristics (or attributes) of the King and of Messiah, yet the psalmist describes them as if they were clothing. The imagery of clothing for characteristics or accomplishments of a great person appears in many works of literature. One reference that comes to mind is a completely opposite image to the one presented in Psalm 45 in which Shakespeare pictures Macbeth's ill-gotten title of king as "hang[ing] loose about him, like a giant's robe / Upon a dwarfish thief";[11] the image suggests that Macbeth is not up to the role of king, and indeed he is not, for he murdered to gain the crown. The robes of majesty and splendor in Psalm 45, however, fit the King perfectly, for they depict his true character. This is no ordinary king; this is Messiah.

The psalm continues the martial imagery of verses 2 and 3 in the next verses, for the King "ride[s] forth victoriously" (v. 4). It is not military victory and the crushing defeat of an enemy on the battlefield, however, that the Davidic King gains. He goes forth "in behalf of truth, humility and righteousness" (v. 4). The purpose of the King's reign is to extend these three godly virtues to all his subjects. In regard to the messianic implications of this passage, only Jesus Christ has perfect truth, humility, and righteousness. The point of the passage is that Christ's divinity, not just his deeds, makes him the Great King. Applied to the Davidic King, Israel will defeat its enemies (v. 5). In reference to Messiah, all nations will eventually bow before Jesus Christ (v. 5), an indication of the certainty of Christ's sovereign rule over all (Phil. 2:9–11).

In verses 6 and 7, the psalmist speaks indirectly of the characteristics of the King by presenting his throne and his scepter. The poet uses a literary device called metonymy when he references the throne and scepter. In this case, the characteristics of the King himself are suggested by association with the throne and scepter. The King's throne evokes ideas of the glory and majesty of a king in his court, surrounded by his courtiers. However, these verses suggest more than the Davidic King's reign, as the writer of Hebrews teaches us by explicitly relating these two verses to Jesus Christ (Heb. 1:8–9). In the case of Jesus Christ as King, the throne represents the eternal rule of Christ over the

---

11. William Shakespeare, *Macbeth,* in *The Riverside Shakespeare* (Boston: Houghton Mifflin, 1974), 1384.

universe (1 Cor. 15:25). We should not miss the profound impression that the psalmist wishes to make in such a matter-of-fact manner. "Your throne, O God, will last for ever and ever" (v. 6), he writes, emphasizing the truth that God exists eternally and Christ's rule will never end (cf. v. 17).

Hand in hand with Christ's eternal majesty as represented in his throne is his righteousness. Here again the psalmist uses a metonymy, this time of a scepter. In ancient times a king on his throne would hold a scepter as a symbol of his authority and power. When he extended it to a subject, the subject was allowed to approach the throne. In the case of Christ as King, as in Psalm 45, the scepter symbolizes something more than power and authority; it represents divine sovereignty. Christ rules over the affairs of nations. This is no ordinary scepter in Psalm 45, for it is associated with Messiah's perfect justice. Christ's reign is just as well as sovereign because he rules with "truth, humility and righteousness" (v. 4). The psalmist emphasizes Messiah's righteousness even more strongly in verse 7 by making the same point twice—once in the positive statement that he "love[s] righteousness," and again in the negative statement that he "hate[s] wickedness." Evil and wickedness will not thrive forever; Jesus Christ will bring them to an end one day, and the righteous will rejoice. Such are the promises of these verses.

Rounding out the picture of the King/Messiah is the next image of him as the bridegroom (vv. 8–9). Again using the literary device of metonymy, the psalmist paints a vivid picture of the royal groom. In language reminiscent of that other great Old Testament wedding song, the Song of Songs (e.g., 4:14), the poet here describes the groom's ceremonial garments and their spices and connects Jesus Christ's role as King (his anointing) with his role as bridegroom to the church (in his wedding garments). The next phrase, "from palaces adorned with ivory" (v. 8), underscores the glory and majesty of Jesus Christ. He comes from the right hand of the throne of heaven as King to become our bridegroom-redeemer. God became man to die to redeem his people and make them his bride.

Beginning with verse 10, the psalmist turns his attention to the bride, referring to her once as a "daughter" (v. 10). While Psalm 45 is rich in its depiction of the ancient wedding customs, particularly the bride's being taken to the house of the groom for the wedding, we will focus specifically on the messianic implications of this section in the psalm. The groom is the Messiah (vv. 6–9), and the bride is shown here to be exalted as well, for she is the church. To begin, Gentile nations as well as Jews will acknowledge the bride; the reference to the "Daughter of Tyre" (v. 12) is a synecdoche for the great Gentile nations that will come to honor the bride. Gentiles too would form part of the bride of Christ, for, as God promised Abraham, "all peoples on earth will be blessed through you" (Gen. 12:3). This promise receives its ultimate fulfillment in Jesus Christ, the Savior of all who believe (Matt. 1:1). Notice also that the bride is invited to leave her people and her father to become the bride of the King (v. 10). Figuratively the psalmist suggests that, when we come in faith to Jesus Christ, we form a new union, which cannot be dissolved. Like the ancient bride who is betrothed to her bridegroom, believers are "married" to Jesus Christ forever, for nothing "will be able to separate us from the love of God that is in Christ Jesus our Lord" (Rom. 8:39).

> *The seventeenth-century English poet John Donne*
> *suggests the same truth in Holy Sonnet 14. In a striking image,*
> *Donne writes that we are "betrothed" to God's enemy (Satan)*
> *and asks God to "divorce" us from Satan and take us*
> *as his own bride.*

The picture of the bride "within her chamber" (v. 13) and then being led to the King (v. 15) emphasizes the important point that it is by virtue of her relationship with the bridegroom that she is being celebrated in this psalm. The "joy and gladness" that occur when the bride is taken to the groom's house (v. 15) is occasioned by the actual marriage itself; the two are one. When applied to the church as the bride of Christ, the wedding imagery in this section of the psalm underscores the rejoicing that takes place when one is united to Christ by faith. Just as a woman becomes a bride and (traditionally) takes a new name by virtue of her relationship with her husband, so are we made believers when we respond by faith to the grace of God in Jesus Christ; we become new (2 Cor. 5:17). Inherent in this image is the fact that our salvation (our marriage to Jesus Christ, in the terms of the imagery here) results in God's glory. The wedding imagery of Psalm 45 is an important part of the messianic allusions in the psalm.

Throughout Psalm 45, the emphasis has been placed on the King-bridegroom. So it is herewith the bride who brings glory to the groom; the church is to honor Jesus Christ.

What Are the Themes and Theology in the Psalm?

The themes of Psalm 45 all relate to the wedding pictured in the psalm. The groom is at one and the same time the ancient king of Israel, David's son, and the Messiah, Jesus Christ, David's "greater Son." The bride is simultaneously the ancient king's bride and the church that is united by faith to Jesus Christ, her bridegroom (Eph. 5:25–27). From the wedding imagery of Psalm 45 come the following themes.

First, the ancient Davidic king was to rule Israel in "truth, humility and righteousness" (v. 4) for the glory of God and the good of the people. He was not to rule selfishly as so many ancient kings did, nor was he to forsake the Lord, for his rule was to figure forth the King to come.

Second, Jesus Christ, who is the Messiah, follows in the line of David as the great King (Matt. 1:1). In Psalm 45, he is also our bridegroom. As such, he establishes a new relationship with those who believe, claiming them as his own. When we respond in faith to the grace of God in Jesus Christ and accept him as Savior and Lord, we are given a new identity, one that can never be taken away. We are eternally the Lord's and will live forever with him in glory.

Third, Christ will return in glory one day and establish a righteous kingdom. All nations will bow before him and acknowledge him as

God's anointed one (vv. 5–6, 17). When he does, "truth, humility and righteousness" (v. 4) will characterize his reign, and all his subjects will enjoy the blessings of his reign.

Inherent in Christ's coming kingdom is the truth that evil and wickedness will not last forever. Christ will put all things right, and Satan will be bound forever. It is comforting to know that good will last forever, but evil will come to an end. There will be justice someday.

Applications

1. Psalm 45 reminds us of a future kingdom when Jesus Christ will rule directly over the earth. As much as possible, we are to try to live our lives in light of the coming King who will rule with justice and righteousness. We are to be just and righteous in this life, even as we are citizens of a righteous kingdom.
2. We are the bride of Christ as well as citizens of a heavenly kingdom. As Christ's bride, we enjoy the blessings of our relationship with him even in this life and anticipate the wedding supper of the Lamb at the end of the ages (Rev. 19:6–9).
3. Also inherent in the wedding imagery of Psalm 45 is the dignity of marriage. God instituted marriage with Adam and Eve before the fall into sin, and he honors it in his people today. Marriage is honorable.

Encountering God as Messiah

If we take a step back from the Messianic Psalms—a step away from David's joys and sorrows, and away from Jesus Christ's suffering and exaltation—we will find God's sovereignty at work. David lived and wrote almost a thousand years before Jesus Christ was born in Bethlehem. After David died, the nation of Israel was split into two kingdoms. Both the northern kingdom of Israel and the southern kingdom of Judah eventually were conquered, and the Jewish people were taken into exile. After all of this, there was a period of silence for over four hundred years before the Messiah was to come. Throughout all of these events, God ruled sovereignly, always preparing his people for the birth of the Messiah.

Of course, the whole Bible attests to God's sovereignty. He alone created the universe and sustains everything in it. He alone prepared a people for his glory, brought them out of Egypt, took them safely across the Red Sea, gave them the Law, and led them into the Promised Land. He alone sent his Son to die on the cross, and he alone will send his Son again to bring history to a close. He alone will destroy this earth and heaven and create a new heaven and earth. If we read the Bible properly, we will see God's sovereign rule implicit in every event in Old and New Testaments alike.

Beyond this general testimony to God's supremacy, however, the Bible reveals the special plan of God's sovereignty in the person and work of Jesus Christ, the Messiah. From the beginning, God was preparing a people for himself. In his covenant with Abraham, for instance, God demonstrates his sovereign plan for the Messiah. God promised Abraham, "all peoples on earth will be blessed through you" (Gen. 12:3). Jesus Christ is the blessing to the nations of the earth, for from the beginning God intended Gentiles to be saved (Rom. 9–11; Eph. 2:11–22). From the beginning, God intended the Messiah to be a King in David's line (2 Sam. 6–7; Matt. 1:1), and from the beginning God intended Messiah to suffer (Isa. 53). It would not be an overstatement to say that the primary purpose of God's sovereign rule over the world is the offer of salvation by grace through faith in Jesus Christ; the Old Testament anticipates Jesus Christ, and the New Testament presents him. If we approach the Scriptures with humility, we will admit that only a God who is sovereign could bring such a thing to pass.

The Messianic Psalms form an important part of the Old Testament testimony to God's special sovereignty in the lives of his people, for they kept the hope of Messiah alive before the people. The ancient Jews used the Psalms in their weekly corporate worship and in their private devotions. When they assembled for worship ceremonies or for special events like the coronation of a king, they would recite the Psalms. They would have memorized many of the Psalms through constant repetition. In singing the Messianic Psalms, they would have been primed to expect the Messiah at any time. Accordingly, we find Messianic Psalms that attest to many aspects of the Messiah's character and function. The Psalms announce, for instance, that the Messiah would be a King (Pss. 2; 45; 72; 89; 110; 132) and that he would suffer (Pss. 22; 55; 69). God shows his sovereignty both in the preparation for the Messiah and in the Scriptures that speak of Messiah—including the Messianic Psalms.

What should we meditate on when we read the Messianic Psalms? In the big picture, we should reflect on the sovereignty of God that planned "such a great salvation" (Heb. 2:3) for all who believe in Jesus Christ. All of the prophecies that Christ fulfills in his incarnation, crucifixion, and resurrection attest to God's sovereign plan of redemption. God planned our redemption from "before the beginning of time" (Titus 1:2), and Jesus Christ provided that redemption. The Messianic Psalms should move us to praise God that he made our salvation the focus of his sovereignty.

Implicit in God's sovereign rule over the world to bring about our redemption in Jesus Christ, the Messiah, are the two subthemes of Psalms 22 and 45. When we read Psalm 22, we remember that Jesus Christ willingly took our sin and its judgment on himself when he died on the cross. The Messiah, prepared for before the worlds began, died for us. Psalm 22 is a Lament, but it should move us to wonder, love, and praise to God for his grace. When we read Psalm 45, we rejoice that Jesus Christ, the King of Kings and Lord of Lords, is our bridegroom. We will join him at the wedding supper of the Lamb (Rev. 19:6–9) and live with him forever. Psalm 45 is a Hymn of Praise, and it cannot help but create a heart of praise in us for Jesus, the Christ. Jesus' suffering and reigning—these are the themes of the Messianic Psalms. What better meditation could there be?

Chapter 9

My Rock and My Redeemer:
God Protects and Delivers

I lift up my eyes to the hills—
  where does my help come from?
My help comes from the LORD,
  the Maker of heaven and earth.
He will not let your foot slip—
  he who watches over you will not slumber;
Indeed, he who watches over Israel
  will neither slumber nor sleep.
The LORD watches over you—
  the LORD is your shade at your right hand;
  the sun will not harm you by day,
  nor the moon by night.
The LORD will keep you from all harm—
  he will watch over your life;
The LORD will watch over your coming and going
  both now and forevermore.

—Psalm 121

WHAT IS OUR FIRST RESPONSE WHEN we are threatened? Behavioral psychologists and evolutionary biologists tell us that many people respond with a threat in kind. Consider the animals, many of which puff themselves up or bare their teeth in the face of a menace. Some people cower in fear, while still others retreat and avoid confrontation at all costs. These are some of the natural responses that danger triggers in us. But how are Christians supposed to respond to threats and enemies? How are they to react when they feel vulnerable and maliciously attacked? The Psalms provide many illustrations of how God's people respond to threats. In the Psalms that show God's people threatened by enemies and slanderers, the psalmists turn to God in praise and petition. Fully one-fifth of the Psalms, in part or in whole, discuss God's protection and provision of his people in difficult times.

For the ancient Israelites, the surrounding nations were always a threat. From the time of the first settlements in the Promised Land, the pagan nations were quick to ally themselves together and attack Israel, for they saw her as a threat to their existence (Josh. 10:1–28). As late as the early tenth century B.C., King David spent much of his reign defending his territory against foreign incursions and securing the safety of his land. In 586 B.C., the Israelites were carried into captivity, and in A.D. 70, Rome sacked Jerusalem and destroyed the temple. The ancient Israelites suffered more than their share of foreign threat and domination. We should not be surprised therefore to find many of the Psalms either asking the Lord for deliverance or praising him for protection.

But how do these psalms apply to us today? Most Christians in Western nations give little thought to foreign attack, and they certainly do not fear for their own safety simply because they are Christians. While we have yet to face a serious persecution of Christians in most modern Western nations, September 11, 2001, served notice that Westerners are no longer invulnerable to foreign aggression. Like everyone else in the United States, Christians must adapt to the new international realities and find ways to live in a state of preparedness in case of terrorist violence. So far terrorist attacks have rarely targeted evangelical Christians specifically, but we share in the national situation along with those of all faiths and those who have no faith.

Beyond terrorist threats, there are enemies that Christians must face, some on a daily basis. Some Christians face daily antagonism in the marketplace from colleagues and employers who have little sympathy for Christians and see them as intolerant bigots. Some Christians must respond to slanderous accusations made by false witnesses who wish to damage their reputations and careers. Still others face daily pressures from family members who are not Christians and resent the faith of those who are. Western culture in general is no friend of Christ. Despite the conservative and patriotic swing occasioned by the terrorist attacks in 2001, an anti-Christian pressure lies dormant in our culture, fueled by those who have no love for the Savior and hate Christians. We should never be lulled into thinking that the United States is essentially a "Christian" nation, for the antagonism in our country toward Christianity increases unabated. Christians may not be under military siege or physical detention in the United States, but many subtle pressures combine to seek to remove Christianity from public life. The Psalms have much to say about suffering and God's protection against such enemies as these.

We will consider two psalms in this chapter on suffering, Psalms 27 and 79. Psalm 79 shows the ancient Israelites under attack because they had sinned against God and been unfaithful to him. Like the Old Testament people of God, Christians sometimes bring suffering on themselves through their own sin or by their thoughtless behavior. Psalm 27, on the other hand, presents a situation in which David does not cause his own suffering by any known sin, but he is still threatened by enemies surrounding him. Both psalms demonstrate God's loving protection and provision. We will examine how Christians are to deal with suffering that their own personal sin causes in chapter 11, where we look at the Penitential Psalms. Here, however, we need to consider how Christians are to respond when they suffer innocently.

The apostle Peter has much to say about the innocent suffering of Christians. In fact, he wrote his first epistle in large part to help Christians understand God's plan in their suffering and teach them how to prepare for it. Peter distinguishes between those who suffer because of sin and those who suffer simply because they are believers:

> If you suffer, it should not be as a murderer or thief or any other kind of criminal, or even as a meddler. However, if you

suffer as a Christian, do not be ashamed, but praise God that
you bear that name.

—1 Peter 4:15–16

We should not miss the implicit point in Peter's words that all Christians will indeed suffer. If Christians suffer because of sin, the proper
response is confession and repentance. If they suffer innocently, or
simply because they believe in Jesus Christ, they should rejoice. Ad-
mittedly, rejoicing in trials is difficult, even impossible, from a human
perspective; it takes the grace of God to obey this command.

It helps to know, however, what God's plan in his people's suffering
is. One reason Christians may suffer for their Christianity is to refine
their faith. One of the first points Peter teaches in the opening chapter
of the epistle relates to this encouragement:

> These [trials] have come so that your faith—of greater
> worth than gold, which perishes even though refined by fire—
> may be proved genuine and may result in praise, glory and
> honor when Jesus Christ is revealed.
>
> —1 Peter 1:7

Christians may suffer innocently for two reasons: so that their faith
may be refined, and so that Jesus Christ might be honored. Though
Peter does not make the point explicitly in this verse, we must remember that God's sovereign reign is the context in which the
Christian's suffering occurs, and we know that God does all things for
his people's good (Rom. 8:28). Even so, how can Christians prepare
ahead of time for the sufferings that will inevitably come? Peter wastes
no time answering this question:

> Therefore, prepare your minds for action; be self-controlled;
> set your hope fully on the grace to be given you when Jesus
> Christ is revealed.
>
> —1 Peter 1:13

Again, the point is twofold. Christians prepare for trials by disciplining their minds to the doctrines of the faith and by looking forward to the blessings they will receive when they are glorified. We need to know these doctrines before we suffer, or we will not be able to rely on the promises of blessing when the trials come.

What is our first response when trials and sufferings come?
When a friend attacks us for our faith, when we are slandered
because we believe in Jesus Christ, or when we receive bad
medical news, how do we respond? How do the psalmists
respond under such circumstances?

Psalm 27
DAVID'S CONFIDENCE IN GOD'S PROTECTION

In Psalm 27 King David sings a song of confident praise to Yahweh for his protection against his enemies. Odd though it appears at first glance, David does not beg God for protection when his enemies surround him; rather, he simply asks for the Lord's presence. This is a psalm for those troubling times when we feel vulnerable.

> [1]The LORD is my light and my salvation—
>   whom shall I fear?
> The LORD is the stronghold of my life—
>   of whom shall I be afraid?
> [2]When evil men advance against me
>   to devour my flesh,
> when my enemies and my foes attack me,
>   they will stumble and fall.
> [3]Though an army besiege me,
>   my heart will not fear;
> though war break out against me,
>   even then will I be confident.

⁴One thing I ask of the LORD,
　　this is what I seek:
that I may dwell in the house of the LORD
　　all the days of my life,
to gaze upon the beauty of the LORD
　　and to seek him in his temple.
⁵For in the day of trouble
　　he will keep me safe in his dwelling;
he will hide me in the shelter of his tabernacle
　　and set me high upon a rock.
⁶Then my head will be exalted
　　above the enemies who surround me;
at his tabernacle will I sacrifice with shouts of joy;
　　I will sing and make music to the LORD.

⁷Hear my voice when I call, O LORD;
　　be merciful to me and answer me.
⁸My heart says of you, "Seek his face!"
　　Your face, LORD, I will seek.
⁹Do not hide your face from me,
　　do not turn your servant away in anger;
　　you have been my helper.
Do not reject me or forsake me,
　　O God my Savior.
¹⁰Though my father and mother forsake me,
　　the LORD will receive me.
¹¹Teach me your way, O LORD;
　　lead me in a straight path
　　because of my oppressors.
¹²Do not turn me over to the desire of my foes,
　　for false witnesses rise up against me,
　　breathing out violence.

¹³I am still confident of this:
　　I will see the goodness of the LORD

>in the land of the living.
>¹⁴Wait for the LORD;
>   be strong and take heart
>   and wait for the LORD.

What Is the Overall Effect of the Psalm?

If we think of Psalm 27 as a painting with a background and a foreground, we can appreciate the overall effect of the psalm. In the background of the psalm are David's enemies, surrounding him on all sides and pressing him hard. The opening verses present a situation that seems hopeless from a human perspective: David is alone, beset everywhere by "enemies," "an army," and "evil men" who wish his defeat and death. In the foreground of the painting, however, is Yahweh. When David looks out and sees his desperate situation, he does not rush to prepare his military defenses. Surprisingly, he simply asks for Yahweh's presence and for the opportunity to worship him in the tabernacle. What a sharp contrast is here—an army ready to attack the king, and the king worshiping God! Psalm 27 strikes a note of great confidence in Yahweh's protection of his people.

> *Psalm 27 is "Theocentric." That is, it is "God-centered."*
> *Yahweh is present in every verse, providing the focus of David's*
> *worship. The only desire of his heart is to worship Yahweh*
> *in his temple.*

What Is the Structure of the Psalm?

Psalm 27 is structured in an A-B-B-A pattern. That is, the first and last sections of the psalm provide statements of confidence in God's ability to help the king; these are the two "As" in the pattern. In the middle of the psalm, between the two statements of confidence, are two prayers to Yahweh; these are the two "Bs" of the pattern. The final statement of confidence in Yahweh's protection, following the desperate situation of the opening verses and the intervening prayers, is even more emphatic than the opening declaration of assurance. The outline of the psalm shows it's A-B-B-A structure:

I.   Verses 1–3:   David's Confidence in Yahweh's Protection
II. Verses 4–6:   David's Prayer for the Presence of the Lord
III. Verses 7–12:   David's Prayer for the Closeness of the Lord
IV. Verses 13–14:   David's Trust in Yahweh's Goodness

The effect of this structure is to emphasize Yahweh's protection of the king over David's fears of his enemies. Beginning and ending in confidence, David learns to place his natural concern about the enemies surrounding him in proper perspective, for God is sovereign in the affairs of nations. Notice the stitching devices that unify the psalm and emphasize Yahweh's protection of David. "Enemies" and "foes" attack David (v. 2), but he will not be surrendered to their evil desires (vv. 6, 12). Early in the psalm, David expresses his "confidence" in Yahweh (v. 3), and he concludes by reasserting his confidence in Yahweh's protection (v. 13). These repetitions serve as stitching devices to emphasize David's confidence in Yahweh in the face of his enemies' threats.

Psalm 27 has elements of three different types of psalms. First, because its subject is King David, it is a Royal Psalm. As the Lord's anointed king in Israel, David enjoys God's special care and protection, or his *ḥesed* love. Of course, God's *ḥesed* love for David extends to the people of Israel as well, for they are a part of God's people; in this way, the psalm is simultaneously a private prayer of David and a public declaration. In the second place, Psalm 27 is a Hymn, or Psalm of Praise. The opening and closing sections of the psalm demonstrate David's confidence in Yahweh's loving protection and praise him for it. The third type of psalm represented in Psalm 27 is the Lament. In a Lament, the speaker identifies his complaint or problem, requests Yahweh for deliverance, and affirms his confidence that Yahweh will answer him. In Psalm 27 David laments his enemies (vv. 2–3), his parents' desertion of him (v. 10), and the false witnesses who have risen against him (v. 12). While the variety of genres in the psalm makes it difficult to categorize the psalm exclusively as one type or another, it is best to think of Psalm 27 as a Royal Psalm that contains elements of praise and lament. Seen from this perspective, King David's cry for God's presence becomes the people's cry—and ours as well.

What Are the Figures of Speech in the Psalm, and What Effects Do They Have?

David begins his psalm with a confident statement of Yahweh's provision and protection. Even in the face of his enemies—whom he does not mention in the opening verse—David knows God will bless him with his covenant, or *hesed,* love. David announces his theme in the initial phrase of the psalm, proclaiming that Yahweh meets his spiritual needs; "light" and "salvation" both refer to the spiritual blessings God gives by his grace to the believer. In the parallel statement that follows this opening declaration, David announces that Yahweh meets his temporal needs, in this case, protection from the armies camped at the gate. Yahweh is David's "stronghold." The repeated rhetorical questions ("Whom shall I fear?" and "Of whom shall I be afraid?") following these two statements demonstrate David's complete confidence in Yahweh, for they are almost like taunts to anyone who would challenge Yahweh. No matter how difficult David's situation is, he trusts God.

When David speaks in the next two verses of his enemies, it is clear that he feels trapped and vulnerable. In an unprovoked attack, "evil men" move forward to "devour" him, and his "enemies" and "foes" attack him (v. 2). These images show David as the innocent one, and the attackers as particularly vicious. By writing these statements in a parallel manner ("when evil men advance against me" and "when my enemies and my foes attack me"), David leads the reader to think that he will repeat the purpose of the attack, "to devour [his] flesh,"[1] in a parallel assertion

---

1. "Devour my flesh" may be a metaphor for slander or oppression in general. Compare the same phrase in verse 12.

after the second statement. However, he does not; instead, after the second statement he makes the confident assertion that "they [his enemies] will stumble and fall" (v. 2). In this antithetic parallelism, David underscores the certainty of his safety in Yahweh. The change of conjunction from "when" in verse 2 to "though" in verse 3 (NIV) further emphasizes David's confidence in God, for, no matter what his enemies do, they cannot defeat him. What gives David this kind of peace is not his military might; it is the Lord who meets his needs spiritually and physically. The Lord has set his love *(ḥesed)* on David. When we witness the armies arrayed against David in these opening verses, we see them against the background of God's all-powerful and sovereign rule over all things. In this light, which of David's enemies can hurt him? If we will meditate on God as David does when our times of trouble come, we too will know David's confidence.

The next section of the psalm, David's prayer for the presence of the Lord (vv. 4–6), begins the main theme of the psalm. In the face of a constant threat of attack, David earnestly desires the presence of the Lord (cf. Ps. 63:2). In a metonymy, David associates the Lord with his "house," or his "temple" (v. 4). For David and the Old Testament Jews, the temple, or tabernacle, was the place where Yahweh met with them; at the least it was a tangible symbol of the presence of God. David's attention to the tabernacle and God's presence there is not a passing fancy or a superficial acknowledgment of God before battle, nor is it a distraught "foxhole prayer." It is the "one thing" David asks of the Lord (v. 4), his all-consuming, heartfelt thought in the face of battle—God's dwelling with men. Note the forms David's prayer takes: he wishes to "dwell in the house of the LORD"; to "gaze upon the beauty of the LORD"; and to "seek him in his temple" (v. 4). David's attention to God, re-peated in these three phrases, is not perfunctory as our worship some-times tends to be, nor is it hypocritical and self-serving. David earnestly wishes to worship the Lord in his tabernacle. The repetition of the "dwelling" of God (v. 5) and his "tabernacle" (vv. 5–6) underscores the *ḥesed* love Yahweh has for David and his people. Yahweh will "hide" David and "set [him] high upon a rock" (v. 5); he will "exalt" him (v. 6). These references are meant to represent Yahweh himself and his care for the king. David shows us that the sovereign Lord of the universe, against whom no army can stand, meets with his people in the temple. What can the king fear? What should we fear?

Verse 7 begins David's second prayer, this one a prayer for the Lord to remain close to him when others desert him and still others attack him. This prayer is the longest and most personal section of the psalm (vv. 7–12), beginning with the entreaty, "Hear my voice when I call, O LORD" (v. 7). In the previous prayer (vv. 4–6), David simply asks for the Lord's presence in the tabernacle and then meditates on him. At the end of the first prayer, David thanks God for his presence "with shouts of joy," making "music to the LORD" (v. 6). In contrast to the few words he addresses directly to God in the first prayer, David speaks to the Lord throughout the second prayer, asking him in multiple ways to remain close to him in his hour of need. In the first prayer, David "gazes" upon the Lord, and God's presence is enough for him. In this second prayer, he addresses God directly. The first image David uses in this section is a personification of God as having a face (vv. 8–9)—a well-known personification found frequently throughout the Scriptures. The image of David face-to-face with God creates a domestic scene in which David speaks tenderly to his "helper" who is also his "Savior" (v. 9). As a young child will seek a parent's attention, sometimes physically turning the parent's face toward himself or herself, so David petitions God personally, asking that he not take his presence away from him. The emotion of the scene deepens when David states that, even if his father and mother were to forsake him, God would remain faithful (v. 10). Like a child too, he asks that God instruct him and "lead [him] in a straight path" (v. 11). Finally, he asks for protection against his "foes," for "false witnesses" have spoken against him (v. 12). Rather than using several figures of speech, David simply presents a domestic scene that any parent or child can appreciate—a child coming to parents for protection from bullies and liars who would cause harm. In David's case, of course, the situation is a matter of life and death for himself and the nation of Israel.

David concludes the psalm as he began, with an unequivocal assertion of his confidence in Yahweh to deliver him from his enemies. When we come to these verses after all that has preceded them, they ring with assurance and hope for David and all those who "wait for the LORD" (v. 14). Earlier in the psalm, David has asked God for help against the enemies at the gate; he has expressed his delight in the Lord when he asks to dwell with him in his temple forever; he has asked for mercy on himself personally; and he has confessed that God is more faithful than father or mother. In the light of all these prayers and expressions of faith, David ends the psalm with a statement of his own confidence in God and an invitation to other believers to share that assurance.

Psalm 27 begins in David's extremity, with the king facing the possibility of military defeat and death and his people facing exile; it ends with the king's absolute confidence that Yahweh will protect him. When we remember that the psalm opens with a description of David's enemies arrayed against him, we might expect a military psalm that presents God as a warrior to defend Israel. Surprisingly, however, David simply presents two scenes in the psalm—one of Yahweh's presence in the temple, and one a domestic scene of a child and parent—that appear to have nothing to do with the military threat at hand. The contrast between David's dilemma and his desire for the Lord emphasizes David's love for Yahweh and Yahweh's sovereign love for David.

What Are the Themes and Theology in the Psalm?

David states the first theme of Psalm 27 in the opening verse: the Lord's unfailing love (*ḥesed*) for his people. God's love is implicit throughout the psalm, because it relates so directly to David's role as king of Israel. The promises God makes to protect David and, in 2 Samuel 6 and 7, to provide a King in his line that will reign forever, extend to all the people of Israel. God's promise never to desert his people and to provide a king in David's line (Jesus Christ) includes believers today as well. The writer of Hebrews quotes Deuteronomy 31:6, "Never will I leave you; never will I forsake you," to Christians as a reminder of God's constant presence with them (Heb. 13:5). Indeed, the closing words of Matthew's gospel are Jesus' promise never to forsake his people: "And surely I am with you always, to the very end of the age" (Matt. 28:20). God's presence provides David with the confidence he expresses throughout Psalm 27, as the presence of Jesus Christ gives Christians an eternal hope.

The second theme of Psalm 27 relates to the attributes of God, three of which David mentions in the psalm. The first attribute of God in Psalm 27 is his sovereignty. God is sovereign and therefore controls the attacks of David's enemies and allows them to advance only so far. He does not permit them to do anything to David that is contrary to his will (vv. 2–3, 6, 12). So too with us: God does not allow anything to happen to us outside of his will. Knowing this truth helps in times of trouble. A second divine attribute the psalm teaches is that God is good to his people, both spiritually and temporally (vv. 1, 13). God's protection of David and the people of Israel demonstrates his goodness, for David knows that he cannot set himself "high upon a rock" (v. 5) and make himself "exalted" (v. 6). Only Yahweh can honor him this way. A third divine attribute Psalm 27 illustrates is God's faithfulness (vv. 5, 10). God's faithfulness is implicit throughout the psalm in his protection of David against his enemies. However, David expresses God's faithfulness to him explicitly when he states that God is closer to him than father or mother ever could be. When faced with enemies and false witnesses, David meditates on the attributes of God, and these bring him encouragement and refreshment.

> *Yahweh's ḥesed love for his people includes his sovereign rule over the circumstances of their lives, his goodness in meeting their daily needs, and his faithfulness to them throughout their lives and into eternity.*

Applications

1. While we may not face military enemies in the direct way that David did, civilized nations do face the threat of terrorist activity close to home. When we experience a terrorist attack, we should turn our thoughts to Yahweh, the one who protects his

people according to his will. This is not to say that governments should not take action against terrorism; they should. It is simply to agree with the words of Scripture:

> No king is saved by the size of his army;
>   no warrior escapes by his great strength.
> A horse is a vain hope for deliverance;
>   despite all its great strength it cannot save.
> But the eyes of the LORD are on those who fear him,
>   on those whose hope is in his unfailing love,
> to deliver them from death
>   and keep them alive in famine.
>   —Psalm 33:16–19

We are to defend ourselves as we need to, but it is finally the Lord who delivers us from our enemies.

2. More often than military or terrorist activity, our enemies are likely to be the false witnesses David mentions in Psalm 27. When we are falsely accused at work, in the office, or perhaps by family members who are not believers, we would do well to turn to Psalm 27, for it speaks to our vulnerability. Like David, we should ask for the Lord's protection in these circumstances. Like David, we should meditate on God's sovereignty (which allows the slander for a purpose), his goodness (which vindicates us), and his faithfulness to us (which restores us). We should remember that an unfounded slur against a believer is a slander against the testimony of God in that believer's life; God has a stake in suppressing the false witness, and we should let him resolve the matter in his way.

3. Where do we turn first when we are threatened or slandered? Do we turn to our own devices first, or to God? Like David, we should meditate on God and know him as he is revealed in Scripture. Then we will be able to turn to him when the troubled time comes. Psalm 27 begins with David facing his enemies (vv. 2, 4) and ends with him face-to-face with God (vv. 13–14). If we do

not study the Scriptures for what they say about God, we will not able to remember what we need in an emergency.

Psalm 79
HOW LONG, O LORD?

Even more than Psalm 27, Psalm 79 turns our attention to Yahweh, not ourselves. More is at stake when enemies threaten God's people than their safety; God's witness is attacked too. When believers ask for God's protection and deliverance, they ask him to defend his testimony in them.

> ¹O God, the nations have invaded your inheritance;
>   they have defiled your holy temple,
>   they have reduced Jerusalem to rubble.
> ²They have given the dead bodies of your servants
>   as food to the birds of the air,
>   the flesh of your saints to the beasts of the earth.
> ³They have poured out blood like water
>   all around Jerusalem,
>   and there is no one to bury the dead.
> ⁴We are objects of reproach to our neighbors,
>   of scorn and derision to those around us.
>
> ⁵How long, O LORD? Will you be angry forever?
>   How long will your jealousy burn like fire?
> ⁶Pour out your wrath on the nations
>   that do not acknowledge you,
> on the kingdoms
>   that do not call your name;
> ⁷for they have devoured Jacob
>   and destroyed his homeland.
> ⁸Do not hold against us the sins of the fathers;
>   may your mercy come quickly to meet us,
>   for we are in desperate need.

⁹Help us, O God our Savior,
    for the glory of your name;
deliver us and forgive our sins
    for your name's sake.
¹⁰Why should the nations say,
    "Where is their God?"
Before our eyes, make known among the nations
    that you avenge the outpoured blood of your servants.
¹¹May the groans of the prisoners come before you;
    by the strength of your arm
    preserve those condemned to die.

¹²Pay back into the laps of our neighbors seven times
    the reproach they have hurled at you, O Lord.
¹³Then we your people, the sheep of your pasture,
    will praise you forever;
from generation to generation
    we will recount your praise.

What Is the Overall Effect of the Psalm?

In Psalm 79 Asaph extends empty hands to Yahweh and asks for help. This is a psalm of petitions in which the writer holds two very different prayers in tension. On the one hand, Asaph acknowledges the sins of God's people and asks for forgiveness and mercy (vv. 8, 9, 11). Asaph does not contend with God and protest that his people are innocent. Rather, the psalm recounts the just judgment of God on the people of Israel for their sins and the sins of their fathers (v. 8). The people's penitence is genuine. On the other hand, the psalm calls down judgment on the pagan nations that Yahweh uses to judge Israel (vv. 6, 7, 10, 12). The attackers have disregarded God, profaned the holy things in Israel, and killed God's people without regard to Yahweh himself (vv. 1–4, 7, 10). Because of their disregard of Yahweh, these people deserve God's judgment. In their attack on Israel, they have impugned God's testimony (v. 10). Habakkuk faced the same problem when he questioned God about how he could use a sinful, pagan nation (in this case, the Babylonians) to judge the Israelites (Hab. 1:12–2:1). In Psalm 79 Asaph contends that the pagans who have killed God's people and profaned the sanctuary deserve to be judged. These two petitions—the one for forgiveness and mercy, the other for judgment of the attackers—alternate throughout the psalm and provide the tension that supports the psalm.

The resolution to the tension of these two apparently antithetical prayers in the psalm lies in the person and work of Yahweh. Psalm 79 turns on two attributes of God, his holiness and his unfailing love for his people. Because Yahweh is holy, he judges the sins of Israel and the other nations. Israel does not escape God's judgment, for his people have suffered his punishment at the hands of the attackers, almost to the point of extinction (vv. 1–4). It is likely that the occasion that prompts this psalm is "Jerusalem's fall and the subsequent exile of Judah (586 B.C.)."[2] Nor do the attackers escape God's judgment. God's judgment of the attackers is implicit in the final verse, where God's people, "the sheep of [his] pasture" (v. 13), will praise God forever. It is God's people who survive this situation, not the attacking nations; God judges the nations for their attack on his people and restores his people to their relationship with him. Because Yahweh loves his people with a *ḥesed,* or unfailing, love, he delivers them from the oppressor and restores them to his favor. Note the terms Asaph uses to describe the Israelites: they are Yahweh's "inheritance" (v. 1), his "servants" and "saints" (v. 2), and his "sheep" (v. 13). All of these terms presume Yahweh's covenant relationship with his people, and they all designate the special relationship the people have with Yahweh. With Habbakuk, Asaph prays to Yahweh, "in wrath remember mercy" (Hab. 3:2). Yahweh is holy and loving in Psalm 79, holy in the judgment of his people and the pagan nations, loving in the forgiveness and restoration of his people. Though Psalm 79 appears to go in two distinct directions at the same time, it is unified by the presence of Yahweh, who is both holy and loving.

---

2. Willem VanGemeren, *Psalms,* vol. 5 of *The Expositor's Bible Commentary,* ed. Frank E. Gaebelein (Grand Rapids: Zondervan, 1991), 519.

What Is the Structure of the Psalm?

Psalm 79 is a Public Lament with every verse spoken to Yahweh. The speaker, Asaph, represents the nation of Israel in confessing national sins and asking for forgiveness and relief. Laments typically contain the elements of complaint (or lament, a description of the problem), petition (or prayer for help), and a final statement of confidence in Yahweh's deliverance. Some Laments contain curses against God's enemies (or imprecations). Other Laments contain the people's confession of their sins. Psalm 79 contains all of these elements, though it is difficult to determine a definitive outline that everyone will accept. Still, the following outline of Psalm 79 captures the speaker's fears and Yahweh's power.

I. Verses 1–4:   Complaint Against the Attackers
II. Verse 5:   Lament About Yahweh's Judgment of His People
III. Verses 6–7:   Yahweh's Judgment of the Nations
IV. Verses 8–11: Yahweh's Forgiveness and Restoration of His People
V. Verse 12:   Yahweh's Punishment of the Nations
VI. Verse 13:   Concluding Statement of Confidence in Yahweh

As this structure readily indicates, Asaph alternates between curses and confessions and between judgment on the unbelieving nations and restoration for God's people. This alternating pattern keeps both God's holiness and his mercy in front of the reader at all times.

What Are the Figures of Speech in the Psalm, and What Effects Do They Have?

Psalm 79 begins with a series of staccato statements that emphasize the desperate situation of God's people. The opening verse comprises three statements that underscore the desolation of the people of God. These three statements, spoken to God, are in synonymous parallelism: the nations have "invaded [Yahweh's] inheritance," "defiled [his] holy temple," and "reduced Jerusalem to rubble." The picture these statements present is one of progressive destruction and profanation. The attackers have disregarded the holy things of God in the temple compound and wantonly destroyed the city of Jerusalem at large. From the temple and city destruction, the writer next turns his attention to the victims of the attack, whose bodies are given to "the birds of the air" and the "beasts of the earth" (v. 2). In a hyperbole, the speaker indicates that the genocide has been so great that there is none left to bury the dead. Of course, there is a remnant, or the final verse of the psalm does not make sense; God keeps a witness to himself at all times. The detail of blood poured out like water (v. 3) completes the picture of wanton destruction and cruel murder of innocent people, reducing the value of life to mere "run-off water."[3] The opening complaint against the attackers, however, does not represent a personal cry for revenge on the part of the speaker, for his primary concern is that the destruction of Jerusalem and the murder of God's people impugn God's testimony. The speaker knows that the people's plight makes of them—and therefore of Yahweh—a "scorn" and "derision" (v. 4) to those who hate Yahweh. God's testimony is at stake, not Asaph's revenge.

Having depicted the destruction of Jerusalem and the murder of God's people, Asaph next addresses God with the rhetorical question, "How long, O LORD?" (v. 5). Taken in its context, this is a desolate cry, for Asaph knows that the destruction and murder are God's righteous judgment against his sinful people, not merely an arbitrary act of aggression on the part of a foreign nation. If God has deserted his people, they are truly alone. Asaph knows that God is sovereign even in this disaster. Asaph uses two figures of speech in this verse, personifying God as being angry and comparing God's jealousy (another familiar human characteristic assigned to God in a personification) in a simile to fire. God's anger against his people's sins underscores his holiness. The simile comparing his jealousy to fire indicates that he will purge the sins of his people to make them holy. This verse is a hinge verse, turning the psalm from God's judg-

---

3. Ibid., 520.

ment of his people (vv. 1–4) into a prayer for him to judge the nations (vv. 6–7).

Verses 6 and 7 represent Asaph's first prayer for God to judge the nations that have attacked Jerusalem and desecrated the temple. In his prayer, the speaker does not show any personal vengefulness against the attackers. His concern in the prayer is Yahweh's testimony. It is because the nations have rejected Yahweh that they deserve judgment. In a synonymous parallelism, Asaph indicates that the nations "do not acknowledge" Yahweh, and they "do not call on [his] name" (v. 6). Nor does their sin end there. Their rejection of Yahweh leads to their attack on his people. The speaker depicts the attack in the imagery of a carnivore eating its prey; the nations "devoured Jacob and destroyed his homeland" (v. 7). It is for these reasons that the nations deserve to be judged, not for personal injuries that the people of God have sustained. They know these to be the just judgment of God on their sin. The first call for judgment on the pagan nations is brief, and it invokes Yahweh's stake in Jerusalem's destruction as the reason for the prayer.

In the next section of the psalm, Asaph prays that Yahweh would forgive and restore his people (vv. 8–11). He begins this section by acknowledging the people's sins and asking God for mercy. To illustrate God's mercy, Asaph uses an image of a runner or a messenger "com[ing] quickly" to Israel's assistance (v. 8). This concrete picture underscores the important truth that God actively and willingly sends his grace to meet our needs, in this case, mercy for forgiveness. God initiates by grace; we respond by faith.

In a series of parallelisms, verses 9 and 10 reiterate the point made earlier (vv. 6–7) that the testimony of Yahweh is at stake in the destruction of his people. Asaph calls on his God and Savior here, putting together God's sovereignty (in *God,* Elohim, the supreme God) and his salvation for his people (in *Savior,* showing his *ḥesed* love). In the synthesis of the two aspects of God's character—his sovereignty over the nations and his covenant love for his people—Asaph unites the two themes of the psalm in one stroke. As sovereign God, Yahweh punishes the nations that attack Israel; as covenant Lord, he forgives the sins of his people and restores them to his favor. Repeated through-out this section is the psalmist's concern for the testimony of God before the pagan nations. In verse 9, he speaks of "the glory of [God's] name" and his "name's sake." In verse 10, he asks God to "make known among the nations that [he] avenge[s] the outpoured blood of [his] servants." Repeatedly, Asaph returns to the glory of God as the basis for his petition for forgiveness and restoration. Just as Jerusalem's de-struction is a reproach to God's name (v. 4), so her restoration mani-fests God's glory. In verse 11, Asaph pleads the pathos of the "groans of the prisoners" to move God's heart to mercy and grace. These verses combine a concern for God's testimony in the restoration of Jerusa-lem with the suffering of the people as a supplication to God for mercy.

In the concluding statement of confidence in Yahweh, Asaph brings the psalm to rest on God's covenant love for his people, here in the familiar image of the "sheep of [his] pasture." The psalmist shows his confidence in God's *hesed* love by the repetition of the promise to praise God "forever" and "from generation to generation." The psalm begins in defeat and death; it ends in rejoicing for God's covenant mercies. Between the opening and the conclusion, the psalmist asks for forgiveness, curses God's enemies, and reminds God of his testi-mony in his people. The psalm begins with a human threat but ends with divine assurance.

What Are the Themes and Theology in the Psalm?

Psalm 79 puts the attacks of the enemies of God against his people in a completely theocentric (God-centered) perspective. That is, the attacks against God's people are ultimately an attack against God. The unbeliever turns his anger at God against his people, just as Satan did in the Garden of Eden in seducing Adam and Eve into sin, in the hope that he might hurt the Lord in spoiling them (and us). By asserting the holiness, sovereignty, and faithfulness of Yahweh, Psalm 79 reminds us that God takes sides in such situations.

The first theme of Psalm 79 is God's holiness. He is justified in his anger (v. 5) against his people because of their sin. If God were not holy, his judgment of sin would be arbitrary and tyrannical. However, because God is holy, his judgment of sin is just and necessary.

The second theme of Psalm 79 is God's covenant love *(hesed)* for his people. God's *hesed* love complements his holiness. While no one is inherently righteous, believers are declared righteous by grace through faith in Jesus Christ. Paul explains the great transaction in which Jesus Christ takes the believer's sin and declares the believer to be righteous:

> This righteousness from God comes through faith in Jesus Christ to all who believe. There is no difference, for all have sinned and fall short of the glory of God, and are justified freely by his grace through the redemption that came by Christ Jesus.
>
> —Romans 3:22–24

In Psalm 79, the covenant love of God for his people is indicated in the relationship they have with him. God's people are called his "inheritance" (v. 1), his "servants" and "saints" (v. 2), and his "sheep" (v. 13). God displays his *hesed* love in the very fact that the psalm was composed at all. Think of it: we have a psalm written by a Hebrew about Yahweh who still sheds his covenant love on his people and whose people still praise him. Where are the pagan nations that attacked Israel? They have passed into the oblivion of history, but Yahweh and his people remain.

The third theme of Psalm 79 also relates to Yahweh. Yahweh is sovereign. Without sovereignty, there would be no psalm. Hard though the thought is, God is sovereign in the Israelites' defeat, the overthrow of Jerusalem, the profaning of the temple, and the exile. No circumstance is outside the sovereignty of God. At the same time, God is long-suffering and redeems his own; not one will be lost. Today, God is calling out a people to worship him, and they do so by responding in faith to God's grace in Jesus Christ and then glorifying him forever. So it was in Asaph's day: God called out his people, in the case of Psalm 79 a remnant, and made them his people (v. 13).

*Psalm 79 is about Yahweh's testimony and his people's suffering.
When God's people suffer through no fault of their own, he will
protect and deliver them according to his will. When he does so,
he demonstrates his holiness, his covenant love, and his
sovereignty. Therefore with Asaph we can say, "from generation
to generation we will recount [God's] praise" (v. 13).*

Applications

1. When we suffer, we must be certain that we are not responsible
   for our own dilemma. If we are living godly lives to the best of
   our ability and we suffer for the name and cause of Christ, we
   are to "consider it pure joy" (James 1:2; cf. 1 Peter 1:6–9). Such
   joy is impossible apart from the grace of God, but with God's
   grace we can triumph even in adversity.
2. When we suffer for the cause of Christ, we can be encouraged
   that the ultimate attack is against the Lord and not us. Yahweh's
   testimony is at stake when his people suffer, and he is committed to honoring his witness in the world. We can take heart in
   Jesus' sufferings when we share them, and we can remember that
   we take part in his glory as well (2 Tim. 2:12; 1 Peter 5:10).

Encountering God as Protector and Deliverer

When the psalmists faced military enemies from without or false
witnesses from within, they turned first to Yahweh, not themselves. In
Psalm 27, David meditates on God's *hesed* love as he contemplates
the problems he faces. Enemies threaten him at the gate, and false
witnesses slander him, yet his one desire is the presence of the Lord in
the temple. Even if parents were to desert him, still God would be
faithful. Faced in Psalm 79 with a military disaster, Asaph meditates
on the *hesed* of God and realizes that an unjust attack on God's people
is an attack on God. As such, God will defend his people. What do we
learn about our suffering from the psalmists?

We learn first that the need for protection may begin with an individual, but it quickly extends to other believers in the community of faith. David's psalm of personal praise in Psalm 27 includes other believers because he is the king, and God's protection for David included the nation of Israel at large. In Psalm 79, Asaph realizes from the beginning that the whole believing community is at stake if God does not intervene on their behalf. When we face personal trials, we should seek God first, as David does by asking for his presence in the temple, and ask for him to protect us according to his will. When we suffer, we should remember that other believers are affected by our trials and ask for their prayers and help. We are not alone, for God is with us, and other Christians can rally to our aid.

The second lesson we learn is that God's testimony is at stake when a Christian is attacked or wrongfully accused. Asaph makes God's testimony the basis of his request for protection. When we are certain that we have not caused our own suffering in a foolish or sinful way, we can ask God to defend us, for in doing so he defends his name. Our suffering is Christ's, and he will be honored at the end. This is not to say that God will remove all Christians from all difficult situations. It is to say, however, that God is faithful and can be trusted to do all things for our good as well as his glory. In fact, his glory is bound up with our good.

Not only do we have the psalmists' testimony that God will defend his people, we have the character and attributes of God as evidence as well. The pagan gods of the nations surrounding Israel were capricious and arbitrary. All the ancient literatures attest to the cruel ways in which gods were known to treat their subjects; they could not be relied upon to behave in any consistent or holy way. Not so with Yahweh. Yahweh's defense of his people relates to the attributes of his character. God behaves consistently with who he is, and the psalmists demonstrate this important truth in the Psalms of protection and deliverance. God is a warrior who defends his people (Ps. 79:9–10).[4] He

---

4. For a full treatment of God as a warrior in the Old Testament, see Tremper Longman and Daniel G. Reid, *God Is a Warrior* (Carlisle, U.K.: Paternoster, 1995).

is sovereign over all nations. The destruction of Jerusalem that Asaph laments in Psalm 79 and the survival of a people of God to this day both fall within the sovereignty of God. When we read Asaph's psalm in modern times, we are reminded that God preserved his people while the pagan nations of the ancient world have passed into history. God restrains the nations and protects his own people. Why? Because he loves them with a *hesed* love that is faithful to them even "in the land of the living" (Ps. 27:13). God is true to his character today as he was in ancient Israel. Reading the Psalms of ancient Israel for what they tell us about Yahweh will help us when we need God's protection and deliverance in our lives today.

Chapter 10

By the Rivers of Babylon: Imprecatory Psalms

Pour out your wrath on them;
　　let your fierce anger overtake them.
May their place be deserted;
　　let there be no one to dwell in their tents.
　　　　　　　　　　　　　—Psalm 69:24–25

The Problem of the Imprecatory Psalms

OF ALL THE EXPRESSIONS OF HUMAN emotion in the Psalms, the curses are the most difficult for many Christians to understand and accept. We find it easy to praise God for the wonders of creation, for they attest to the matchless glory of the Creator. Add to God's creation of all things his *hesed* love for his people, and we should be moved to celebrate God's grace. Knowing that Jesus Christ is the King of Kings who will return one day to reign in righteousness forever encourages Christians to persevere, for their faithful service is not in vain. The Messianic Psalms show us the love of God in sending his Son, Jesus Christ, and remind us that God is sovereign, for he fulfilled his promises in his Son. When difficult times come and we are slandered or even attacked, we learn to turn to God for protection and assurance that nothing can happen to us that he does not allow. We acknowledge all of these blessings and more in the Psalms, but how do we relate to the Psalms that call on God to curse other people with suffering and even eternal judgment? What can we make of the Imprecatory Psalms?

An imprecation is "an invocation of judgment, calamity, or curse uttered against one's enemies, or the enemies of God."[1] In the Imprecatory Psalms, the psalmists curse their enemies, sometimes wishing evil on them in this life (e.g., Pss. 35; 58; 59; 69; 83; 109; 139) and even in the life to come (e.g., Pss. 69; 109). Because of God's covenant with his people, the enemies of the psalmist are also the enemies of Yahweh—hence the prayers to Yahweh to participate in their judgment. When we read these psalms, however, we find it difficult to reconcile the psalmists' attitude, which at first glance appears so vindictive, with our understanding of the Christian life. Why are the Imprecatory Psalms in the Bible? How are we to handle them? Because these psalms are among the most problematic for modern Christians, we will consider the dilemma they pose before we analyze an Imprecatory Psalm later in the chapter.

The New Testament requires us to love our enemies; how can we relate to the psalms that tell us to curse our enemies?

The first place most Christians will turn for instruction on how to live a life that pleases the Lord is the New Testament. What does it say regarding the imprecations in the Psalms? The New Testament provides clear ethical teaching about how Christians should treat others. Jesus himself teaches that the summary of the commandments is to love God and our neighbors as ourselves (Mark 12:29–31). There is not much room for cursing in these two commands. The commands become even more specific when Jesus teaches his disciples about cursing and revenge:

---

1. J. Carl Laney, "A Fresh Look at the Imprecatory Psalms," *Bibliotheca Sacra* 138, no. 549 (January–March 1981): 35.

> But I tell you who hear me: Love your enemies, do good to those who hate you, bless those who curse you, pray for those who mistreat you.
>
> —Luke 6:27–28

Jesus' teaching is quite clear: if we are his disciples, we are to love our enemies and bless those who curse us. We are not to curse our enemies. How do we reconcile this clear teaching with the curses in the Psalms?

It is not just New Testament teachings on love that cause a problem for the modern Christian, for the Old Testament enjoins believers to love their enemies as well. The covenant laws God gives the people of Israel at Mount Sinai, which include the Ten Commandments, require merciful treatment for enemies. For instance:

> If you come across your enemy's ox or donkey wandering off, be sure to take it back to him. If you see the donkey of someone who hates you fallen down under its load, do not leave it there; be sure you help him with it.
>
> —Exodus 23:4–5

Even the Old Testament instructs us not to hate our enemies. Why do the psalmists sometimes curse their enemies?

Here among the laws relating to justice in interpersonal relations, God tells his people to treat their enemies with kindness and mercy. Again in the Proverbs, the writer enjoins God's people to help their enemies:

> If your enemy is hungry, give him food to eat;
>   if he is thirsty, give him water to drink.
>
> —Proverbs 25:21

These are not the only Old Testament commands to treat an enemy kindly, but they serve to make the point that God has expected such merciful behavior toward enemies from earliest times. The psalmists, even those who wrote the imprecations, were well aware of the injunctions in the covenant laws to treat an enemy in a kind way, yet they nevertheless curse their enemies.

The problem seems to be more acute when we discover that the New Testament insists that the whole Bible is inspired, including the Psalms. When the Sanhedrin release Peter and John and command them not to speak again in Jesus' name, the disciples immediately give thanks to the Lord in prayer. The prayer is instructive, for in it the disciples acknowledge God's sovereign acts of creation and go on to affirm their belief in the divine inspiration of Scripture, citing Psalm 2:1–2 as an example (Acts 4:24–26). Here are two of the grand themes of the Bible as a whole: God created everything that exists, and he inspired the Scriptures. God has given himself a witness every time we look at the created world and whenever we open the pages of the Bible. Would it surprise us to learn that the disciples turn to the Old Testament, specifically the Psalms, when they consider Judas's betrayal of Christ and the vacancy he left among the apostles by his betrayal (Acts 1:20)? There is no way around it: the New Testament teaches the inspiration of the Psalms and even refers to the Psalms in its denunciation of Judas. The problem of the curses in the Psalms is more serious for Christians who believe in the inspiration and inerrancy of Scripture than it is for those who do not have a high view of the Bible.

C. S. Lewis explains the dilemma for modern-day Christians when he remarks that we must face two facts squarely when we wrestle with the problem of the Imprecatory Psalms. First, the hatred is there in the Psalms; there is no way around it. Second, we would sin if we ourselves condone such hatred or use it ourselves.[2] How then are we to respond to the curses in the Psalms?

---

2. C. S. Lewis, *Reflections on the Psalms* (New York: Harcourt, Brace, Jovanovich, 1958), 22.

Purposes of the Imprecatory Psalms

If we acknowledge that God inspired the imprecatory sections of the Psalms and realize that their inspiration requires us to come to terms with them, then we can begin to understand their place in Scripture. Though we cannot provide a full treatment in this chapter of the theology related to the Imprecatory Psalms, we can begin to recognize their use and identify four points that will help us see what the Holy Spirit is doing with the curses in the Psalms.

The first purpose for the imprecations in the Psalms is that they remind us that some things are indeed evil, and we are to hate such evil. C. S. Lewis makes this point in *Reflections on the Psalms*, stating, "the ferocious parts of the Psalms serve as a reminder that there is in the world such a thing as wickedness and that it (if not its perpetrators) is hateful to God."[3] God hates sin, and Christians ought to do the same. Patrick Henry Reardon takes the point even further:

> To relinquish any one of the Psalms on the excuse that its sentiments are too violent for a Christian is a clear sign that a person has also given up the very battle that a Christian is summoned from his bed to fight. The psalms are prayers for those who are engaged in an ongoing spiritual conflict.[4]

While Reardon's comment may strike some Christians as strongly worded, it nonetheless does address an issue modern Christians, especially in the Western nations, have not always had the courage to face: when we sweep sin under the rug, we compromise the testimony of Christ to unbelievers. If an unbeliever looks at Christianity and sees that Christians take sin lightly, what reason would he have to be converted? The Old Testament writers of the Psalms abhorred evil because they understood the holiness of God; David, for one, hated

---

3. Ibid., 33.
4. Patrick Henry Reardon, *Christ in the Psalms* (Ben Lomond, Calif.: Conciliar, 2000), 6.

his sins of adultery and murder and confessed them to the Lord (Ps. 51:3, 9).[5] We too need to appreciate the holiness of God if we are to understand the outrage the psalmists express in the face of their enemies. At the same time we hate sin, however, we cannot become hateful ourselves. VanGemeren reminds us:

> But indiscriminate hatred is wrong. The psalmists wrote under the inspiration of God regarding the nature of evil. They . . . were concerned with the manifestation of God's righteousness and holiness on earth.[6]

We must learn how to hate sin without sinning. If we tolerate sin, we will lose our testimony before nonbelievers, for they will see little difference between themselves and Christians. While we are to hate sin, however, we are to love our neighbors. We should pray for the vindication of God's testimony and not be vindictive ourselves. The Imprecatory Psalms remind us of the difficult balance we must maintain.

A second purpose for the imprecations in the Psalms is that they can help us identify sin in our own lives and confess it. When we read the curses in the Psalms, we might recognize a hateful attitude on our own part; if we do, we should confess such hatred as sin. C. S. Lewis describes this use of the imprecations in his chapter "The Cursings" in *Reflections on the Psalms* and suggests this purgative use of the imprecations as one of their applications for the modern Christian. Seeing the sinful hatred in these psalms, Lewis writes, will help us see "the same thing in [our] own heart[s]"[7] and lead us to root it out. Not everything written in Scripture is there for our approval: consider Lot's treatment of his daughters as an example of sinful behavior that we should condemn (Gen. 19:6–8). So too with the curses that are sinful (and not all are); they can help us face our own hate. Willem

---

5. Laney, "A Fresh Look at the Imprecatory Psalms," 42.

6. Willem VanGemeren, *Psalms,* vol. 5 of *The Expositor's Bible Commentary,* ed. Frank E. Gaebelein (Grand Rapids: Zondervan, 1991), 831.

7. Lewis, *Reflections on the Psalms,* 23.

VanGemeren takes the spiritual implications of this use of the imprecations one step further, writing, "These psalms help us to pray through our anger, frustrations, and spite to a submission to God's will."[8] It is not simply a matter of our deciding to "do better" and not hate anyone. The issue here is obedience to the Lord, and it takes prayer and confession to resolve the problem; we need God's grace to obey him in this regard as we do with all his other commands. The Imprecatory Psalms can help us examine ourselves and purge any hate we may have.

A third purpose for the imprecations is their benefit to unbelievers. Reading the psalmists' curses on God's enemies may well warn the non-Christian to turn from unbelief. The Holy Spirit certainly can use any part of Scripture to convict unbelievers of their sin and their need for the grace of God in Christ (Isa. 55:11). He may bring a great conviction of sin into a person's heart when that person hears or reads one of the Imprecatory Psalms. Carl Laney identifies this evangelistic use of the imprecations in his article, "A Fresh Look at the Imprecatory Psalms." Laney writes that the curses may "cause the wicked to seek the Lord," and he cites Psalm 83:16–18 as a case in point.[9] Like many of the Imprecatory Psalms, Psalm 83 expresses the hope that unbelievers will turn to God when they see his justifiable wrath. These psalms go in two directions, encouraging the Christian to root out hate from his or her life, and drawing the unbeliever toward faith. At least, the psalmists thought so.

A final purpose for the imprecations in the Psalms is that they teach us about the sovereignty of God.[10] Simply stated, the doctrine of God's sovereignty teaches that God rules the universe. While some people, even some Christians, find it difficult to believe that God controls all events and knows the future in its entirety, the Bible teaches a high view of God's sovereignty over all things. The Bible knows nothing of "openness theology," which teaches that God does not know all future

---

8. VanGemeren, *Psalms*, 5:832.

9. Laney, "A Fresh Look at the Imprecatory Psalms," 41.

10. Cf. ibid.

events and hence is not absolutely sovereign. Unbelievers hate the doctrine of God's sovereignty, for it attacks their pride and reminds them that they can never be free of God's claims on their lives. Christians, on the other hand, should rejoice in God's sovereignty, for it includes his *hesed,* saving love, and grace in their lives. Still, when we consider God's sovereignty from our limited human perspective, there are times it is difficult to discern what God is doing, especially when we are tested or attacked.

One reason we sometimes do not understand God's sovereignty is that we necessarily look at events in our lives from only one perspective—our own. The problem with our limited vision is that we do not always see what God is doing in others' lives to bring about his will. God's sovereignty in our lives often involves his leading in other lives in ways we may never know. As a part of his sovereignty, God judges sin. When God condemns, he does so justly; such judgment expresses his righteousness and sovereignty. The Imprecatory Psalms face us with the sobering reality that there are those who hate God and his grace in Jesus Christ. When we think of the price of our sin, the sacrifice of the sinless Son of God on the cross, we cannot impugn God's justice in the Imprecatory Psalms. To find fault with God's sovereignty tempts us to Satan's sin and places us above God. The Imprecatory Psalms are an antidote to such presumption.

> *Like Adam and Eve in the Garden, we challenge God's*
> *sovereignty when we question him about his judgments.*
> *Such are the imprecations in the Psalms.*

Psalm 59
GOD'S PROTECTION OF DAVID
AGAINST HIS ENEMIES

We turn to Psalm 59 as an example of an Imprecatory Psalm, for it shows so many of the themes that characterize these psalms elsewhere in the Psalter. Psalm 59 is one of King David's laments when Saul was attempting to kill him. Saul had sent spies to watch David and plot his death. It is in these circumstances that God inspires David to write a psalm that should comfort us when God's enemies threaten us today.

> [1]Deliver me from my enemies, O God;
>   protect me from those who rise up against me.
> [2]Deliver me from evildoers
>   and save me from bloodthirsty men.
>
> [3]See how they lie in wait for me!
>   Fierce men conspire against me
>   for no offense or sin of mine, O LORD.
> [4]I have done no wrong, yet they are ready to attack me.
>   Arise to help me; look on my plight!
> [5]O LORD God Almighty, the God of Israel,
>   rouse yourself to punish all the nations;
>   show no mercy to wicked traitors. *Selah*
>
> [6]They return at evening,
>   snarling like dogs,
>   and prowl about the city.
> [7]See what they spew from their mouths—
>   they spew out swords from their lips,
>   and they say, "Who can hear us?"
> [8]But you, O LORD, laugh at them;
>   you scoff at all those nations.
>
> [9]O my Strength, I watch for you;
>   you, O God, are my fortress, [10]my loving God.
>
> God will go before me
>   and will let me gloat over those who slander me.
> [11]But do not kill them, O Lord our shield,
>   or my people will forget.

In your might make them wander about,
and bring them down.
[12]For the sins of their mouths,
for the words of their lips,
let them be caught in their pride.
For the curses and lies they utter
[13]consume them in wrath,
consume them till they are no more.
Then it will be known to the ends of the earth
that God rules over Jacob. *Selah*

[14]They return at evening,
snarling like dogs,
and prowl about the city.
[15]They wander about for food
and howl if not satisfied.
[16]But I will sing of your strength,
in the morning I will sing of your love;
for you are my fortress,
my refuge in times of trouble.

[17]O my Strength, I sing praise to you;
you, O God, are my fortress, my loving God.

What Is the Overall Effect of the Psalm?

To appreciate Psalm 59, we must see the subject matter from the perspective that David, inspired by God to write the psalm, saw it.[11] Saul hunted David because he was jealous of the people's love for David. In killing David he thought he would secure his throne. Saul's attack

---

11. Some scholars question Davidic authorship of Psalm 59. See the discussion in the note to Psalm 59 in Kenneth Barker, ed., *The niv Study Bible* (Grand Rapids: Zondervan, 1995), 838. I accept Davidic authorship and the context of Saul's attacks on David for Psalm 59.

on David, however, was also an attack on God, for God's purpose was to put David on the throne and bless his family (1 Sam. 15–16), and the psalmist knows this when he writes. Those who oppose the psalmist in effect oppose God himself. When David asks the Lord in Psalm 59 to defend him against his enemies and destroy them, he does not do so out of personal vindictiveness against Saul or anyone else. In fact, David tried to honor Saul as king (1 Sam. 16–18) and did not kill him even when he had the opportunity to do so (1 Sam. 24; 26). David's prayer for protection and the judgment of God on his enemies represents the covenant king's prayer on behalf of his people for God to protect them and honor his word by fulfilling his promises. Seen in this light, the curses of Psalm 59 take on national significance for the people of Israel and covenant importance for all of God's promises to David. Even more significant is the fact that those who would attack God's people attack God himself. God's testimony is at stake in the Imprecatory Psalms.

What Is the Structure of the Psalm?

Psalm 59 is a personal Lament Psalm with national overtones. It is difficult to classify its genre any more precisely than this,[12] but it is clear that David's Lament stems from personal vulnerability that simultaneously includes the whole nation's security. If David were to be killed, the people would be defenseless before the Philistines. What is more, God's covenant with David (2 Sam. 7:8–16) could be compromised if David were to die at this time. As with many other Laments, Psalm 59 does not follow a prescribed structure, but it does include the elements characteristic of a Lament. Psalm 59 is structured in a bifid (two-part) pattern that turns on a hinge verse as follows:

I. Verses 1–7:   Part One: The Problem
II. Verse 8:   Hinge: God's Reaction
III. Verses 9–17:   Part Two: The Solution

---

12. VanGemeren, *Psalms*, 5:409.

We can subdivide the two parts of Psalm 59 more precisely in the following manner:

A. Verses 1–2:   First Petition to Yahweh for Protection
B. Verses 3–5:   Reasons for the Imprecation
C. Verses 6–7:   First Lament: The Malice of David's Enemies
D. Verse 8:   God's Reaction
E. Verses 9–10:   Assurance of Yahweh's Protection
F. Verses 11–13:   Petition to Yahweh Along with Reasons for
                   the Imprecation
G. Verses 14–15:   Second Lament: The Malice of David's Enemies
H. Verses 16–17:   Final Statement of Confidence in Yahweh

From this structure we see Saul's attack on David and David's petitions for help against the backdrop of God's covenant with his people, Israel. Psalm 59 maintains the twin emphases we see so often in the Psalms: human problems seen against the background of God's sovereignty and covenant love for his people. The structure of the psalm reflects these two emphases—David's problems and God's answers.

What Are the Figures of Speech in the Psalm, and What Effects Do They Have?

David opens the psalm by asking Yahweh to protect and deliver him from those who threaten him. He begins in a personal way by asking for help against his "enemies" and "those who rise up against [him]" (v. 1). In the second verse, however, David calls his enemies "evildoers" and "bloodthirsty men," implying that they are more than just his enemies; they are inherently evil men. From the beginning of the psalm, David makes it clear that he is not asking for personal revenge. These people are evil men whose attacks are vicious and unjustified.

When he names the reasons for his imprecation (vv. 3–5), David explicitly protests his innocence. A hint of animal imagery appears in these verses in the picture of David's enemies preparing an ambush as a big cat would quietly wait to attack its prey (v. 3). The enemies are "fierce," suggesting their subhuman, animalistic hatred of David. The combination of the animal imagery with the fact that these men "conspire against [David]" (v. 3) shows their deep ill will toward David, for only humans plot maliciously to hurt another. David's enemies represent the worst of humanity combined with animal ferocity and cunning. Against these enemies, David calls on God as his covenant King ("LORD") and the omnipotent Ruler of the nations ("God Almighty"), uniting the absolute power of God with his *hesed* love for his people—an unbeatable combination.

David continues the animal imagery in his first Lament (vv. 6–7), though he depicts his enemies in this section as vile "dogs," reducing them to the contempt their malice deserves. David's enemies are like dogs who come out under cover of night ("They return at evening") to scavenge for food in the city (v. 6). They are underhanded and vicious, for their words are like "swords" (v. 7). Often in the Old Testament, dogs are symbols of contempt, as is the case in King Ahab's death, when the dogs licked his blood, "as the word of the LORD had declared" (1 Kings 22:38). Rejected as king by God, Ahab dies an ignominious death, and the picture of the dogs licking his blood serves to underscore God's repudiation of him. In Psalm 59, the dogs have the temerity to be arrogant, thinking no one can call them to account for their evil behavior; "Who can hear us?" they ask in their pride (v. 7). The irony is, however, that God not only hears their boasts, he laughs them to scorn (v. 8). The close juxtaposition of the enemies' boastful mockery in verse 7 with God's derisive laugh at the futility of their hatred for him and his people in verse 8 underscores God's sovereign power over them and David's security in God's love. The contrast between the psalmist's enemies as animals and God as the sovereign Ruler of the universe could not be sharper. David always sees his enemies' threats in the context of God's sovereignty, and his praise for God is not far beneath the surface even of the lament sections of the psalm.

After his lament, David declares his confidence in Yahweh's protection (vv. 9–10). In the imagery of God as a "fortress" (v. 9), David expresses the protection God provides for him. He has just described the enemies as dogs, spewing malicious words against him from their mouths (vv. 6–7), and now he presents himself as protected inside a fortress. What dog can threaten him there? The absurdity of the image emphasizes God's omnipotence and the enemies' powerlessness. It is in this context that we are to understand the speaker's "gloat[ing]" over his enemies (v. 10), for he has not protected himself; it is God who has frustrated the plans of the enemies and put David in such a strong position of defense. He boasts in God, not himself.

The psalmist's desire to see his enemies routed and cursed receives full expression in the next section, the petition to Yahweh to curse the enemies (vv. 11–13). David asks Yahweh to judge his enemies but not to annihilate them immediately. Rather, David wishes Yahweh to draw out his judgment and thereby prolong his enemies' suffering. "Do not kill them," David asks, "make them wander about, and bring them down" (v. 11). On a first reading, this request sounds vengeful and vindictive. Such a reading, however, takes this petition out of context and even misreads it. David asks this judgment of God for three reasons, none of which betray a vengeful spirit on his part. David's full request is that his enemies might suffer over an extended period of time so that God's people will not forget his righteous judgment of the nations and gracious mercy to them (v. 11).

The Imprecatory Psalms look in two directions simultaneously—
the radical sinfulness of sin and the absolute holiness of God.

The first reason for David's wish is the testimony of Yahweh among his people. The second reason for David's curse is that his enemies have indeed sinned in their attack on him (v. 12), and sin should not go unpunished. This reason for the curse makes sense only if David is not pleading revenge in it but asking that God's righteousness not be impugned by such sin going unpunished. This is an example of the psalmist's zeal for God's holiness to be recognized in this world. The third reason for David's curse is the testimony of Yahweh throughout the world (v. 13). If God punishes the enemies' sin and rescues his people from their traps, the nations will recognize that Yahweh is the one true God, worthy of praise. These verses (vv. 11–13) are the clearest imprecation in Psalm 59, but they do not show David to have a vengeful spirit. Rather, they show God's righteousness in the face of sin, his *ḥesed* love for his own people, and his concern for the lost. We might go so far here as to say that God's judgment is missionary minded.

In the second Lament of the psalm (vv. 14–15), the psalmist returns to an image he had used earlier to describe his enemies as dogs prowling about the city under cover of darkness. The repetition of this image at this point in the psalm, however, is ironic. The initial reference to the enemies as dogs follows David's first petition to God for help when he was vulnerable. The second reference to this image falls between David's invocation of God's testimony (vv. 11–13) and his final statement of confidence in God (vv. 16–17). Appearing in this context, the doglike enemies are not a serious threat. They may "wander about for food" (v. 15), but they do not pose a serious threat to David.

In the final section of the psalm, David provides a glorious statement of his confidence in God to defend him against all enemies (vv. 16–17). Here, David brings together all of the images of God used throughout the psalm in a final declaration of God's sovereignty. David describes God as his "strength," his "fortress," and his "refuge" (v. 16), all terms that express God's protection of the king and remind us of their use earlier in the psalm (v. 9), when David first declares his confidence in Yahweh's protection. Here too the psalmist calls on God's *ḥesed* love (v. 16), once again invoking God's covenant promises to King David and his people. As a final reminder of God's grace and protection to the people, David calls God his "strength" and "fortress" and concludes the Psalms with the words, "loving God" (v. 17). While the dogs prowl about the city at night (vv. 6, 14), David sings of God's love "in the morning" (v. 16). In Psalm 59, the night passes, but the day remains as the final expression of God's *ḥesed* love in the psalm.

What Are the Themes and Theology in the Psalm?

Psalm 59 is a typical Imprecatory Psalm. It invokes God's judgment of Israel's enemies, pronounces curses on them (esp. vv. 11–13), and ends in the confidence that God will protect his people. Like most Imprecatory Psalms, this one goes in two directions at the same time, for God's blessing on his people necessarily involves his defeat of their enemies. In situations like David's in Psalm 59, enemies must suffer for God's people to be protected. This is the conundrum that creates the problem for us today. Like the other Imprecatory Psalms, however, Psalm 59 provides the answer to our dilemma, for it shows us the sinfulness of sin and the holiness of God in close juxtaposition with each other. Psalm 59 reminds us that there is an evil that must be rectified, and only God is justified in judging it.

David's imprecations in Psalm 59 do not represent a vengeful attitude on his part. Under the inspiration of the Holy Spirit, David is careful to place his request for his enemies to be cursed in a context that reflects God's glory, not his own. From the beginning of the psalm, David realizes that a desire for revenge on his part would make him as guilty of sin as his enemies (v. 4), and it is clear in the psalm that David's enemies are conducting an evil attack for sinful reasons (v. 2). Psalm 59 reminds us that there is evil in the world, but God will not tolerate sin in the end. We must be careful, however, that we do not presume to avenge ourselves against our enemies as if we were God. "It is mine to avenge," God declares, "I will repay" (Deut. 32:35).

Behind God's judgment of the sin of David's enemies lie two of the most important truths of Psalm 59: God's righteousness and his covenant love. God's judgments are just, for he is holy. Because God does not judge indiscriminately or with partiality, we know that his judgment of sin reflects his holiness. Were he not holy, his judgments would be suspect, as ours sometimes are. God's righteousness guarantees his justice. God's judgment of his people's enemies in Psalm 59 also presumes his covenant love for King David and the people. In this psalm, David speaks as the representative of the people, not just as an individual seeking redress for an injury. Throughout the psalm, David is careful to place his petitions in the context of God's covenant love for his people and reminds God that it is his testimony that is at stake if the Israelites were to be annihilated (vv. 9–13, 16–17). The imprecations in Psalm 59 say something about the holiness and love of God, not David's personal attitudes.

In particular, David provides three reasons why God should be concerned about his situation. First, God's judgment of sinful enemies will remind his people of his holiness and *hesed* love (v. 11). Second, David is zealous for God's holy name and recognizes sin and pride for what they are, asking for justice in dealing with them (v. 12). Third, David wishes God to vindicate himself in judging his enemies so that others will bow their knees to Yahweh (v. 13). Ironically, God's mercy is demonstrated in his justice, not despite it; if God were not to judge sin, sinners would continue in their rebellion and never come to know the salvation God offers by grace in Jesus Christ. Though it may be hard for us in our limited perspective to recognize it, God's holiness confronts man's sinfulness and invites him to accept God's mercy.

Applications

1. When we are attacked or slandered, we are to let God vindicate us. We should not react angrily and be guilty of sin ourselves.
2. At the same time, we should hold a high standard of God's holiness and deal with sin when we see it. It may be that our loving confrontation of sin in a brother's or sister's life would bring about confession and restoration (Gal. 6:1).
3. When believers do not tolerate sin, unbelievers may be confronted with their need of God's grace and be converted.

Encountering God in the Imprecatory Psalms

Many Christians find the imprecations in the Psalms difficult to reconcile with their faith in Jesus Christ. Some are deeply troubled by what they perceive to be an inconsistency in Scripture between the admonition to love our neighbors and the curses in the Psalms and elsewhere in the Bible. When unbelievers read the Imprecatory Psalms, and they may do so in a world literature class at college, they may be quick to condemn Christianity and its Old Testament roots as a barbaric, vindictive religion. Indeed, I have heard an unbeliever call God a "bloody butcher" just days before she died. We must admit that these psalms raise difficulties.

The difficulties granted, however, we must recognize that the Holy Spirit inspired these psalms initially and preserved them throughout the ages for our edification and God's glory. They glorify God and edify us by demonstrating God's holiness, grace, and sovereignty in the affairs of men. They remind us of God's holiness because he will judge sin. They assure us of God's grace because he offers mercy to those who repent. They demonstrate his sovereignty because he alone has the power to judge and forgive. The Imprecatory Psalms are much like the book of Job, for they bring us face-to-face with the reality that we are not God (e.g., Job 38–42). With Job, we need to be reminded at times that Yahweh alone is God; when we remember who we are, we will be grateful for God's grace and glorify him for his unfailing love.

"Do I take any pleasure in the death of the wicked?" declares the Sovereign LORD. "Rather, am I not pleased when they turn from their ways and live?" (Ezek. 18:23)

Chapter 11

Against You Only: God Forgives the Penitent

O LORD, hear my prayer,
    listen to my cry for mercy;
in your faithfulness and righteousness
    come to my relief.
Do not bring your servant into judgment,
    for no one living is righteous before you.
                    —Psalm 143:1–2

The Penitential Psalms

JOHN CALVIN CALLED THE PSALMS AN "anatomy of the soul."[1] For Calvin, as for most believers throughout the ages, the Psalms give expression to every major aspect of the human experience. Of course, the great literature of the ages also reports the experiences of the human condition, so why should we be more concerned with the voices of the Psalms than with other expressions of our humanity? The most obvious response to such a question is that God inspired the Psalms, and they

---

1. John Calvin, *Commentary on the Book of Psalms,* trans. James Anderson (Grand Rapids: Baker, 1998), 1:xxxvii.

are therefore inerrant in all they say about our human condition. Because they are inspired, the Psalms give us God's words, not just our own, to express our human experiences. They help us tune our lives to God's will. We certainly need God's words and will when we sin. The Penitential Psalms help us confess our sin to Yahweh and ask him for forgiveness. We should be ready to turn to these psalms when we sin.

Early Christian tradition named the seven psalms that focus primarily on the problem of sin and the guilt it brings the Penitential Psalms—Psalms 6; 32; 38; 51; 102; 130; and 143. In each of these psalms, the writer acknowledges his sin to Yahweh and asks for forgiveness. Hence the term *Penitential:* these psalms voice the repentant attitude of the speakers and demonstrate God's loving forgiveness when sin is confessed. In identifying these seven psalms, early Christian writers recognized the use of Scripture in helping us repent and ask for forgiveness. Today in the early twenty-first century, we still can find solace in the inspired words of these Penitential Psalms to help us confess our guilt and ask for pardon.

When the words are hard to find, how do we confess sin to God?

As believers in Jesus Christ today, we have the New Testament teachings about sin and forgiveness to guide us in dealing with our sin. The apostle John instructs believers in the proper way to deal with their sin in his simple admonition, "If we confess our sins, he is faithful and just and will forgive us our sins and purify us from all unrighteousness" (1 John 1:9). All that is required of Christians is repentance, or a godly sorrow, for sin, confession, and a turning to God to ask for forgiveness. God will never reject the penitent (John 6:37). It seems so simple. Why do we need the Psalms to remind us of our sin in such painful detail when we already know what we have to do?

There are at least three reasons for the Penitential Psalms. This first relates to our experience of guilt and forgiveness. Knowing what to do when we sin and doing it are often two different matters. Foolish and unwise though it is, we sometimes find it difficult to confess our sins to God. It is easy to say to someone whom we have wronged, "I am sorry," but it is much more difficult to say to God, "I have sinned against you and ask for your forgiveness." C. S. Lewis has the right understanding of repentance when he writes in *Letters to an American Lady*, "forgiveness by its nature is for the unworthy."[2] We cannot repent until we acknowledge that we do not deserve forgiveness. We know we need to confess our sins to God, but sometimes we feel so overwhelmed by them that we do not know how to express our repentance adequately to a holy God. This is the first reason for the Penitential Psalms: using God's words, they walk us through the experience of guilt, confession, and forgiveness, thereby helping us to participate experientially in the process of forgiveness.

The other reasons why we need the Penitential Psalms relate directly to God's perspective on sin. The Penitential Psalms show us how necessary God's righteousness and his unfailing love (*hesed*) are for cleansing human sin. God's righteousness is necessary for forgiveness because, if he were not entirely holy, his judgments could be arbitrary and even unjust. *Hesed* love is essential for forgiveness because, if God did not initiate mercy, we would not seek to be forgiven. There is nothing in us that would naturally repent of sin; it is only by God's grace in us that we wish to confess our sins. God's righteousness and mercy form the context of confession.

Closely related to God's righteousness and mercy, and the third reason for the Penitential Psalms, is the way God sees sin. We might ask the question this way: "How sinful is sin?" The answer is that sin is infinitely sinful. The reason for such an answer is that the price of sin is inestimable—the sacrifice of the Son of God, Jesus Christ, at Calvary. Salvation, which is free to all who by God's grace believe in Jesus Christ, cost God the Father the highest price that could be paid—the death of his Son. How does God look at sin? Through Calvary—mercy for all who by faith accept Christ's sacrifice and judgment for all who reject it. What is the cost of sin? More than we can pay. The Penitential

---

2. C. S. Lewis, *Letters to an American Lady* (Grand Rapids: Eerdmans, 1967), 82.

Psalms put sin in divine perspective, giving us a glimpse of how God sees sin. Sin is not just a surface blemish; it marks the whole person and must be dealt with accordingly.

Psalm 51
DAVID'S PENITENTIAL PRAYER

The best-known Penitential Psalm is Psalm 51, David's profound confession following his adultery with Bathsheba and the murder of her husband, Uriah the Hittite. There is no doubt in this psalm of David's godly sorrow for his sin. As C. S. Lewis reminds us, "a man who admits no guilt can accept no forgiveness."[3] If God can forgive a man for two such heinous crimes (adultery and murder), he can forgive us for our sins.

> [1]Have mercy on me, O God,
>   according to your unfailing love;
> according to your great compassion
>   blot out my transgressions.
> [2]Wash away all my iniquity
>   and cleanse me from my sin.
>
> [3]For I know my transgressions,
>   and my sin is always before me.
> [4]Against you, you only, have I sinned
>   and done what is evil in your sight,
> so that you are proved right when you speak
>   and justified when you judge.
> [5]Surely I was sinful at birth,
>   sinful from the time my mother conceived me.
> [6]Surely you desire truth in the inner parts;
>   you teach me wisdom in the inmost place.

---

3. C. S. Lewis, *The Problem of Pain* (New York: Macmillan, 1967), 110.

[7]Cleanse me with hyssop, and I will be clean;
   wash me, and I will be whiter than snow.
[8]Let me hear joy and gladness;
   let the bones you have crushed rejoice.
[9]Hide your face from my sins
   and blot out all my iniquity.

[10]Create in me a pure heart, O God,
   and renew a steadfast spirit within me.
[11]Do not cast me from your presence
   or take your Holy Spirit from me.
[12]Restore to me the joy of your salvation
   and grant me a willing spirit, to sustain me.

[13]Then I will teach transgressors your ways,
   and sinners will turn back to you.
[14]Save me from bloodguilt, O God,
   the God who saves me,
   and my tongue will sing of your righteousness.
[15]O Lord, open my lips,
   and my mouth will declare your praise.
[16]You do not delight in sacrifice, or I would bring it;
   you do not take pleasure in burnt offerings.
[17]The sacrifices of God are a broken spirit;
   a broken and contrite heart,
   O God, you will not despise.

[18]In your good pleasure make Zion prosper;
   build up the walls of Jerusalem.
[19]Then there will be righteous sacrifices,
   whole burnt offerings to delight you;
   then bulls will be offered on your altar.

What Is the Overall Effect of the Psalm?

Psalm 51 affects the reader in two ways at the same time. The first impact of Psalm 51 on the reader is the intensity of David's godly sorrow for his sin. No less than nine times in the psalm, David asks for forgiveness. In every section of the psalm, in one way or another, David asks for God's mercy (v. 1), or to be cleansed (vv. 2, 7) and washed (vv. 2, 7). He is always conscious of his sin (v. 3) and is racked with guilt for his transgressions and iniquity. It may have taken Nathan the prophet to confront David with his sin, but when he did, the Holy Spirit brought deep conviction on David, and he repented immediately (2 Sam. 12:1–14). Psalm 51 provides ample testimony to the true repentance David felt for his sins of adultery and murder.

The second effect of Psalm 51 is its expression of the absolute righteousness and mercy of Yahweh. While acknowledging his sin throughout the psalm, David does not dwell on his sin in an unhealthy, morbid introspection. Rather, at the same time that he recognizes his sin, he glorifies God in what he says about him. In fact, the reason David sees his sin to be so offensive is because, by God's grace, he sees God for who he is. Psalm 51 is as much a Hymn of Praise to God as it is a Lament for David's sin. In the psalm, David reminds us of God's compassion and mercy (vv. 1, 11–12, 13), righteousness (vv. 3–4, 14), *ḥesed* love (vv. 1, 18–19), and immanence (vv. 11–12). The psalm strikes a balance between David's repentance and God's glory, showing us in its overall effect how important it is in every aspect of our lives for us to know God as he reveals himself in the Bible. When he asks for forgiveness, David does not brag to God about the good things he has done, hoping to win God's favor that way. Rather, he reminds God of his righteousness and mercy and throws himself at God's feet.

Psalm 51 is shot through with the righteousness and compassion of God; in turn, God's righteousness and compassion provide the background to David's sin and assure the reader of forgiveness.

What Is the Structure of the Psalm?

Psalm 51, along with the other Penitential Psalms, is a type of Lament Psalm. As such, it identifies a problem (in this case, the speaker's sin) and calls on God to solve the problem (in this case, forgiveness and cleansing). Lament Psalms typically include sections of praise along with petitions for help. Psalm 51 follows the typical Lament Psalm structure, though it does not include a request that Yahweh judge the psalmist's enemies. In his circumstances, King David has no right to curse anyone; indeed he needs God's great mercy to restore him to fellowship with the Lord. Here is the structure of Psalm 51.

    I. Verses 1–2:   David's Introductory Petition to Yahweh
    II. Verses 3–6:   David's Statement of His Sinfulness
    III. Verses 7–9:   David's Prayer for Forgiveness
    IV. Verses 10–13: David's Prayer for Cleansing
    V. Verses 14–17: David's Vow to Praise Yahweh
    VI. Verses 18–19: David's Concluding Confidence in Yahweh

The structure of Psalm 51 reflects the dual effects of the psalm we noted earlier. David begins and ends the psalm emphasizing Yahweh's holiness and mercy (vv. 1–2, 14–17). Beginning the psalm this way focuses our attention on God before we see David's sorrow for his sin. Ending the psalm by returning to God means that the final reminder in the psalm is that God is faithful to his people, even when they sin. In the middle section of the psalm, David confesses his sin and asks for forgiveness and cleansing (cf. 1 John 1:9). This middle section is carefully patterned in that it begins with an admission of sin (vv. 3–6), proceeds to a prayer for forgiveness (vv. 7–9), and concludes with a request to be cleansed and made fit for further service (vv. 10–13). The frame structure of Psalm 51—God/David/God—reinforces the important point that David is entirely dependent on God for forgiveness and restoration. This structure further underscores the twin emphases of the psalm by keeping God before our eyes, even when David laments his sin and asks for mercy.

What Are the Figures of Speech in the Psalm, and What Effects Do They Have?

In his introductory petition to God in the first two verses, David casts himself entirely on God. The first verse forms a chiasmus that begins and ends in two pleas for forgiveness. David cries, "Have mercy on me, O God" and "blot out my transgressions." By "transgressions" in the plural, it is likely that David means his particular sins of adultery and murder. Between the two petitions, David invokes God's "unfailing love" (or *ḥesed*) and his "great compassion." Here is the psalm in miniature: David asks for forgiveness and calls on the unfailing love of God, not his own righteousness, as the basis on which he hopes for an answer. David knows, as we do when we sin, that he deserves justice, but he asks for mercy. In *Letters to an American Lady*, C. S. Lewis remarks, "I'd sooner pray for God's mercy than for His justice on my friends, my enemies, and myself."[4] This is the spirit of David's opening, though it is far more intense than C. S. Lewis's comment.

In the second verse, David again uses repetition to emphasize his repentance and sorrow. "Wash" is followed by "cleanse," and "iniquity" is paralleled by "sin." The reader cannot miss David's abject dependence on God alone for forgiveness. It may be that the sin referred to in this verse represents his sin nature. If this is so, David admits in verse 1 that he has committed sins (plural) and in verse 2 that he is sinful by nature. He has no ground of his own on which to turn to God; he must rely entirely on God's mercy. In this confession, David uses the familiar Old Testament imagery of washing to indicate forgiveness, as he will later in the psalm (cf. v. 7). Willem VanGemeren reminds us, "The OT sacrifices and ritual washing symbolized the removal of sin and the renewal of fellowship with the Lord. The sacrifices by themselves could not affect so great a salvation (v. 16), but God is free to give his grace to whomever he wants. The prayer is for forgiveness and cleansing."[5] By repeating his request to be washed and cleansed, David assures God of his repentance.

---

4. Lewis, *Letters to an American Lady*, 14.
5. Willem VanGemeren, *Psalms*, vol. 5 of *The Expositor's Bible Commentary*, ed. Frank E. Gaebelein (Grand Rapids: Zondervan, 1991), 379.

The second section of the psalm, David's statement of his sinfulness, goes a long way toward showing us how God sees sin. In these four verses David's sin and God's righteousness are alternated. David admits his sin in verse 3; he testifies to God's righteousness in verse 4; he returns to his sin in verse 5; and finally he repeats God's righteousness in verse 6. This alternating pattern keeps human sin and divine righteousness before our eyes as we read, highlighting again the twin emphases of the psalm.

David further underscores his sin by the parallelism of verse 3, which moves from his acknowledgment of his sin ("For I know my transgressions") to the statement that he can never forget it ("and my sin is always before me"). The second statement heightens the first, accentuating how profoundly David feels the guilt of his sin. In the same way, verse 4 shows how keenly David feels God's righteousness. David acknowledges that God is "proved right" (in general) when he speaks; he then confesses that God is "justified" (in particular) when he judges sin.

Verses 5 and 6 bring the sinner's dilemma into even sharper relief. The two verses are paralleled in an antithetic manner, verse 5 speaking of human sin and verse 6 of God's righteousness and truthfulness. David accentuates the contrast even further by beginning both verses with "Surely." These verses could not make the predicament any clearer: man is sinful by nature (v. 5), and God is righteous (v. 6). What makes the situation even worse for the sinner is that God "desire[s] truth in the inner parts," and none of us in ourselves can provide such truthfulness. These verses make it painfully clear that we are desperately sinful before a holy God. Jeremiah explains the dilemma even more clearly:

> The heart is deceitful above all things
> and beyond cure
> Who can understand it?

> "I the LORD search the heart
>   and examine the mind,
> to reward a man according to his conduct,
>   according to what his deeds deserve."
> —Jeremiah 17:9–10

We are hopelessly sinful, but God demands truthfulness and holiness. In ourselves, we have no escape. This is David's predicament in these verses.

Charles Haddon Spurgeon expresses the same dilemma David feels in his comment on this psalm:

> The love of the heart, the mystery of its fall, and the way of its purification—this hidden wisdom we must all attain; and it is a great blessing to be able to believe that the Lord will "make us know it." No one can teach our innermost nature but the Lord.[6]

Spurgeon recognizes our inability to solve the problem by ourselves, and he realizes that God alone knows our hearts. By paralleling his statements and intensifying the experience of his guilt in these middle verses of Psalm 51, David confesses his own sinfulness and acknowledges God's righteousness. This dual admission is the beginning of forgiveness. This is the starting point for David and Spurgeon alike.

The third section of the psalm, David's prayer for forgiveness (vv. 7–9), represents our proper posture when we have sinned. We must ask God for mercy, for he alone can forgive sin. In asking for forgiveness, David makes three specific requests of God, and he makes each request using two different verbs.

Using the verbs *cleanse* and *wash,* David first asks for purification from his sin. Hyssop was used in ritual cleansing in the Old Testament, most notably in the first Passover as Yahweh was about to take the people of Israel out of their slavery in Egypt (Exod. 12:22). The

---

6. Charles Haddon Spurgeon, *The Treasury of David* (Grand Rapids: Baker, 1983), 2:452.

association of hyssop with the Passover suggests God's gracious, unfailing love *(ḥesed)* toward his people, for only he could redeem them from their bondage. It is this love that David invokes with the reference to hyssop. Washing, as we have already noted, "symbolize[s] the removal of sin and the renewal of fellowship with the Lord."[7] The act of washing itself does not bring forgiveness, for it is God's mercy that grants forgiveness and redeems his people from their sins. Still, the symbolism of water for spiritual cleansing runs throughout the Old and New Testaments. Pontius Pilate comes to mind as the most important example in the New Testament of a man who tried in vain to wash his hands of guilt (Matt. 27:24). Shakespeare's Lady Macbeth could not wash her guilt away with water, for in her famous sleepwalking scene she vainly rubbed her hands in an attempt to do so. In fact, Shakespeare shows Lady Macbeth desperately trying to wash the crime from her conscience by washing the blood from her hands (Act 5, Scene 1). Lady Macbeth can find no forgiveness, but David finds God's mercy. In Psalm 51, David emphasizes the depth of his sorrow for his sin by repeating his request for forgiveness twice, first in the petition to be cleansed and then in the request to be washed.

David's second prayer in this section is a wish to be certain that God has indeed forgiven him. He asks that he might "hear joy and gladness" and then that his "bones" might "rejoice" (v. 8). David does not mean either of these expressions literally; he does not wish merely to hear joyful songs, and his bones certainly cannot rejoice. What he is suggesting by these expressions is that he wishes to have assurance from God that he has forgiven his sins and restored him to fellowship. Joy and gladness characterize those who are not burdened by guilt. The image of the bones suggests the depth of David's sorrow for his sin, which in turn calls for a deep-seated conviction that he will be forgiven. In effect, David is asking that he might know God's forgiveness in the deepest parts of his being and be able to rejoice in that knowledge.

The third request in this section of the psalm is that God would

---

7. VanGemeren, *Psalms,* 5:379.

remove the record of David's sin altogether (v. 9). David suggests this idea in two ways. He requests that God might "hide [his] face" from his sins, or that he would turn away from them. The imagery here personifies God in his turning his back on sin and thereby not being able to see it again. David intensifies the prayer by asking God to "blot out all [his] iniquity" (v. 9). David uses the same terminology in verse 1 of the psalm, where it presents the image of God removing a record in a scroll.[8] The repetition at this point in the psalm of the imagery of erasing the scroll underscores how preoccupied David is with his need for forgiveness.

With these three requests in mind, we can see the progression of David's prayer. He first asks for forgiveness ("cleanse" and "wash" me), then for assurance of forgiveness ("let me hear joy and gladness" and "bones . . . rejoice"), and finally for God's removal of the record of David's sin from his scroll ("hide your face" and "blot out all my iniquity"). David's prayer for forgiveness (vv. 7–9) is as thorough and intense as his admission of his guilt (vv. 3–6). The one complements the other.

The fourth section of the psalm is David's second petition. In verses 7–9, he asks for forgiveness; in verses 10–13, he asks for cleansing. This prayer is a petition for purity of heart (cf. v. 10); it parallels 1 John 1:9 in the New Testament. David's prayer for forgiveness corresponds to God's first act of grace in 1 John 1:9 ("[he] will forgive us our sins"), and the prayer for cleansing God's second act on our behalf ("and purify us from all unrighteousness"). As in the earlier prayer for forgiveness, David makes use of three parallel pairs of verbs to ask for cleansing. He asks God to "create in [him] a pure heart" and "renew a steadfast spirit" in him (v. 10), both deeds that only God can accomplish. Next he asks that God might not "cast" him away, nor "take [his] Holy Spirit from [him]"; both are requests for God to remain close to him. Finally, he asks that God might "restore" spiritual joy to him and "grant [him] a willing spirit" so he might continue to serve him. As in the earlier section, David's requests here progress, in this case from

---

8. Kenneth Barker, ed., *The niv Study Bible* (Grand Rapids: Zondervan, 1995), 831.

purity (v. 10), to God's presence (v. 11), and finally to service (v. 12). The parallel verbs emphasize how serious David is about his petitions, and the incremental nature of David's requests suggests his progress toward restoration with God.

Following David's two petitions, he vows to praise God and thank him for his grace (vv. 14–17). It is clear in these verses that David has learned his lessons well. Only God can forgive sin, and when we sin we need to ask him for mercy. In verses 14 and 15, David knows that he can only respond to what God has already done for him. In verse 14, David asks specifically to be cleansed of the murder of Uriah (cf. 2 Sam. 12:9) when he asks to be released from his "bloodguilt." Assured of God's forgiveness of this sin, he can declare God's righteousness. In verse 15, he asks God to give him a witness to others and then acknowledges that he will be able to praise God with his words. The pattern is the same in both verses: God acts graciously toward the penitent, and the penitent is enabled to respond.

After these admissions, David demonstrates a mature spiritual understanding of God's dealing with sinners. External sacrifices do not suffice (v. 16); only heartfelt sorrow for sin pleases God. David understands too that his confession does not compel God's forgiveness; rather, God graciously moves the penitent to godly sorrow and then accepts his confession and forgives. David has cast himself on God's mercy, and the result is glorious indeed.

David finishes the psalm with a concluding statement of his confidence in God (vv. 18–19). At first glance, these verses appear to take a new turn, for nowhere else in the psalm does David mention Zion or the people of Israel in general. Up to this point, the psalm has expressed David's personal guilt and prayer for forgiveness; it seems strange, then, that he should conclude the psalm with a reference to Israel at large. Upon further reflection, however, it is clear that these verses not only fit the psalm, they conclude it properly. The closing verses remind us that sin is not just a personal matter; it has consequences in other lives. David's sin affected Bathsheba personally, Uriah's family, David's family, the armies of Israel, and the nation of Israel at large. All sins affect others, though David's two sins—adultery and murder—do so particularly. By returning to the community of Israel, as symbolized in Zion, David concludes his psalm with the confidence that God will bless Israel again, now that he has confessed his sin. David is the king of Israel, and the relationship of Yahweh with his covenant people is represented in his relationship with the king. The king's sin stood in the way of Yahweh's blessing his people. David's confession removes the impediment, and Yahweh's blessing flows again to his people. The community of believers benefits from confession of sin. Hence it is appropriate that David ends the psalm with a reference to the larger community and the anticipation of God's blessing on his people.

What Are the Themes and Theology in the Psalm?

The themes of Psalm 51 fall into two broad categories. The first of these is the character of God, the second the sinfulness of man. Taken together in such close proximity as they are in this psalm, they highlight each other in bold relief. Yahweh is seen to be entirely righteous and merciful, man as desperately sinful. It is these two general themes that provide the theology of the psalm.

Like all the Penitential Psalms (and all of Scripture, for that matter), Psalm 51 teaches us about the attributes and actions of Yahweh. To begin, David emphasizes God's righteousness along with his mercy. Burdened with the guilt of his sin and unable to remove his guilt, David bathes his confession in a rich expression of the attributes of God, particularly his righteousness and mercy. In the opening verse David falls at God's feet asking for mercy. As he does so, he calls on God's "unfailing love" (*ḥesed*) and "great compassion" as the only reasons he has to expect mercy; there is nothing in him that would compel or invite God's forgiveness.

Modern Christians are quick to claim God's mercy and compassion, but they are not always as quick to admit his righteousness. How often do we hear someone speak of God's love? By contrast, how often do we hear about his righteousness? We do an injustice to God's self-revelation in Scripture if we separate his love from his righteousness this way; the Scripture presents both of these attributes of God and does not separate them as we sometimes do. David understood that, if we want God's mercy, we must begin with his righteousness. Almost immediately after he calls on God's mercy, he admits that God is "proved right when [he] speak[s] and justified when [he] judge[s]" (v. 4). David is not afraid to confess God's righteousness even when he repents of his sin. In fact, when we sin we need God's righteousness as much as we do his mercy, for God's righteousness guarantees that his mercy is not arbitrary. We can never take God's forgiveness lightly, for the truth is that, every time God forgives a repentant sinner, he does so on the basis of the righteous judgment of sin on Christ.

Closely related to David's understanding that he can bring nothing to the table but repentance is his admission that only God can forgive sin. David acknowledges this truth in the way he asks for mercy at the beginning of the psalm. Nowhere in the opening verses does he claim anything but godly sorrow on his own behalf. In fact, he even admits that he has sinned against God alone (v. 4). If it is God he has wronged with his sin, only God can forgive him. In Jesus' time, the Pharisees knew that only God could forgive sin, and they accuse Jesus of blasphemy when he says to the paralytic, "Take heart, son; your sins are forgiven" (Matt. 9:2). Jesus' statement amounts to a claim to be God. In Psalm 51, David admits that only God can forgive sin, but for a far different reason: David acknowledges that he needs to be forgiven and cleansed, whereas the Pharisees do not confess either their sinfulness or Christ's divinity.

When God forgives sin, he removes it from the record. David's repeated request for God to "blot out" his "transgressions" (v. 1) and his "iniquity" (v. 9) is that God would wipe out the register of the sin. Can we ask for anything more? God moves the sinner to repentance, forgives the sinner when he does repent, and then removes the record of the sin from the scroll. It is all of grace. How unlike us! We sometimes forgive and remember. The truth of the matter is that we cannot forgive someone apart from God's grace in our lives, any more than we can confess our own sin apart from his grace. David understands that forgiveness and cleansing are all of God.

The second general theme of Psalm 51 is man's sinfulness. In Adam we are sinful by nature, and in ourselves we choose to sin willfully. There is nothing in us that would move us to confess our sin. We are radically sinful. Why then does David confess his sin so poignantly in this psalm? The answer lies in the "pure heart" (v. 10) that God gives the repentant sinner. Paul tells us in the New Testament, "For as in Adam all die, so in Christ all will be made alive" (1 Cor. 15:22). Only by regeneration can we desire to repent of our sin. We need the Word of God to show us our sin (Ps. 51:10–12) and the Spirit of God to convict us of our sin (vv. 2–6). How sinful are we? We are so sinful we cannot repent apart from the grace of God.

The second subtheme in Psalm 51 relating to man's sinfulness is that our sin affects others around us. David's sin affected Bathsheba and resulted in the murder of Uriah, her husband. Nothing would ever be the same for her after David saw her on the rooftop that day. A family was destroyed, a man was murdered, and a child died—all for the lust of a man whom no one could refuse because he was the king. More generally, however, Psalm 51 teaches us that all sin affects others. We may think we are sinning by ourselves, but our transgressions ultimately affect those around us. The concluding verses of the psalm underscore the point that David's sin affected the nation of Israel, and his confession results in the return of God's blessings to the people of Israel. While we are not kings, and Christians are not the nation of Israel, the principle holds true today as it did then. When we sin, others around us suffer. They may be family members, coworkers, or church people. Whatever else our sin is, it is selfishness too, for we involve others in our choices.

The third theme about man in Psalm 51 develops directly out of the first two. Because we do not naturally desire to repent, and because our sin affects others, it is important that we confess sin. Psalm 51 teaches us that confessing our sin is important for at least three reasons. First, not to confess our sin gives us a skewed and inaccurate view of God. When we refuse to repent of our sin, we fail to acknowledge God's righteousness and mercy. The Scriptures indicate repeatedly that God alone forgives sin; if we do not confess this truth, we misrepresent God. Not confessing our sin, then, damages our relationship with God. Second, not to confess our sin hardens our hearts toward the lost (vv. 12–13). When we have unconfessed sin in our lives, we lose our desire to evangelize. In fact, in Psalm 51, one of the first results of repentance for David is a renewed desire to see sinners converted. Third, not to confess sin robs us of joy and peace (v. 12). Only the Lord can provide spiritual peace, and he makes us restless when we refuse to repent.

We need Psalm 51 more than we may know. We sin by thought, word, and deed on a daily basis. While we might confess some sins quickly, there are times we would do well to use David's words in Psalm 51 to help us confess our sin and rid ourselves of the guilt that bothers us.

Psalm 51 has a double emphasis. It keeps both God and man before our eyes. In doing so, the psalm shows us how serious sin is and how gracious God is to forgive it. Psalm 51 shows the righteous judgment of God on our sin and the gracious forgiveness of God in moving us to repentance and then wiping the sin from the record. Our first thought when we read Psalm 51 is no doubt David's great confession, but our overwhelming response to the psalm should be the glory and grace of God.

We should come away from Psalm 51 with a high view of God and a proper understanding of our complete dependence on him.

Applications

1. Sometimes when we sin, we find it difficult to confess our sin to God, even though we know we must. God already knows our sin, of course, but he commands us to confess our sin to him. Psalm 51 gives us the words to say to confess our sin, to be forgiven, and to be released from guilt. Meditating on this psalm and the other Penitential Psalms like it will move us to want to ask for forgiveness when we find it difficult to do so in ourselves.

2. To be truly sorrowful for our sin, we need to see it as God sees

it—as a thoroughgoing stain that separates us from God. In turn, when we confess our sin with godly sorrow, we acknowledge God's truthfulness and place ourselves at his mercy. This is what David does in Psalm 51, and he is gloriously forgiven.

3. We must recognize that all sin attacks God as well as other people. This is reason enough for us not to deal lightly with our sin.

4. Not to confess sin implies that God is a liar and will not forgive us. In effect, impenitence compounds the sin; an unrepentant spirit doubles the sin.

5. One result of confession of sin is a healthy wish to see others brought to faith in Christ. Sin hardens the heart not only against God but against the lost. Do you long to see family members, friends, colleagues, and even strangers converted?

Encountering God in the Penitential Psalms

What more practical psalm could there be than one like Psalm 51, which helps us see our sin? Sinners by nature and by choice, we need to come to Christ by faith and accept God's pardon of our sin and gift of eternal life. Once we are justified by grace through faith in Jesus Christ, we need to keep "short sin accounts" with God. Psalm 51 gives us God's words for us to speak back to him when we are truly repentant. David sinned grievously; if God can forgive him when he repented, he will forgive us when we repent.

There are some sins that affect us so deeply that we cannot seem to shake them off. We want to confess them, but they haunt our memory and imagination. Our desire to repent is genuine, but we cannot voice our prayer. When we find ourselves at such an impasse, Psalm 51 walks us through the experience of repentance, confession, and forgiveness. To be certain, we need to know the theology of repentance. To be forgiven, however, we need to be moved to repentance and take the active step of asking for forgiveness. We need the experience of confession and forgiveness, not just its theology. Psalm 51 and the other Penitential Psalms provide the experience in words that the Holy Spirit inspired. These psalms help us confess sin in a way that honors the Lord.

Finally, Psalm 51 not only reveals our sin to our eyes, it proclaims God's glory and grace to us. One of the reasons we sin so easily is because we often focus our lives on ourselves alone and not on God. In Psalm 51, David discloses his heart to us, to be sure. More than that, however, he reveals God to us. This in itself is an antidote to sin: if we will concentrate our lives on God, not ourselves, we will be less inclined to sin. When David sees God's righteousness and mercy, as he does in Psalm 51, he can be cleansed from sin and bolstered against further sin. So it will be with us. In Psalm 51, David gives us the words to put God back at the center of our lives, even when we sin.

Chapter 12

The Way of Wisdom: Psalms 111 and 112

Blessed is the man
who does not walk in the counsel of the wicked
or stand in the way of sinners
or sit in the seat of mockers.
But his delight is in the law of the LORD,
and on his law he meditates day and night.
—Psalm 1:1–2

The Way of Wisdom

IN THIS CHAPTER, WE TURN TO TWO companion poems, Psalms 111 and 112, both of which are Psalms of Praise, or Hymns. Psalm 111 is a great Hymn to Yahweh, celebrating his attributes and his great deeds on behalf of his people. Psalm 112 is a Hymn to the godly man, showing how his life is patterned after the attributes of Yahweh. These two psalms teach us that the practical aspects of our daily Christian lives ought to be grounded in the character of Yahweh. They are companion poems because Psalm 112 is based on Psalm 111 and is structured in a parallel fashion. The one psalm focuses on God, the other on the godly man. Together, they show us the way of wisdom, or how to live a godly life.

Both psalms begin with a "Hallelujah," or "Praise the Lord." The first verse of each psalm then introduces the main subject—Yahweh in Psalm 111 and the godly man in Psalm 112. The concluding verse of each psalm emphasizes the wisdom motif in the psalm—the beginning of wisdom is the fear of the Lord in Psalm 111, and the contrasting comment on the godless man in Psalm 112. The frames of the opening and concluding verses in each psalm indicate the twin emphases of the Psalms on the person and work of Yahweh and the wisdom of the godly man in patterning his life on the divine attributes enumerated in Psalm 111.

Psalms 111 and 112 can be described further as character studies or character sketches because they present two portraits with a view to providing wisdom for godly living. Psalm 111 presents a portrait of God's character, Psalm 112 a study of the godly man's character. Leland Ryken calls the literary form of such character studies simply "the character" and cites Psalm 10 as an example of the genre.[1] Several other psalms, among them 1; 14; 15; 36; 49; 52; and 54, are character sketches; each one focuses on the wisdom necessary to live a life pleasing to the Lord. It is noteworthy that the book of the Psalms begins in Psalm 1 with a character sketch that contrasts the godly man to the ungodly and admonishes readers to godly living. So too Psalms 111 and 112: Psalm 111 shows us God's character, and Psalm 112 calls upon us to live in such a way as to reflect the character of God. The character sketches and the parallel structures underscore the wisdom themes of the two psalms.

The two psalms taken together as companion poems
show us the biblical pattern of wisdom.

---

1. Leland Ryken, *Words of Delight: A Literary Introduction to the Bible* (Grand Rapids: Baker, 1992), 242.

Psalm 111
THE RIGHTEOUS GOD

[1]Praise the LORD!

I will extol the LORD with all my heart
    in the council of the upright and in the assembly.

[2]Great are the works of the LORD;
    they are pondered by all who delight in them.
[3]Glorious and majestic are his deeds,
    and his righteousness endures forever.
[4]He has caused his wonders to be remembered;
    the LORD is gracious and compassionate.
[5]He provides food for those who fear him;
    he remembers his covenant forever.
[6]He has shown his people the power of his works,
    giving them the lands of other nations.
[7]The works of his hands are faithful and just;
    all his precepts are trustworthy.
[8]They are steadfast for ever and ever,
    done in faithfulness and uprightness.
[9]He provided redemption for his people;
    he ordained his covenant forever—
    holy and awesome is his name.

[10]The fear of the LORD is the beginning of wisdom;
    all who follow his precepts have good understanding.
    To him belongs eternal praise.

What Is the Overall Effect of the Psalm?

Psalm 111 is doxological; that is, it praises Yahweh for who he is and what he has done for his people. This is one of those psalms we need to read slowly if we are to appreciate the many reasons it cites for praising the Lord; eight of its ten verses name either an attribute of God or a deed he has done for his people. When we look for what the psalm says about Yahweh, we find ourselves celebrating his glory and majesty. He is high and lifted up, but he accommodates himself to his people and meets their needs in every way. Psalm 111 takes us outside of ourselves and brings us face-to-face with Yahweh and the blessings he gives his people.

What Is the Structure of the Psalm?

Scholars have noted that Psalm 111, along with 112, is an acrostic on the Hebrew alphabet.

"Each (Hebrew) half line," we are told, "advances the alphabet" and thereby provides the overall pattern for the psalm.[2] Apart from its acrostic patterning, however, Psalm 111 is structured like a typical Hymn, or Psalm of Praise. Accordingly, it is structured much like other Hymns:

I. Verse 1:   A Call to Praise
II. Verses 2–5:   Yahweh's Great Provision for His People
III. Verses 6–9:   Yahweh's Great Redemption of His People
IV. Verse 10:   Concluding Confidence in Yahweh

The psalm begins with the poet's announcement that he will declare God's glory in the congregation. It concludes with the psalmist's acknowledgment that the wise man will hear the words of the psalm and apply them to his life. These opening and closing verses provide the frame for the psalm and emphasize the public declaration that the psalm will make. Forming the body of the psalm, the intervening verses fall into two sections: first, praise to God for his provision of his people's needs, and, second, praise to God for his self-revelation and the redemption he provides for his people. As this brief outline suggests,

---

2. Kenneth Barker, ed., *The niv Study Bible* (Grand Rapids: Zondervan, 1995), 900. Compare with Willem VanGemeren, *Psalms,* vol. 5 of *The Expositor's Bible Commentary,* ed. Frank E. Gaebelein (Grand Rapids: Zondervan, 1991), 700.

the psalm is focused entirely on Yahweh. It is radically theocentric until the final verse, which in its turn admonishes the reader to learn true wisdom from the psalm and study the character of God as a pattern for wisdom.

What Are the Figures of Speech in the Psalm, and What Effects Do They Have?

Psalm 111 is an unusual psalm in that it contains few figures of speech, such as images and metaphors. It is simply a series of propositional statements, or assertions, about God or his actions. The lack of figures of speech in the psalm may be attributable to the fact that it is an acrostic poem, with each half verse beginning with a letter of the Hebrew alphabet. The acrostic pattern in such a short psalm makes it difficult for the psalmist to elaborate on his subject at length. Consequently, the psalm reads like a litany, or list, of God's characteristics in rapid-fire order. This sequence of propositional statements is intended to impress readers with the majesty and glory of God so profoundly that, when they read the concluding verse, they desire the wisdom the psalmist describes.

While it is true that the psalmist does not use figures of speech in Psalm 111, he does make effective use of parallelisms to describe the character of God. The poetic parallelisms help the reader focus attention on each of the characteristics of God as they are presented in turn, beginning with the section on God's great provision for his people (vv. 2–5). Verse 2 uses a synthetic parallelism to create a double focus for the reader. In this verse, the writer states in the first colon (or phrase) that Yahweh's works are "great," and then parallels this statement in the second colon by testifying that those who delight in his works "ponder" them. The verse moves from God's works to their effect on his people. The subtlety of this parallelism lies in the suggestion that God's works are not only great in themselves, but they are great because they encourage believers to meditate on him. Two verses later, the psalmist reverses the order, placing the "wonder" of believers before the statement of God's grace and compassion (v. 4). Another example of synthetic parallelism, verse 4 serves the double purpose of forming a frame with verse 2 and reiterating the blessing believers receive when they reflect on God's kindness to them. The parallel patterning of these verses functions as a mnemonic device, helping the reader to meditate on Yahweh.

Again in the section on Yahweh's great redemption for his people (vv. 6–9), the psalmist utilizes parallelism to encourage the reader to contemplate God's glory and majesty. Verse 6 begins with an emphatic affirmation of how great God's works are. In a synthetic parallelism, the second colon of the verse illustrates just how great God's works are by reminding the Israelites that he gave them the lands of other nations. With Yahweh on their side, the Israelites conquered Canaan and settled in the land of promise. How "great" is God? He is sovereign over the nations and blesses his own people with good things, for they could not have conquered Canaan without God's defeating their enemies for them. Speaking further of God's redemption of his people, verse 9 begins with a general statement about God's "redemption" and completes it in the second colon with a synthetic parallelism that declares God's redemptive covenant with his people is eternal. In both of these verses, the psalmist reminds believers how glorious and majestic God is and then exhorts them to reflect on him for themselves.

Between the frame verses of 6 and 9, the psalmist further demonstrates God's glory by paralleling his works and words. Verse 7 introduces the double emphasis on word and works by paralleling the faithfulness and justice of God's works (v. 7a) with the trustworthiness of his words (v. 7b). The point is that God's Word is shown to be "trustworthy" in that God fulfills the promises he makes in his Word. His actions on behalf of his people corroborate his Word. The conclusion of this section is the meditation on how "holy and awesome" Yahweh is (v. 9); he is holy and awesome because of his Word and works.

Verse 10 concludes the psalm in a final parallelism that defines wisdom as understanding who Yahweh is and obeying his precepts. What is wisdom? It is to know Yahweh for who he is and what he does (v. 10a) and to obey him in all things (v. 10b). The psalm ends as it begins, with an ascription of praise to God. This is not merely a conventional framing device to bring the psalm to full closure. Rather, it emphasizes the fact that the only way we can obey God is to know him and his words. Psalm 111 praises God for revealing himself to us so that we can apply wisdom to our lives.

> *Framed in praise, Psalm 111 shows us the "character" of Yahweh by showing us who he is and what he does.*

What Are the Themes and Theology in the Psalm?

Because Psalm 111 presents a list of statements of facts about Yahweh, it is a thoroughly theocentric psalm. That is, it focuses entirely on Yahweh until its final verse, which in turn exhorts the readers to apply the wisdom of the psalm to their own lives.

The first theme of the psalm is the self-revelation of God to us in his deeds and in Scripture, which is his Word. Had he not revealed himself to us in these ways (and he reveals himself to us in Jesus Christ and the Holy Spirit as well), we could never know him correctly, for he is too far above us for us to learn about him on our own (cf. Isa. 55:8–9). God's revelation of himself is yet one more instance of his grace, for we could not know him if he had not shown himself to us.

Related to the theme of God's self-revelation is the psalm's emphasis on the importance of Scripture. Verses 7 and 8 declare that everything God says is true, faithful, and just. God's Word is normative, setting the standard by which everything else is judged. God's Word is reliable because it communicates God's character and in turn is verified by the truthfulness and holiness of God. Psalm 111 attests to the fact that Christians ought to hold a high view of Scripture, for the testimony of God's character is at issue in the Bible. Think of the changing seasons as an illustration of how God's works corroborate his Word. God tells Noah that he will give the seasons in their due course until he destroys this heaven and this earth (Gen. 8:20–22). Has he not been faithful? Word and work prove each other true. Scripture teaches us how to see God's fingerprints in everything that happens. We can never overlook the importance of God's Word if we wish to understand God correctly.

The third theme of Psalm 111 is its list of God's attributes. He is holy (v. 3). He is gracious and compassionate (v. 4). He provides for the needs of his people (v. 5). He is sovereign over the affairs of the nations (v. 6). He is truthful in all he says (v. 7). He redeems his people (v. 9). We could meditate on each of these attributes—and should do so. Brought together in such close proximity as they are in this psalm, the attributes of God should move us to praise him, for this is how the psalmist responds to such a glorious and majestic God.

Applications

1. We are to praise God for who he is. Knowing who God is and what he is like is the beginning of all wisdom. If we do not know Jesus Christ as our Savior, we must begin there. If we have already trusted Christ as Savior, we need to study the Scriptures with an eye to learning what God is like. The Psalms are a rich source of information about Yahweh.

2. We are to praise God for what he has done. God's character is expressed in part in the way he relates to his people. As Psalm 111 shows, God has been gracious to us spiritually and temporally. We ought to meditate daily on God's goodness to us.

3. We are to praise God for revealing himself to us. Though this application may appear self-evident at first glance, we ought not to take it for granted that God has chosen to reveal himself to us. He is so far above us that we could not know him if he had not chosen to show himself to us. The Bible is an evidence of God's grace. Do we honor it by reading it and meditating on it?

4. We are to be grateful that God has redeemed us from our sins and declared us righteous in Jesus Christ. Do we thank God often for his salvation in Jesus Christ?

Psalm 112
THE GODLY MAN

When we turn from Psalm 111 to Psalm 112, we turn from a concentrated meditation on Yahweh himself to a consideration of the godly
man who longs after Yahweh and wants to be like him. Like Psalm
111, Psalm 112 is a character study—this one on the godly man.

¹Praise the LORD.

Blessed is the man who fears the LORD,
    who finds great delight in his commands.

²His children will be mighty in the land;
    the generation of the upright will be blessed.
³Wealth and riches are in his house,
    and his righteousness endures forever.
⁴Even in darkness light dawns for the upright,
    for the gracious and compassionate and righteous man.
⁵Good will come to him who is generous and lends freely,
    who conducts his affairs with justice.
⁶Surely he will never be shaken;
    a righteous man will be remembered forever.
⁷He will have no fear of bad news;
    his heart is steadfast, trusting in the LORD.
⁸His heart is secure, he will have no fear;
    in the end he will look in triumph on his foes.
⁹He has scattered abroad his gifts to the poor,
    his righteousness endures forever;
    his horn will be lifted high in honor.

¹⁰The wicked man will see and be vexed,
    he will gnash his teeth and waste away;
    the longings of the wicked will come to nothing.

What Is the Overall Effect of the Psalm?

In a word, Psalm 112 shows the manifold blessings Yahweh gives the godly man. Psalm 111 sketches a glorious portrait of God; as its companion psalm, Psalm 112 portrays the great benefits the godly enjoy. Meditating on this psalm encourages the reader with the many different ways God blesses the godly in both temporal and spiritual terms. After reading the psalm, only a fool would choose the curses of the godless in exchange for the blessings of the godly. Of course, it is God's grace that brings the godless into union with Jesus Christ and changes their lives from cursing to blessing. This psalm praises God by showing how the godly man patterns his life after the character of God himself.

Though Psalm 112 portrays the godly man, it is still a Psalm of Praise to Yahweh, for the godly man is made in Yahweh's image.

What Is the Structure of the Psalm?

Psalm 112 is a Hymn, or Psalm of Praise, to the godly man. Its structure parallels the structure of its companion psalm, Psalm 111, though its final verse stands in stark antithesis to the rest of the psalm.

   I. Verse 1:   A Call to Praise Yahweh
  II. Verses 2–5: The Character of the Godly Man
 III. Verses 6–9: The Blessings of the Godly Man
 IV. Verse 10:   The Fate of the Ungodly Man

The psalm begins by defining the godly man as one who "fears the LORD" and "finds great delight in his commands." It ends by declaring the curses a godless man brings upon himself by refusing to honor the Lord. Between the opening and closing verses, the remaining eight verses begin by defining the godly man as one who follows God and then enumerate the many ways God blesses the godly. The sharp contrast in the frame verses between the one who fears the Lord (v. 1) and the one who rejects God (v. 10) serves to underscore God's grace in bestowing blessings upon the godly. It is God who redeems us and creates in us a pure heart (Ps. 51:10), and it is by their willful rejection of Christ that the godless bring curses upon themselves. The structure of Psalm 112, so closely paralleled to the structure of Psalm 111, reflects the truth that Christians are to become more Christlike as they mature in their faith (Rom. 12:1–2) and ends with a stark reminder that not everyone will choose to honor God.

What Are the Figures of Speech in the Psalm, and What Effects Do They Have?

Like Psalm 111, Psalm 112 uses frequent parallelisms to illustrate the blessings the godly man enjoys. In contrast to the earlier psalm, however, Psalm 112 uses figures of speech to make important associations between the godly man's actions and the character of God. The figures of speech are appropriate in this psalm because no human can be like God; all we can do is reflect him in our limited way. Images and metaphors provide appropriate language devices to portray the fact that a Christian's godly character is only a resemblance of God. The combination of parallelisms and figures of speech in this psalm establishes the godly man's character for the reader.

Psalm 112 begins with a synthetic parallelism that shows how completely the godly man loves the Lord. After the liturgical call to praise, verse 1 begins with the godly man's reverential fear of the Lord. The next phrase in the verse intensifies this awe by showing his delight in the law ("commands") of the Lord. Here is a man who obeys God out of love. He does not merely obey God's law out of a sense of duty; he actually enjoys God's law. Christians can enjoy God's law when they realize that it reflects the character of God and develops godly character in them. Such is the "character" sketched in Psalm 112—a man who delights in God's character and word.

Using a combination of figures of speech and parallelisms, the psalmist depicts the character of the godly man in verses 2 to 5 and demonstrates that his blessings come from God's grace, not his own strength alone. These verses parallel the same verses in Psalm 111, where the psalmist depicts the character of God. The early verses of Psalm 111 state that God is righteous (v. 3), gracious, and compassionate (vv. 4–5). The parallel verses in Psalm 112 show the godly man to have the same characteristics as God: he is righteous (vv. 2, 3, 4), gracious, and compassionate (vv. 4, 5). The first phrase of verse 2 states that the godly man's children will be "mighty in the land." In a synthetic parallelism, the second phrase makes it clear that their success does not come from their own efforts but from the Lord, for it is his blessing that upholds them. In the next verse, the psalmist uses another parallelism to name two categories of God's blessings—temporal ("wealth and riches are in his house") and spiritual ("and his righteousness endures forever"). In short order, these two verses make it abundantly clear that the godly man enjoys the fruits of his labor, but that it is God who provides the increase both temporally and spiritually for the godly man.

Matching the structure of Psalm 111 again, Psalm 112 states that the godly man is "generous" and that he "lends freely" to those in need (v. 5); Psalm 111 states that God "provides food for those who fear him" (v. 5). In Psalm 112:4, the writer uses a synthetic parallelism to expand our understanding of what it means to be "upright" (v. 4a): it is to be "gracious and compassionate and righteous" (v. 4b). As in the character of God, righteousness and mercy are not antithetical, for in the godly man kindness and generosity are proofs of righteousness; the two go hand in hand. In this same verse, the psalmist deepens our appreciation of God's blessings on the godly man in his use of the familiar biblical image of darkness and light. He states, "Even in darkness light dawns for the upright" (v. 4a). Light is a conventional image of good in the Bible, as darkness is of evil. In this reference, the psalmist nuances the familiar imagery in his implication that there will be dark times for the godly man; difficulties are to be expected. When they come, however, God will provide what the godly man needs to get through the dark hours. Again, the psalmist wants to make it clear that the godly man's "success" comes from God's grace, not his own efforts alone.

In verses 6–9, the psalmist turns from the character of the godly man to the blessings of the godly man. As in the earlier section, this part of Psalm 112 (the character of the godly man) matches its parallel section in Psalm 111 (the character of God). In Psalm 111:6–9, the psalmist declares God's great power and his use of that power to bless his people; in Psalm 112:6–9, the psalmist shows how the godly man is blessed by God's power in the difficult times (vv. 6–8) and in God's protection against his enemies (v. 8b). God's kindness to his people (111:6, 9) is reflected in the godly man's generosity to those in need, for "he has scattered abroad his gifts to the poor" (112:9).

Verses 7 and 8 of Psalm 112 are further structured to show the confidence the godly man has in God even in the face of difficulties. These verses are patterned in an A-B-B-A arrangement. The godly man "will have no fear of bad news" (A); "his heart is steadfast, trusting in the LORD" (B); "His heart is secure" (B); and "he will have no fear" (A). This tight structure underscores the certainty that the godly man will not be removed from all difficult circumstances; he will even face enemies (v. 8b). He will not fear bad news or his enemies, however, for God will protect him and give him victory over those who would do him harm.

In verse 9 we are reminded of the godly man's generosity to those in need. In turn, the Lord rewards this kindness with honor. We must always remember that the blessings God gives to the godly do not come because they have earned righteousness by good deeds. Remember verse 1, in which "godly" is defined as the one who "fears the LORD" and "finds great delight in his commands." A person is godly only when God imputes his righteousness to him or her by grace. Another indication that good deeds do not make a person godly is the parallel with Psalm 111. There, God is identified as righteous; here in Psalm 112, righteousness is derived from God only by grace. Blessings follow righteousness; they do not produce it.

This section of God's blessings on the godly man ends with the image of his "horn" being "lifted high in honor" (v. 9c), emphasizing again that it is God who blesses him, not the godly man who secures his own success. Throughout this section, the psalmist takes pains to praise God who blesses him. All the gifts the godly man enjoys come from God; even his generous character is made in God's image (cf. Ps. 111:5–6, 9).

The last verse of the psalm provides a sharp contrast with the rest of the poem. Here we see the unrighteous, or ungodly, man as the opposite of the godly man. The contrast of the two is called a foil. In this case, as in Psalm 1, the foil serves to show how utterly blessed the godly man is and how profoundly cursed the ungodly man is. The first image in the verse is of the wicked seeing the blessings of the righteous and being unable to enjoy those blessings, even when he schemed to do so. This image is followed by an even more appalling picture of the wicked "gnash[ing] his teeth." The image presents the horror of a person gnawing or chewing his own gums in utter agony because he cannot participate in the good things he had hoped for. How intense is such jealousy! The final image of the wicked "wast[ing] away" suggests how completely he is consumed by his own evil desires and malice when God leaves him to the results of his own sin. How unlike the godly is the godless man.

How does the final verse of the psalm, so obviously opposite to the godly man's character, relate to the rest of the psalm?

In this final verse, the psalmist obviously means to strike a sharp contrast with the godly, who "will never be shaken" (v. 6) and is stable even in the face of difficulties. C. S. Lewis agrees with the psalmist when he writes, "There are only two kinds of people in the end: those who say to God, 'Thy will be done,' and those to whom God says in the end, 'Thy will be done.'"[3] The wicked reap the results of their own will; the godly reap the blessings of God's grace. To add insult to injury for the wicked person, he will not see his desires fulfilled. He will always long for more and never be satisfied. Contrast this with the peace and contentment the godly enjoy in God.

The concluding verse of Psalm 112 is not a cry for vengeance on

---

3. C. S Lewis, *The Great Divorce* (New York: Simon & Schuster, 1996), 72.

enemies or malice toward them. Rather, it is a confirmation of the horrors that attend a rejection of God, a refusal to "fear the LORD" and find "great delight in his commands" (v. 1). It confirms these horrors for a particular reason: this verse is a warning to readers to avoid the fate of the wicked. God does not unjustly condemn anyone; by rejecting God, the ungodly condemn themselves. By contrasting the righteous man with the unrighteous at the conclusion of the psalm, the writer underscores God's grace and compassion toward those who trust in him (cf. Ps. 111:4 and Ps. 112:4). Finally, the last verse of Psalm 112 invites another contrast with the final verse of Psalm 111. In Psalm 111:10, the godly enjoy God forever; in Psalm 112:10, the wicked are everlastingly cast away from God. Can the teaching be any clearer? The psalm ends in a solemn warning to any ungodly person who will "hear" what the writer has to say. The psalmist leaves the reader in a position of decision. Which way will he turn?

What Are the Themes and Theology in the Psalm?

The themes of Psalm 112 relate to the character of the godly man and the blessings he enjoys. We might summarize the character of the godly man in Psalm 112 with the three attributes of righteousness, graciousness, and compassion. He is upright in his character and actions; he lends to those in need; and he does not fear evil men. The important point about these characteristics of the godly man is that he derives them by grace from God. God works in us to sanctify us, or to set us apart, for his glory. Paul elaborates this idea in the list of the fruit (or graces) of the Spirit, which are "love, joy, peace, patience, kindness, goodness, faithfulness, gentleness and self-control" (Gal. 5:22–23). The Holy Spirit produces these characteristics in believers; we do not develop them ourselves. So too with the godly man in Psalm 112—God sanctifies him and then blesses him.

The second theme of Psalm 112 relates to the blessings God showers on the godly man. He is made stable in the face of bad news (vv. 6–7). He does not fear enemies who wish to harm him (v. 8). He is generous to the needy (v. 9). And he enjoys God's favor forever (vv. 6,

9). Contrast these blessings with the instability, jealousy, and vanity of the wicked in verse 10, and the wise reader will make the right choice. Indeed, Psalm 112 paints a portrait of wisdom, and it is the godly person who fears the Lord and delights in his commands.

Applications

1. We always must remember that God is the only one who is righteous in himself. He declares us righteous in Jesus Christ when we receive his saving grace by faith. Our righteousness is not our own; it is Christ's righteousness imputed to us (Rom. 4:23–5:2).

2. Godliness shows itself in action, not just theological knowledge. Christ commands us, "'Love the Lord your God with all your heart and with all your soul and with all your mind.' This is the first and greatest commandment. And the second is like it: 'Love your neighbor as yourself'" (Matt. 22:37–39). C. S. Lewis once said, "Christian love is an affair of the will";[4] that is, godly love is not mere emotion, it is action on behalf of the beloved.

3. Though God nowhere promises to remove us from all difficulties and sufferings, he does promise to sustain us always. Christ himself says, "Come to me, all you who are weary and burdened, and I will give you rest" (Matt. 11:28). Though it may be difficult, we must learn to cultivate an awareness of the presence of God so that he can sustain us in the dark hours.

4. As we read the horrible, and horrifying, fate of the ungodly in Psalm 112, we should redouble our desire for sinners to be converted by God's grace into believers. We should pray more fervently to this end—both corporately in our churches and individually in our private prayers.

5. We should seek to be "transformed by the renewing of [our] mind" to the image of Jesus Christ (Rom. 12:2). We must cultivate godliness.

---

4. C. S. Lewis, *Mere Christianity* (New York: Simon & Schuster, 1996), 117–18.

Encountering God in the Wisdom Psalms

Simply put, biblical wisdom has two dimensions to it: knowledge and action. The first aspect of godly wisdom is knowledge; we must know Yahweh. We must know who he is and what he is like. How can we know God? Such knowledge is too great for us; it is only by God's grace that we can know him. In the first place, knowing God means having a personal relationship with him by grace through faith in Jesus Christ. To know God, we must be saved; put in theological terms, we must be justified. Second, knowing God means developing godly characteristics in ourselves, or, more properly put, allowing the Holy Spirit to develop a godly character in us. If we wish to be conformed to the image of Jesus Christ, as the New Testament admonishes us, we must be "transformed by the renewing of [our] mind[s]" (Rom. 12:2). To have our minds renewed, we must study the Scriptures diligently for what they say about Jesus Christ, and we must ask the Holy Spirit to transform us into Christ's image. In fact, the transformation of our sinful desires into Christlike character is one of the goals of the Christian life. Biblical wisdom begins in knowing God.

The second dimension of biblical wisdom is action. That is, we must put our knowledge into practice in our daily lives. Put in theological terms, we must be sanctified. We must allow the Holy Spirit to transform our actions, as well as our minds. The biblical pattern is always the same: action reflects belief. Who we are determines what we do. If we wish to develop godly character, we must first be changed on the inside; then we must demonstrate the inner difference by outward actions. James reminds us that true religion involves godly action, not just knowledge (James 1:26–27).

As companion poems, Psalms 111 and 112 show us the biblical pattern of wisdom. Psalm 111 presents the attributes and actions of Yahweh, and Psalm 112 demonstrates that the godly man is the one who allows the Holy Spirit to develop Godlike character in him. Godly wisdom begins in the reverent study of Scripture for what it says about

Yahweh. Such study results in godly behavior, which, in turn, glorifies the Lord.

> *Biblical wisdom produces sanctification.*

Chapter 13

What Have We Learned?

OUR READING OF THE PSALMS IN THIS book has had two underlying assumptions. The first of these is that God reveals himself to his people in the Psalms. Christianity begins with the truth that God has told us about himself and that everything we know about him comes from his self-revelation. In turn, God's self-revelation puts us in a position of choice: we either accept God's self-disclosure by faith, or we reject him. From this beginning point, we can draw several conclusions, the first of which is that God has given us the means of knowing him. God has revealed himself in a variety of ways—in nature (Rom. 1:20), the human conscience (Rom. 2:15), the Bible (2 Tim. 3:16–17), and Jesus Christ (John 10:30). God details his many attributes and perfections most completely in the Bible, and we must turn to the Bible if we wish to know God and obey him. This is the reason we began with the story of Moses' life in Genesis and the ways God revealed himself to Moses. The Psalms reflect the same attributes that God revealed to Moses and recount his actions on behalf of his people. The Psalms bring God close to his people; this is reason enough to study them carefully.

The second assumption behind this book is the understanding that the Psalms are written as poems and must be read that way. The Holy Spirit inspired the forms, as well as the content, of the Psalms. The content of the Psalms is what we learn about God and ourselves. The form is the way the Psalms express the content; form involves the poetry of the Psalms, including their figures of speech, parallelisms, and genres. If we wish to know God for who he is and what he does, we must read the Psalms as poems, paying due attention to their poetic features.

In the Introduction, we proposed three questions to guide our study. We now return to them to consider what we have learned.

What Have We Learned About Reading the Psalms?

Our first question relates to how we read the Psalms. All good reading of Scripture is an active process in which the reader is engaged mentally, emotionally, and spiritually. We must read Scripture slowly if we are to appreciate all that the Holy Spirit wants us to learn; a five-minute devotional is good, but it is simply not enough. If we wish to enjoy the full spiritual benefit of the Psalms, we will read them slowly and carefully. Because the Psalms are poems, we must read them particularly closely, for poems involve the senses and emotions, not just the intellect. Poetry is more intense than prose and demands that we pay close attention to each word, not just the sentence sense. The four questions we have used throughout the book to approach the Psalms are designed to help us read Hebrew poetry accurately and to encourage us to read actively. The first question draws attention to the overall effect of a given psalm and provides the appropriate context and tone for our reading. The second question considers the genre and structure of the psalm and aligns our expectations with the intentions of the psalmist. The third question provides the opportunity to understand and appreciate the details of the psalm on its own terms. The final question draws the others together by asking about the theology and themes of the psalm. Taken together, these four questions help us read slowly and actively for our spiritual benefit. In short, they help us read the Psalms the way they were written.

Many modern literary and biblical critics do not think we can recover the original intention of an ancient writer, and many think that, even if we could recover the original intention, it is not particularly relevant to us today. They deny that we can read the Psalms the way they were written. Such a position is naive, for it ignores the primary ground we have for understanding Scripture—the texts themselves. If we hold a high view of the inspiration of Scripture, we must acknowledge that the Holy Spirit certainly has a purpose in inspiring and preserving the Scripture as we have it today. The assumption throughout this book therefore has been that we must do our best to come as closely as we can to an accurate reading of the texts of the Psalms themselves if we are to receive their full spiritual benefit. To read the Psalms accurately, we must understand them in their own terms, their poetic form included.

Reading the Psalms the way they were written helps us understand that the form and style of the Psalms are as inspired as their content. That is, the Holy Spirit inspired the poetry of the Psalms as much as he did their theology and themes. We should not be intimidated by Hebrew poetic devices on the one hand, nor should we ignore them on the other, for we cannot appreciate the full impact of the Psalms until we learn to ask the questions appropriate to their poetic form. This is why we have paid so much attention to genres, figures of speech, and parallelisms in the Psalms. It is these features that make the Psalms distinct from other types of biblical writings, and it is these features that help open up the psalmists' original intentions for us today. Simply put, we ask different questions of biblical poems than we do of biblical narratives, epistles, or the Gospels.

When we read Hebrew poetry, we ask specifically about genre, structure, figures of speech, and parallelisms. These are the literary features of the Psalms that distinguish them from other writings, and we have directed our attention toward these features throughout the book. The two primary impulses of the Psalms are praise and prayer. The Hymns and the Psalms of Thanksgiving focus primarily on praise, while Laments and Penitential Psalms offer prayers for help or forgiveness. Genre helps us understand the purposes and tones of the Psalms. Structure helps us analyze the Psalms by providing the subdivisions each psalm contains. In effect, structure divides the Psalms into manageable pieces that help us recognize the individual sections and how they relate to each other and to the psalm as a whole. Structure is the framework of the psalm and gives it shape.

Figures of speech—such as similes, metaphors, and images—carry much of the meaning in a psalm. Far from being decorations to embellish the meaning, they frame and limit the meaning. Consider again the image of the shepherd in Psalm 23; all that the psalm teaches about Yahweh comes from, and is framed by, the picture of the shepherd who protects his sheep, provides abundantly for them, delivers them in death, and ultimately takes them to heaven to be with him forever. Figures of speech carry a great deal of meaning in a few words, for it is the single image of the shepherd in Psalm 23 that supports all of these truths about Yahweh.

Finally, parallelism is the principal means by which Hebrew poetry is easily memorized; believers throughout the ages have memorized large portions of the Psalms and have been able to recall them in the dark hours of life. Parallelism functions much like paragraphs do in prose; it indicates the individual thoughts of the psalmist and their connections, helping the reader to do what we have suggested is so necessary in reading the Psalms—to read them actively for spiritual benefit. Asking questions related to these literary features of the Psalms takes us a long way toward understanding them properly.

> *If we believe that Scripture is inspired, we will recognize that the Holy Spirit inspired the poetry of the Psalms as much as he did their theology. If we wish to read the Psalms the way they were written, we will learn how to read their poetry as well as their theology. We read the theology of the Psalms through their poetry.*

What Have We Learned About Yahweh?

Our second and third questions relate to what we learn in the Psalms, not how we read them. The Psalms maintain a twofold, or binocular, focus; that is, we are always thinking in two directions when we read them. The twin emphases of the Psalms are what they teach us about

Yahweh and what they tell us about ourselves. Our second question asks what we have learned about Yahweh from our reading of the Psalms.

Whether they are praising or praying, the psalmists direct our attention toward God. When they praise God, the psalmists do so directly in Hymns, Messianic Psalms, and Psalms of Thanksgiving. When they pray, the psalmists praise God indirectly because their prayers tacitly acknowledge that only he can meet their needs. The psalmists often mix prayer and praise, as they do in the Lament Psalms, turning them into an occasion to acknowledge God's goodness. The psalmists begin with God, and so should we.

The Psalms show God as he reveals himself to his people. Of the many names of God in Scripture, the Psalms reference God most often as Yahweh, "God's personal name to Israel."[1] The next most frequent name of God in the Psalms is Elohim. The ratio of the two names is 3 to 1—698 references to God as Yahweh, and 265 to God as Elohim.[2] Overwhelmingly, the psalmists see God in his relationship with his covenant people. The psalms reveal God principally as he wishes himself to be known by his own people. They are the "family talk" for Christians—a personal "conversation" with Yahweh, the covenant God.

The basis of God's relationship with his people is his *hesed* love. God's *hesed* love is his special love for his people, an "unfailing love" (NIV) he expresses in a variety of ways. To name just a few examples of this covenant love, God demonstrates his unfailing love for us when he forgives our sins, when he provides what we need in this life, and when he protects us from slander and from wicked men. We have seen this unfailing love in many of the Psalms we have studied, and it forms the foundation of everything God does for his people. In fact, it would not be an exaggeration to say that God superintends everything in the universe, from natural events to the actions of the nations and the events of individual lives, for the good of his people and for his glory. Indirectly, then, his unfailing love stands behind all of his actions, not

---

1. Tremper Longman, *How to Read the Psalms* (Downers Grove, Ill.: InterVarsity, 1988), 43.
2. Ibid., 44.

just those related directly to his people. Such a realization should provide encouragement and hope in the face of international terrorism and personal tragedy alike. If we have trusted Jesus Christ by faith through grace, we can be certain with Paul that "in all things God works for the good of those who love him, who have been called according to his purpose" (Rom. 8:28). God's sovereignty guarantees his unfailing love for his people.

Of course, the Psalms illustrate countless other characteristics of God. In the few psalms we have analyzed, we have seen God's sovereignty emphasized numerous times, for in his providence God controls all of nature, the affairs of the nations, and the events of individual lives. If he did not, he would not be omnipotent and omniscient. The references in the Psalms to the history of God's people testify to God's sovereignty working on behalf of his people. From the Exodus, through the wilderness wanderings, and into the Promised Land, the psalmists testify to God's sovereign management of the affairs of the nations to accomplish his will for his people. Other frequent attributes of God in the Psalms we have studied include his faithfulness, his goodness, his omnificence, his protection, and his provision. The reader is referred to the Appendix, "Major Attributes of God in the Psalms," for a psalm-by-psalm list of God's attributes.

The way we have read the Psalms reflects the intentions of the psalmists to praise Yahweh, whether in thanksgiving or lament, hymns or penitence. We need to develop the habit of reading the Psalms for what they say about Yahweh.

What Have We Learned About Living the God-centered Christian Life?

The third question turns to what the Psalms teach us about ourselves. The Christian life is all of grace. God saves us by grace, and he sanctifies us by grace. As one preacher put it, "We can do nothing of eternal importance apart from God." In fact, apart from God, we could not take the next breath necessary for life itself. Paul tells us as much, for he says of Christ, "in him all things hold together" (Col. 1:17). By the word of his power, Jesus Christ sustains the universe; without his power, everything would disintegrate instantly. Reading the Psalms should give us a high view of Yahweh and an understanding that he sustains us physically and accomplishes his work through us by the Holy Spirit. We are entirely dependent on him.

The Psalms teach us that to live the Christian life we need God's grace to develop godly wisdom in us. The wisdom of the Psalms has two dimensions—knowledge and action. It begins in our knowing God—who he is and what he does—and results in godly behavior on our parts. In our reading of the Psalms, we have concentrated on the attributes and actions of God as our primary emphasis. We have discovered that every psalm teaches us something about the character or work of God. Knowing God as he reveals himself in the Scripture is the starting point of godly wisdom, and we would do well to begin our study of the Psalms looking for the attributes and actions of God. Of course, intellectual knowledge from the Psalms about God is inadequate in itself to produce godly wisdom; we must live in such a way that we reflect the character of God in our daily lives. The first psalm is a Wisdom Psalm that contrasts the godly man with the ungodly, making the choice between the two obvious. Psalms 111 and 112 provide a clear indication that the man who wishes to be godly must develop a Godlike character, and to do that he must know God. Psalm 111 therefore teaches that God is righteous, gracious, and compassionate; Psalm 112 shows that the godly man needs to develop righteousness, graciousness, and compassion in his character. A Christian is to reflect Jesus Christ.

The seventeenth-century English poet George Herbert understood godly wisdom, and he wrote "The Windows" to demonstrate our need of God's grace if we are to demonstrate godly wisdom in our lives. In this poem, Herbert uses the image of Christians as panes of stained glass in a cathedral window; as the light shines through them, they refract the light and show their beautiful picture.[3] Because we are im-

---

3. George Herbert, "The Windows," in *The English Poems of George Herbert,* ed. C. A. Patrides (Totowa, N.J.: Rowman & Littlefield, 1978), 84–85.

perfect, we cannot shine the light of Christ perfectly; however, the refraction of the light of Christ through our personalities and character, like light through stained glass, should adorn the gospel and make it attractive to unbelievers. That is, we should live in such a way that people are attracted to Christ (2 Cor. 5:20). When Christians honor the Lord in their lives, the light of the gospel is easy to see. Herbert's image captures the essence of godly wisdom in the Psalms, for we are to radiate his grace for the world to see.

Even the uniquely divine qualities of God that we cannot develop in our own character—such as his omnipotence, omniscience, and omnificence—have implications for living the Christian life. God created everything out of nothing, an action only God can perform. In a derivative sense, however, all people are creative, for they are created in the image of God. All human beings are creative in one way or another, and such creativity is not limited to Christians. Even so, Christians can do their work well to the glory of God, reflecting in some small way the creativity that God gave each one of us. More than our creativity, God's work as Creator of the universe guarantees his promises to us. God's creation demonstrates his sovereignty, and his sovereignty guarantees his promises. There is a practical dimension to God's creative activity, for it encourages us to use our own creativity for his glory and assures us of his power to fulfill his promises to us.

The same can be said of the many promises of protection and provision in the Psalms. These promises reflect God's unfailing love for his people and again demonstrate his sovereignty. The many assurances in the Psalms of God's protection should encourage us in our everyday trials because an unjust attack on one Christian is an attack on others; we are part of the community of faith, and others are affected by our suffering (1 Cor. 12:26). We should ask for the help and prayers of other Christians when we are unjustly attacked. We should not think of God's promises of protection in the Psalms in a purely academic or intellectual manner, for they help unite the community of believers in their testimony for Jesus Christ. In the same way, God's promises of provision should encourage us, especially when we experience financial difficulties. God's testimony is that he will provide for his own, and, provided that we have not created our problem by financial mismanagement or inappropriate behavior, we can expect that he will meet our needs (Ps. 37:25). Far from being general promises for others, God's promises of protection and provision should encourage our daily praise even when we do not feel threatened or lack any necessity. When we thank God for a meal, we testify to his goodness, grace, faithfulness, and power. We should thank God for all his provisions in the same way.

When the psalmists take the next step beyond asking for protection and provision and curse their enemies, we may wonder what benefit there could be for Christians in these psalms. Even these Imprecatory Psalms, however, have practical application to our lives as believers today. As we read these psalms, we should be looking for what they say about Yahweh. If we do so, we will find that behind all the imprecations is Yahweh's holiness and righteousness. None of us can attain to God's holiness, and the Imprecatory Psalms therefore encourage us to examine ourselves to see if we have a vengeful or self-righteous attitude; if we do, we should confess it as sin and ask for forgiveness. A second practical benefit of the Imprecatory Psalms is that they should help encourage us to evangelize the lost. When we read of the curses called down on God's enemies and realize afresh that God is justified in his judgments, we should wish to see loved ones, friends, and colleagues converted. As the old saying has it, "There but for the grace of God go I." The Imprecatory Psalms remind us who we are—sinners by birth and choice—and should develop in us a godly concern for the conversion of unbelievers.

Finally, the Psalms teach us how to ask for forgiveness when we sin. We know we should repent when we sin, but we sometimes find it difficult to do so. The Psalms, especially the Penitential Psalms, provide God's words for us to confess our sins, ask forgiveness, and purge our guilt. When we do not repent of a known sin, we usually are impenitent or proud; reading the Penitential Psalms will show us God's perspective on our sin (all sin is abominable to God) and his willingness to forgive us if we will repent. We should not minimize this benefit of the Psalms, for we all sin daily. The more we leave sin unconfessed, the harder our hearts become to the grace of God. Psalms like David's great confession in Psalm 51 can help us keep "short sin accounts" with God and our hearts sensitive to his grace for daily living. How can we possibly think the Psalms are not relevant to us today—this very day?

Final Remarks

To speak metaphorically (as the Psalms so often do), we are all soils of one kind or another. The picture of people as different types of soils is the image Jesus Christ uses in the Parable of the Sower (Matt. 13:2–23; Mark 4:1–20; Luke 8:11–15). In us, the Word of God either takes root, or it withers and dies. Those in whom the Word of God thrives are those who by grace have placed their faith in Jesus Christ—Christians. Those in whom the Word of God withers are those people who reject Jesus Christ. The purpose of this book has been to help the Word of God take root in our hearts by encouraging us to read the Psalms the way they were written—as poems—and by learning about their primary subject—Yahweh. My hope for this book is that it becomes a tool to prepare the soil.

Appendix

Major Attributes of God in the Psalms

1. This appendix is a list of the major attributes of God in each psalm. By "major" is meant the attributes that each psalm emphasizes; the list is not exhaustive.
2. Some attributes of God are ascribed explicitly to him (e.g., Ps. 111), while in many places, we understand the attributes of God indirectly as they are applied to "the godly man" or God's covenant people (e.g., Pss. 1; 112).
3. Psalm 119, the longest psalm in the Psalter, praises the Word of God. In ascribing characteristics to the Word of God, the psalmist describes the attributes of God indirectly. Psalm 119 is an acrostic, organized in twenty-two stanzas according to the letters of the Hebrew alphabet. At times, whole stanzas describe one primary attribute of God, while mentioning others in specific verses; we note the stanzaic ascriptions in these cases.

Psalm	Title	Attributes of God
1	The Godly and the Ungodly	righteous (v. 1), provider (v. 3), omniscient judge (vv. 4–6)
2	The Son's Sovereign Reign	sovereignty (vv. 4–6), judge (vv. 10–12), revelator (vv. 7–9), redeemer (vv. 7, 12), covenant maker (vv. 6–9)
3	God's Protection of David	righteous (v. 4), protector (vv. 3, 8), covenant maker (v. 8)
4	David's Confidence in God	righteous (v. 1), merciful (v. 1), sovereign (v. 3), provider (vv. 6–7), protector (v. 8)
5	The Tent of God's Protection	righteous (vv. 4–6, 10), merciful (vv. 7–8), covenant (vv. 11–12), protection (v. 11)
6	God's Mercy	mercy (v. 2), covenant (v. 4), protector (vv. 8–10)
7	God Our Shield	protector (vv. 1–2, 10), just (vv. 6–7), righteous (vv. 9, 11, 17), omniscient (v. 9), sovereign (vv. 15–16)
8	The Majestic Creator	glorious (vv. 1–2), ruler (vv. 5–8)
9	God's Sovereign Mercy and Justice	righteous (v. 8), eternal (v. 7), merciful (v. 18), protector (vv. 4, 9)
10	God's Defense of His People	omniscient (v. 14), helper (v. 14), sovereign (vv. 16–18), eternal (v. 16)
11	God's Righteous Rule	provider, protector (vv. 1, 3–4), righteous (vv. 4, 7), omniscient (v. 4)

		sovereign (vv. 7–10), warrior (vv. 7–10)
25	God's Mercy and Love	merciful (vv. 6, 11, 18), *ḥesed*/loving (vv. 6, 10, 14), righteous (vv. 8, 21), gracious (v. 16), faithful (v. 10)
26	A Prayer for God's Mercy	omniscient (v. 2), loving (v. 3), righteous (vv. 4–6, 9–11), merciful (v. 11)
27	David's Confidence in God's Protection	redeemer (vv. 1, 9), protector (vv. 5, 12), merciful (v. 7), faithful (v. 10)
28	The King's Prayer for Protection	righteous (v. 2), merciful (v. 6), protector (vv. 7–9)
29	The Splendor of Holiness	strong (vv. 1–2), holy (vv. 1–2), omnipotent (vv. 3–9), covenant (vv. 10–11)
30	Rejoicing Comes in the Morning	holy (vv. 4–5), covenant (vv. 5, 7), faithful (v. 9), merciful (v. 10)
31	A Spacious Place	protector (vv. 2–4), love (vv. 7, 16, 21), good (v. 19), sovereign (v. 15)
32	A Hiding Place	forgiving (vv. 1–2, 5), counselor (vv. 8–10)
33	A Psalm of Praise for God's Unfailing Love	righteous (vv. 5, 21), covenant (vv. 5, 12, 18, 22), Creator (vv. 6–19), sovereign (vv. 10–11), omniscient (vv. 13–15)
34	Taste and See	good (v. 8), protector (v. 7), compassionate (v. 18)
35	A Prayer for Relief	mercy (v. 10), righteousness (vv. 24,

		28), omniscient (v. 22a), immanent (v. 22b), good (v. 27)
36	Under the Shadow of God's Wings	loving (vv. 5a, 7, 10), faithful (v. 5b), righteous (vv. 6, 10), provider (vv. 8–9)
37	The Wicked Fall, but the Righteous Stand	righteous (vv. 6, 17, 25, 28, 37, 39), generous (vv. 11, 21), faithful (vv. 25, 28), protector (vv. 28, 37–40)
38	Guilt and Repentance	righteous (vv. 1, 5, 18), merciful (vv. 15–16, 21–22)
39	David's Sinful Silence	righteous (vv. 1, 8, 11), merciful (vv. 7, 10, 12–13)
40	David Proclaims God's Grace	savior (vv. 1–3, 10), righteous (vv. 9–10), faithful (v. 10), love (vv. 10–11)
41	A Cry for Mercy	compassionate (v. 1), merciful (vv. 4, 10), eternal (v. 13), righteous (v. 4)
42	Longing for God	savior (vv. 5, 11), love (v. 8), sustainer (v. 9)
43	A Cry for Vindication	righteous (v. 1), protector (v. 2), guide (v. 3), truth (v. 3), holy (v. 3)
44	A Prayer for Restoration	faithful (vv. 1–3), *ḥesed* (vv. 1–3, 26), sovereign (vv. 1–3, 4–8), covenant (vv. 2, 4, 23–26)
45	The Royal Bridegroom	king (v. 3), righteous (vv. 4, 7), sovereign (vv. 5–6), just (v. 6)
46	Listening for God	omnipotent (vv. 1–3, 7, 8–10, 11), covenant

59	God's Protection of David Against His Enemies	sovereign (vv. 5, 11–13), covenant (vv. 5, 10, 11, 13, 16, 17), protector (vv. 9, 16, 17)
60	God Gives Victory	protector (v. 5), covenant (vv. 3–4, 6–7), sovereign (vv. 6–12)
61	The Rock That Is Higher Than I	protector (vv. 2, 3, 4), covenant love (v. 7), faithful (v. 7)
62	Strength and Love	protector (vv. 1, 2, 5, 6, 8), loving (v. 11), savior (vv. 1, 6), truthful (v. 5)
63	The King Praises God	provider (vv. 1, 5, 7), majestic (v. 2), covenant love (v. 3)
64	Wicked Men and a Holy God	protector (vv. 1, 7–8, 10), holy (vv. 7–8), righteous (v. 10)
65	God's Generous Provision	forgiving (v. 3), covenant (v. 4), righteous (v. 5), provider (vv. 11–13)
66	Great Things God Has Done	sovereign (vv. 5–7), providential protector (v. 9), holy (v. 10), love (vv. 19–20)
67	May the Lord Bless Us	gracious (v. 1), just (v. 4), guide (v. 4), provider (v. 6)
68	God's Awesome Power and Unfailing Love	sovereign over nature (vv. 4, 8–10, 15–17), sovereign over nations (vv. 1–2, 11–14, 18, 21–23), righteous (vv. 3, 5, 21–23), provider (vv. 5–6, 7–10), covenant (vv. 26–27, 34–35)
69	A Prayer for Deliverance	omnipotent (vv. 6, 34), covenant (vv. 6, 8–9,

91	The Shelter of the Most High	protector (vv. 2, 4–6, 14), faithful (v. 4), immanent (v. 15), sovereign (v. 8)
92	Like a Cedar of Lebanon	sovereign (vv. 6–7, 9–11), caring (vv. 1–5, 8, 12–15), faithful (v. 2), righteous (vv. 12–15)
93	The Majestic Creator	eternal (vv. 2, 5), holy (v. 5), majestic (vv. 1, 4), revelator (v. 5a)
94	God, a Refuge for His People	sovereign (vv. 4–7, 8–11, 20–23), covenant (vv. 12–15, 16–19), faithful (v. 14), refuge (vv. 20–22)
95	The Great King Above All Gods	Creator (vv. 3–6), redeemer (v. 7), righteous (vv. 9–11)
96	Let All the Nations Praise Yahweh	Creator (vv. 5, 10–13), glorious (vv. 3–6), holy (vv. 9, 13), sovereign (v. 10)
97	Let the Earth Be Glad	sovereign (vv. 1–6, 9), righteous (vv. 2–3, 6, 10, 12), redeemer (vv. 8–9)
98	An Invitation to Praise God	loving and faithful (vv. 1–3), sovereign over nations (vv. 4–6), sovereign over world (vv. 7–9), righteous, holy (vv. 1–2, 9)
99	Enthroned Between the Cherubim	ruler of his own people (vv. 2, 4, 6–7), forgiving (v. 8), holy (vv. 3, 5, 9), revelator (vv. 6–8a)
100	The Goodness of the Lord	love for Israel (vv. 3, 5), good (throughout), faithful (v. 5)

101	A Righteous King	loving (v. 1), just (vv. 1, 7), holy (vv. 2–8)
102	A Prayer That God Will Protect His People	compassion (vv. 13, 17, 20), Creator (v. 25), eternal (vv. 26–27)
103	Bless the Lord for His Unfailing Love	forgiving (vv. 3, 4, 9), love (vv. 4, 8, 13), good (v. 5), righteous (vv. 1, 6, 17)
104	A Creation Hymn	Creator, sustainer (throughout), omnificent (vv. 10–18), majestic (vv. 1, 31–32, throughout)
105	God's Faithfulness to His People	holy (v. 3), covenant (vv. 5–11, 42–45), faithful (vv. 12–45)
106	God's Mercy to His People	faithful (vv. 8–12, 43–46), love (vv. 1, 4–5, 44–46)
107	God's Covenant Love Demonstrated	loving (vv. 1, 8, 15, 21, 31, 43), good (vv. 2–9, 33–42), protector (vv. 23–32), forgiving (vv. 17–22)
108	God Is a Warrior	loving (v. 4), faithful (v. 4), covenant (vv. 6–9), sovereign (v. 9)
109	A Prayer for Deliverance	good (v. 21), sovereign (v. 21), love (v. 26), compassion (v. 31)
110	Messiah-King and Priest	sovereign (vv. 1, 2), holy (v. 3), warrior (v. 5), judge (v. 6)
111	The Righteous God	compassionate (v. 4), provider (v. 5), redeemer (v. 9), revelator (vv. 7, 8), righteous (vv. 3, 8)
112	The Godly Man	righteous (v. 3), generous (v. 5), sovereign (vv. 7–8)

Select Bibliography

Books

Achebe, Chinua. *Things Fall Apart.* New York: Random House, 1992.

Allen, Ronald. *And I Will Praise Him: A Guide to Worship in the Psalms.* Grand Rapids: Kregel, 1999.

Alter, Robert. *The Art of Biblical Poetry.* New York: Basic Books, 1985.

Arp, Thomas R. *Perrine's Literature: Structure, Sound and Sense.* 7th ed. Fort Worth: Harcourt Brace College Publishers, 1998.

Augustine. *Confessions and Enchiridion.* Vol. 7, *The Library of Christian Classics.* Translated and edited by Albert C. Outler. Philadelphia: Westminster, 1955.

Barker, Kenneth, ed. *The niv Study Bible.* Grand Rapids: Zondervan, 1995.

Blanchard, John. *Does God Believe in Atheists?* Auburn, Mass.: Evangelical Press, 2000.

Calvin, John. *Commentary on the Book of Psalms.* Vol. 1. Translated by James Anderson. Grand Rapids: Baker, 1998.

Conrad, Joseph. *Heart of Darkness.* New York: Penguin, 1983.

Davies, Paul. *God and the New Physics.* New York: Simon & Schuster Touchstone Books, 1984.

Frye, Northrop. *The Educated Imagination.* Toronto: CBC Publications, 1963.

Hurston, Zora Neal. *Their Eyes Were Watching God.* New York: Perennial Classics, 1998.

Lewis, C. S. *The Great Divorce.* New York: Simon & Schuster, 1996.

————. *Letters to an American Lady.* Grand Rapids: Eerdmans, 1967.

————. *Mere Christianity.* New York: Simon & Schuster, 1996.

————. *The Problem of Pain.* New York: Macmillan, 1967.

————. *Reflections on the Psalms.* New York: Harcourt, Brace, Jovanovich, 1958.

Longman, Tremper. *How to Read the Psalms.* Downers Grove, Ill.: InterVarsity, 1988.

————. *Literary Approaches to Biblical Interpretation.* Grand Rapids: Zondervan, 1987.

Longman, Tremper, and Daniel G. Reid. *God Is a Warrior.* Carlisle, U.K.: Paternoster, 1995.

Luther, Martin. *Works.* Vols. 10–14. Edited by Hilton C. Oswald. St. Louis: Concordia, 1974.

Reardon, Patrick Henry. *Christ in the Psalms.* Ben Lomond, Calif.: Conciliar, 2000.

Ryken, Leland. *Words of Delight: A Literary Introduction to the Bible.* 2d. ed. Grand Rapids: Baker, 1992.

The Scientific American Science Desk Reference. New York: John Wiley & Sons, 1999.

Spurgeon, Charles Haddon. *The Treasury of David.* 7 vols. Grand Rapids: Baker, 1983.

VanGemeren, Willem. *Psalms.* Vol. 5 of *The Expositor's Bible Commentary.* Edited by Frank E. Gaebelein. Grand Rapids: Zondervan, 1991.

Westermann, Claus. *Praise and Lament.* Translated by Keith R. Crim and Richard N. Soulen. Atlanta: John Knox, 1981.

————. *The Psalms: Structure, Content and Message.* Minneapolis: Augsburg, 1980.

Articles

Laney, J. Carl. "A Fresh Look at the Imprecatory Psalms." *Bibliotheca Sacra* 138, no. 549 (January–March 1981): 35–45.

Lewis, C. S. "Meditation in a Toolshed." In *God in the Dock: Essays on Theology and Ethics*, 212–15. Grand Rapids: Eerdmans, 1970.

———. "Transposition." In *The Weight of Glory*, 72–89. New York: Simon & Schuster, 1996.

Patterson, Richard D. "A Multiplex Approach to Psalm 45." *Grace Theological Journal* 6, no. 1 (1985): 29–48.

Hymns

"All You That Fear Jehovah's Name." In *Trinity Hymnal*, 9. Philadelphia: Great Commission, 1990.

Grant, Robert. "O Worship the King." In *Trinity Hymnal*, 2. Philadelphia: Great Commission, 1990.

Havergal, Frances R. "Who Is on the Lord's Side?" In *Trinity Hymnal*, 587. Philadelphia: Great Commission, 1990.

Lyte, Henry F. "Praise, My Soul, the King of Heaven." In *Trinity Hymnal*, 76. Philadelphia: Great Commission, 1990.

Neander, Joachim. "Praise to the Lord, the Almighty." In *Trinity Hymnal*, 53. Philadelphia: Great Commission, 1990.

Watts, Isaac. "The Heavens Declare Your Glory, Lord." In *Trinity Hymnal*, 138. Philadelphia: Great Commission, 1990.

Wesley, Charles. "Rejoice, the Lord Is King." In *Trinity Hymnal*, 309. Philadelphia: Great Commission, 1990.

Poems

Blake, William. "Tyger, Tyger." In *The Poetical Works of William Blake*. Edited by John Sampson. London: Oxford University Press, 1941.

Donne, John. "Holy Sonnet 10." In *Donne Poetical Works*, 297. Edited by Sir Herbert Grierson. London: Oxford University Press, 1933.

Eliot, T. S. "Little Gidding." In *T. S. Eliot: The Complete Poems and Plays, 1909–1950,* 144. New York: Harcourt Brace, 1980.

Frost, Robert. "Mending Wall." In *The Poetry of Robert Frost,* 33–34. Edited by Edward Connery Lathem. New York: Henry Holt, 1969.

Herbert, George. "Antiphon I." In *The English Poems of George Herbert,* 72–73. Edited by C. A. Patrides. Totowa, N.J.: Rowman & Littlefield, 1974.

Hopkins, Gerard Manley. "God's Grandeur." In *The Poems of Gerard Manley Hopkins,* 66. 4th ed. Edited by W. H. Gardner and N. H. MacKenzie. Oxford: Oxford University Press, 1967.

Kipling, Rudyard. "The Ballad of East and West." In *Works of Rudyard Kipling.* Vol. 10. New York: National Library, 1909.

Milton, John. *Paradise Lost.* In *John Milton: Complete Poems and Major Prose.* New York: Odyssey, 1957.

Shakespeare, William. "Sonnet 116." In *The Riverside Shakespeare.* [1864]. 2d ed. Boston: Houghton Mifflin, 1997.

Tennyson, Alfred, Lord. "The Charge of the Light Brigade." In *The Complete Poetical Works of Tennyson,* 226–27. Edited by W. J. Rolfe. Cambridge, Mass.: Riverside, 1898.

Wordsworth, William. "Sonnet XXX." In *Poetical Works: Wordsworth,* 205. London: Oxford University Press, 1967.

Plays

Shakespeare, William. *Macbeth.* In *The Riverside Shakespeare.* 2d. ed. Boston: Houghton Mifflin, 1974.